THE CUTTING EDGE

50 Years of British Fashion 1947-1997

Mulberry
ENGLAND

THE CUTTING EDGE

50 Years of British Fashion

1947-1997

EDITED BY AMY DE LA HAYE

V&A Publications

First published by V&A Publications, 1996
V&A Publications
160 Brompton Road
London SW3 1HW
Text and photographs © The Board of Trustees
of the Victoria and Albert Museum 1996

Amy de la Haye asserts her moral right to be
identified as author of this book

ISBN 1 85177 199 9

A catalogue record for this book is available from the British Library

Designed by Area

Photography by Richard Davis (Tailoring, Bohemian, Country); Sara Hodges (Hats,
Shoes, Bags); Daniel McGrath (Romantic); James Stevenson (Knitwear, Underwear)

Printed in Singapore by C.S. Graphics

FRONT COVER PICTURE: 'Watteau' evening dress, 1996, by Vivienne Westwood.
BACK COVER: Lulu Guinness handbag, 'Florist's Basket', 1996; Tommy Nutter Suit, 1983; Charles and Patricia Lester
ensemble, 1994; Hackett shooting suit, 1996.
FRONTISPIECE: Detail from Worth evening dress, 1955. Pink beaded silk satin with floral appliqué embroidery.

ACKNOWLEDGEMENTS

Published to coincide with the opening of the exhibition 'The Cutting Edge: Fifty Years of British Fashion', at the Victoria and Albert Museum in March 1997, this book was made possible by the generosity and support of a great many people.

We are indebted to all the British fashion designers, tailors, manufacturers and their clients who consistently support and boost the holdings of the Twentieth Century Dress Collection. This retrospective would not have been possible without their generous donations. Individual donors are credited in the captions which accompany each photograph. Sincere thanks are also extended to everyone we pursued by letter, telephone calls or visits; all were enthusiastic and generous in their response. We are also most grateful to the many designers who provided insights into their own work as well as their experiences of working within the British fashion industry.

For providing additional information and support, we especially thank Nina Campbell, Tony Glenville, Bobby Hillson, Peter Hope-Lumley, Marion Hume, Charles Lester, Clinton Silver, Manny Silverman, Professor Lou Taylor and Annette Worsley Taylor. Further acknowledgements conclude each chapter.

Photographs of all clothing and accessories which feature in this book were taken by V&A photographers Richard Davis, Sara Hodges, Daniel McGrath and James Stevenson, Head of the V&A Photo Studio. Thanks are due to Sue Müller from Stockman London Ltd., who provided the mannequins, which were dressed and styled for photography by Sue Milner, Emma Damon and Fiona Anderson.

We are enormously grateful to Mary Butler, Miranda Harrison and Clio Whittaker of V&A Publications; Paul Greenhalgh, Head of Research; Linda Lloyd-Jones, Head of Exhibitions and Juliette Foy, Exhibitions Officer for The Cutting Edge exhibition. The contextual picture research was undertaken by Emma Damon, who studied original works housed by the V&A's Department of Prints, Drawings and Paintings and by the Archive of Art and Design. We would like to thank colleagues from these departments as well as the staff of the National Art Library and the Picture Library. In addition, we are grateful for the support of all members of the Textiles and Dress Department, especially Avril Hart, Susan North and Jane Dutil for providing additional research, and Debbie Sinfield who calmly responded to numerous pleas for administrative support.

Celebrating the V&A's unique collection of twentieth-century British fashion, this volume is the first extensive exploration of British designer-level fashion and its identifying traits.

The introduction provides a contextual appraisal, followed by chapters highlighting areas in which the British excel: Romantic, Tailoring, Country, Bohemian and Accessories. These five thematic areas, in place of a strict chronological survey, offer the most appropriate and exciting framework for both the book and the exhibition.

Gathered together from a variety of fashion-related professions, the team of authors give valuable insights based upon their particular fields of expertise – dress and social history, fashion journalism, design education and curatorship. Their sometimes candid assessments consider the Britishness of British fashion; the tensions between tradition and modernity; the strength of the nation's fashion education and the industry's undernourished sub-structure.

The chapters reveal that there is no single British fashion identity. Many looks have been labelled 'British', which change and cross-fertilise to create a thriving diversity of styles. The output of established designers as well as students feeds into the continuing international cycle of innovation and inventiveness. The world comes to London to replenish its wardrobe with 'the best of British', including fine tailoring, country and sporting classics, hand-knits, fantasy hats, bespoke shoes and romantic ball gowns. The picture is kaleidoscopic. British fashion readily embraces extremes, from utility and seemly conformity to fairy-tale romance and the downright outrageous.

Valerie D. Mendes
Chief Curator, Department of Textiles and Dress

Introduction

AMY DE LA HAYE

The glass of fashion and the mould of form,
The observ'd of all the observers.

(Act III, Scene I, *Hamlet,* Shakespeare)

BRITAIN AND FASHION

PREVIOUS
PAGES:
PLATE 2. Detail
of Hussein
Chalayan suit,
spring/summer
1995. Jacket,
photographi-
cally printed
paper with floral
design, trousers,
gold paper
hipsters. Given
by Mr Hussein
Chalayan.
(T.679:1&2-1995.)

LEFT:
PLATE 1. Detail of
Utility suit by
Digby Morton,
1942. Grey
herringbone
wool. Given by
the Board of
Trade. (T.45:
A&B-1942.)

ABOVE:
PLATE 5. Michael
of Carlos Place
two-piece suit,
1968. Suit,
black silk and
rayon, black
leather belt,
black-and-
white print silk
scarf. Given by
Mr Michael
Donellan.
(T.314&A,B,C-
1974.)

It could be argued that high fashion has been Britain's most successful visual art form since the Second World War. In this area Britain is comfortable in the company of its major competitors: France, the US, Italy and Japan. The Britishness of British fashion determines its inspirational role, sets it apart and establishes its identity. British fashion is peculiar to itself.

This is a most surprising success story, as many facets of British culture would appear to be antipathetic to the idea of high fashion. The powerful Protestant ethic traditionally militates against show and excess and willingness to invest capital, or to indulge in élite luxury, have hardly been national characteristics. The frivolity and hedonism associated with fashion goes against the perceived grain of Britishness. This partly explains why the British have never fully recognized, in the way that others have, the commercial potential and cultural cachet of the high-fashion industry.

British high fashion has been little supported by government and industry, nor has it enjoyed the patronage of the wealthy. Paradoxically, state-funded art schools provide the finest fashion training in the world. But, once qualified, British designers are tempted to show abroad, have their clothes made abroad and establish their reputations abroad. High fashion in Britain is a maverick industry populated with individual high-achievers, but there is precious little infrastructure.

Exploring the Britishness of British high fashion, this chapter considers the industry in its historical context and looks at its structure and status. Additionally, it points up the significance of British art-school training and considers the shift from *haute couture* to designer-level ready-to-wear clothing in the post-war years. British fashion textiles, a topic that deserves its own study, are also mentioned.

It is clear that in recent decades British peculiarities have been brilliantly exploited by fashion designers. Fashion is a mirror of socio-cultural trends, reflecting nuances of the culture from which it emerges. Whether inadvertently absorbed or fully exploited by fashion designers, national identity offers a route to product differentiation and makes

ABOVE:
FIG. 1. *Avebury after Thomas Hardy* by Bill Brandt, 1945. (CIRC.563A –1975 x911/H.) Reproduced courtesy of Bill Brandt estate.

good business sense. In order to persuade buyers and press to include London on their seasonal tour, designers have to present distinctive collections.

It is worth pondering what constitutes the Britishness of British fashion. From the 1870s, when Britain's role as the 'workshop of the world' was undermined, the British have increasingly projected a national identity dominated by history and custom. Some have suggested that the quip about all the oldest British traditions being invented at the end of the nineteenth century has a lot of truth in it. Britain's profile was created not by looking to the future, but to its illustrious past: when the present is unstable, the past is an obvious refuge.

Britain has effectively been in economic and imperial decline for the whole of the twentieth century, the period that corresponds with the rise of most cultural forms of modernism. It was inevitable that the British would attempt to combine tradition with modernity in order to present themselves in the contemporary world. A quintessential feature of British fashion is its preoccupation with historical style; the past is reworked and re-presented as the future.

The characteristics of a nation's cultural products are partly determined by geography and climate. In his famous study *The Englishness of English Art* (1956) Nikolaus Pevsner cites landscape and climate as determinants in the psychological formation of the population. It is perhaps natural that a nation that constantly complains about its wet weather should become a market leader in rainwear. The landscape and climate are conducive to sheep farming; it is no coincidence that woollen textiles and yarns are central to Britain's sartorial identity. These factors also shape colour preferences. As Pevsner states, 'Animals of cold climates are grey, brown and black – tigers and parrots live in hot climates. So too art will take on a different hue in the mists of the north and under clear blue skies.'[1]

Explorations of socio-cultural conditions can provide more solid insights, while highlighting apparent conundrums. As W.D. Rubenstein, in *Past and Present* (no.76, 1977) points out, Britain is in many ways an anomalous country, being 'the first with a bourgeois revolution, the last with an aristocracy; the earliest with a modern working-class revolution, yet manifesting the least working-class consciousness; the earliest with industrialisation, yet the last among the advanced countries to witness a merger of finance and industry, and so on'. Being the first country to industrialize, Britain became obsessed with the integrity of the non-industrial environment. Before the end of the eighteenth century Romantic poets were ruing the effects of an industrial activity that had barely begun, and the British have been preoccupied with perceptions of rural life ever since. Britain has been thoroughly urbanized since the late nineteenth century, yet authentic country clothing and its spin-offs have remained a staple feature of fashion. The homogenizing effects associated with industrial development have led to a constant desire for individuality, underpinning 200 years of romantic escapism. Bohemian styles and romantic eveningwear, areas in which British fashion designers excel, eloquently reflect this spirit. Conversely, the British love of understatement has been perfectly served by a tailoring tradition.

In the same way that Britain's passage through the twentieth century has been an uneasy one, as it struggles to cope with the modern world while carrying the baggage of the old, so fashion sits uncomfortably among other forms of cultural production. It appears to fit simultaneously within the spheres of art, design and craft, yet it belongs to none of these. The coming-together of Britain and fashion is therefore most intriguing.

'THE UNFORGIVABLE DISADVANTAGE OF BEING ENGLISH IN ENGLAND'

The high-fashion industry as we know it today, with seasonally presented, designer-led fashions was established in Second Empire Paris (1852-70). British-born Charles Frederick Worth and his partner Otto Bobergh have been widely credited with establishing the dominance of the designer, when they founded their fashion house in 1858. Worth conceived and imposed his own design ideas and in so doing created fashion unequivocally determined by the designer. Prior to this, highly skilled dressmakers had carried out the dictates of their clients. With great aplomb and a shrewd business head, Worth emphasized that his taste was the final word.

Worth's legendary rise to fame, from fabric salesman at the London department store Swan & Edgar to the couturier responsible for the sumptuous crinoline gowns worn by the Empress Eugenie, has been examined in depth.[2] It is important here simply to record that Worth acquired a prestigious international clientele and attracted other designers and specialist craftspeople into the area surrounding his premises in the rue de la Paix. He established good links with the finest silk manufacturers in Lyons, and this symbiotic relationship between fabric-makers and fashion designers has continued to the present day. In 1868 the Chambre Syndicale de la Couture Parisienne, still highly influential, was founded in order to co-ordinate, study and defend the economic, industrial and commercial interests of this prestigious, burgeoning industry.

From the outset, Parisian *haute couturiers* were the undisputed international arbiters of women's fashion. The wealthiest European and American women purchased their clothing direct from the couture houses and the rest of fashionable society looked to Paris for stylistic guidance. This supremacy was promoted at all market levels: the most exclusive small dress shops and department stores proudly advertised that they stocked the very latest models from Paris, while others boasted of their fine copies, available at a fraction of the original price. Highly talented British designers including Redfern, Lucile and Molyneux were to follow in Worth's footsteps, opening branches in Paris and working as part of the *haute couture* industry.

In contrast, the top end of the British fashion trade, based in London's West End, was dominated by court dressmakers. The very term 'court dressmaker' emphasized links with the monarchy, the pinnacle of Britain's social hierarchy. The Edwardian period witnessed the heyday of London's social life surrounding the court. Queen Alexandra and King Edward Vll, even from the days when he was the Prince of Wales, were great socialites and fashion-setters and did much to consolidate the importance of court social life.

The coterie of court dressmakers was well-versed in the minutiae of etiquette and in the rigorous sartorial codes of high society. However, it was widely accepted that on the whole they copied and adapted Parisian models for an élite British clientele. The 'Season' played a central role and continues to exert a powerful influence on British social life and the domestic fashion industry, even though 1958 was the last year that the daughters of the aristocracy were formally presented to the monarch. This high-profile ceremony served to introduce the young débutante into high society and, ideally, to find her a suitable husband. From 1928 Queen Charlotte's Birthday Ball, a charity event to raise money for the hospital named after its patron, became an essential event in the débutante's calendar. This occasion has effectively taken over the role of the court presentation. The carefully appointed young ladies, all dressed in white, curtsey to a huge iced cake in honour of Queen Charlotte. The Balls ceased in 1976 but were revived in 1989.

The Season runs from May to the end of July and formally opens with the private view of the Royal Academy Summer Exhibition. Key social occasions include the Chelsea Flower Show and the Fourth of June at Eton, the most rarefied school speech day in the world. British pageantry can be seen at its most magnificent each June with the Trooping of the Colour, staged to mark the Queen's Official Birthday. Central to the Season are sporting events, including the Royal Ascot Race Meeting, Wimbledon Lawn Tennis Championships and the Henley Regatta. Racing at Goodwood used to mark the official end of the Season, but it now extends to sailing at Cowes Week. Ascot is patronized by the royal family, and is the most significant event in terms of fashion. Ladies' Day is an ostentatious celebration of eye-catching dress. These events are interspersed by a glittering array of garden parties, luncheons and balls for Britain's social élite. Foreign travel often follows after the Season. Then, during the autumn and winter months, country houses are given over to hunting, shooting and fishing parties – the clichés of aristocratic British life. Each of these occasions has specific dress codes, which are met by specialist clothing companies, tailors and high-fashion designers. Apparent anachronisms, these activities have pretty much survived two world wars and major socio-cultural shifts.

The First World War formed a watershed, after which there was a gradual demise of London's court dressmakers. In the 1920s and '30s a new school of British designers emerged. They worked along similar lines, although on a much smaller scale, to the French couture houses. Many became dominant forces in British high fashion in the years after the Second World War.

Norman Hartnell opened his Bruton Street salon in 1923, Peter Russell opened during the late 1920s, Victor Stiebel in 1932, Molyneux opened a London branch the same year and Mattli set up in 1934. The House of Lachasse was formed in 1928 as the sportswear offshoot of Gray & Paulette Ltd. Under the design leadership of Digby Morton, Lachasse became renowned for tailored tweed suits. When Digby Morton left to set up on his own in 1934, Sir Hardy Amies took over. London also experienced an influx of Parisian fashion houses during these inter-war years, as designers sought to expand markets.

During the early years of their careers, many British couturiers struggled to assert themselves as creative forces in their own right. In his autobiography Norman Hartnell describes how, during the early 1920s, clients would often come into his salon and, having chosen a dress, would enquire whose design it was. Hartnell would proudly say that it was his own. 'Oh, is it not a Patou or a Lelong? Not a French model? Then, I think I will reconsider it. No, on reflection I won't take it.' Hartnell states unequivocally, 'I suffered from the unforgivable disadvantage of being English in England'.[3] In 1927 he took his collection to Paris, where it was well received. This earned him a highly desirable Parisian cachet and he went on to become Britain's most famous fashion designer.

In 1937 the Council for Art and Industry published the report *Design and the Designer in Industry*, which stressed how reluctant Britain was to exploit domestic fashion talent because of the prestige associated with Parisian design. Likewise, America's fashion industry,

BELOW: FIG. 2. *Between the showers at Henley.* Barbara Goalen photographed for the *Daily Express* by John French, 1950. (PL5 1491-1541-F1491/2.)

located around Seventh Avenue in New York, was also eclipsed by Paris. As in London, highly talented designers catered for the domestic market but few were known internationally. It was not until the Second World War that the hegemony of Parisian fashion came to a temporary halt.

CO-ORDINATION AND CONSOLIDATION

When hostile German forces entered Paris in June 1940, communications with the outside world were temporarily severed. The prestigious *haute couture* industry was encouraged to function during the Occupation and styles continued to evolve, but these were no longer instantly communicated to the outside world. Paris-based British designers Edward Molyneux and Charles Creed returned to London. This break from Paris was to provide an unprecedented opportunity for designers in London and New York. Britain and America were compelled to realize the potential of domestic fashion talent.

On 1 June 1941 clothes rationing was introduced in Britain to ensure an even distribution of scarce resources, to control consumer expenditure, to release clothing workers and to make factory space available for the war effort. In the first year sixty-six clothing coupons were allocated to each adult: a pair of men's trousers represented eight coupons; an overcoat sixteen; a woollen dress, eleven; and a pair of women's shoes, five. As shortages became more pronounced, this allowance decreased.

Britain's fashion designers were fully occupied throughout the war, within the services, creating special collections for export and conceiving clothing designs for the civilian population under the auspices of the Incorporated Society of London Fashion Designers. Founded early in 1942, Inc. Soc., as it popularly became known, was the first organization to consolidate and co-ordinate the activities of Britain's high-fashion industry. During the early years of the war, the government was keen to raise foreign revenue, especially dollars, and recognized the commercial potential of exporting designer-level fashion and textiles. This was facilitated by working through Inc. Soc.

The Hon. Mrs Reginald Fellowes, a fashionable society beauty, was appointed President of Inc. Soc., Mrs Ashley Havinden as Chairman and Miss Lillian Hyder as Executive Director. Peter Russell provided premises within his fashion house, at 2 Carlos Place. Inc. Soc.'s founding aims were:

a) To maintain and develop the reputation of London as a centre of fashion.
b) To collaborate with groups of fabric and other manufacturers, and with companies, forms and individuals, with a view to increasing the prestige of British fashions, and promoting the sales of British fashions in home and overseas markets.
c) To assist fashion designers by protecting their original designs; enabling them to exchange information to their mutual advantage, arranging dates for their respective showings; fostering the professional and trade interests of persons engaged in creating British fashions; developing the standards of skilled workmanship and representing the views of government and trade bodies to the press.[4]

From its inception, Inc. Soc. forged excellent links with UK textile manufacturers and trade bodies, including the National Wool Textile Export Corporation, the Cotton Board and the Rayon Export Group, presenting shows of clothes made from their fabrics. In 1940 the Manchester-based Cotton Board established its influential Colour, Design and Style Centre, which campaigned for higher standards of design in printed cotton fabrics. With the aid of government subsidies and enlightened leadership, the Cotton Board commissioned artists such as Ben Nicholson, Duncan Grant, John Piper and Graham Sutherland to inject a lively, modern impetus into their British-made cottons.

In March 1942 Inc. Soc., at the invitation of Sir Thomas Barlow, President of the Board of Trade, accepted responsibility for the design of wartime civilian clothing. The Board of Trade recognized the virtues (in terms of economics and public morale) of inviting top fashion names to design this range. However, in tune with the times, they chose to call it Utility, the very antithesis of fashion. Sir Thomas emphasized that while the clothes were to be desirable, they should not overly stimulate demand.

Hardy Amies, Digby Morton, Bianca Mosca, Peter Russell and Worth (London) Ltd, agreed to create a basic wardrobe consisting of an overcoat, suit (with shirt or blouse) and a day dress, which would serve throughout the year. Each designer received a fee of ninety guineas, with the garments being the property of the Board of Trade. All clothes were made from Utility cloth and had to conform to strict regulations issued by the Board. The specifications for womenswear required that a dress must have no more than two pockets, five buttons, six seams in the skirt, two inverted or box pleats or four knife pleats, 160 inches of stitching and no superfluous decoration. Thirty-two designs were selected for manufacture and templates of these were made available to manufacturers for a small fee. The designers responsible for individual items were not publicized, instead all garments bore the CC41 Utility label. The prototypes were donated to the V&A, and in some cases the designers are identified (plate 1).

These restrictions continued into peacetime, impacting upon clothing expenditure and design choices. Consumer rationing did not end until March 1949 and Utility clothes remained in large-scale production until 1952. Freed from the tyranny of constantly changing fashions, manufacturers focused upon improving production techniques, which stood the ready-to-wear industry in good stead in the post-war years. With the end of rationing, new manufacturers were permitted to enter the industry and fashion became an important determinant of demand once more.

Britain's economic and social landscape changed dramatically in the post-war years. In 1945 the first majority Labour government was elected, with Clement Atlee as Prime Minister. Morale was high and the populace looked forward to the future with optimism. Britain was victorious, but emerged almost bankrupt from the war. Acute shortages presented the government with the difficult task of extending the ethos of wartime sacrifice into peacetime.

Britain's confidence was severely dented, and the promotion of design and cultural activities provided one way to redress this. In 1946 the Council for the Encouragement of Music and the Arts (CEMA) was reorganized to form the Arts Council. The Council of Industrial Design (COID), whose remit included fashion, was founded in 1944. One of COID's first major activities was the staging of the 'Britain Can Make It' exhibition, which opened at the V&A in September 1946. Unlike many multimedia exhibitions, it featured sections on women's high fashion, top-quality menswear and accessories. The exhibition was rapidly dubbed 'Britain Can't Have It' as most of the goods, including fashion, were either prototypes or for export. None the less, it attracted 1.4 million visitors, all keen to catch a glimpse of the future as defined by domestic design.

Not only were consumer goods in short supply, but money was very tight. Many men returning home were without jobs, while many women resumed their traditional roles as non-earning housewives. The 1947 budget dealt Britain's aristocracy a severe blow by considerably raising levels of income tax and dramatically increasing the duty payable on large estates (although eliminating death duties on small inheritances) from 10 per cent to 75 per cent. As a result many families with landed wealth could no longer afford to maintain their country estates. Critics of the new tax laws emphasized that it was not only the architectural fabric of these houses that was at peril, but also the social status quo. In spite of some impoverished aristocrats, however, appearances were maintained. While the lavish evening courts of the pre-war years were not revived, from 1947 the Season continued to offer its traditional entertainments and in so doing boosted the fortunes of London's couturiers.

Having tasted wartime independence, British designers were eager to assume a dominant position in future world markets. Leading fashion writer Alison Settle explored this issue in her influential article, 'London: Can it Become a World Fashion Centre?' published in *Picture Post* on 6 January 1945. She issued a warning that is still valid fifty years later:

Success cannot come to English fashions, so long as men of the country treat fashion as being essentially frivolous and even laughable…Only when fashion trends, colours and the whole philosophy of clothes is talked about – as films, pictures or…music are discussed – can the textile trades of Britain regain their merited superiority in the eyes of the world.

British (and American) hopes of leading world fashion were instantly dashed when new Parisian couturier Christian Dior presented his first collection, the Corolle line (the New Look), in the spring of 1947. In stark contrast to Utility, which still prevailed in Britain, Dior's designs revelled in unashamed luxury and traditional notions of femininity. Backed by textile magnate Marcel Boussac, Dior exploited huge quantities of costly fabrics. Today, it is unimaginable that a fashion collection could cause such a sensation. Stafford Cripps, President of Britain's Board of Trade at this time, recognized that this new fashion spelt economic disaster and he was vocal in his condemnation. The intensity of feeling was eloquently expressed in a *Picture Post* article of that year, 'Paris Forgets This Is 1947', criticizing the New Look's profligate use of fabric and anachronistic styling:

Straight from the indolent and wealthy years before the 1914 war come this year's much-discussed Paris fashions. The styles are launched upon a world which has not the material to copy them – and whose women have neither the money to buy, the leisure to enjoy, nor in some designs even the strength to support these masses of elaborate material.[5]

None the less many women were captivated, and orders by Princess Margaret and the Duchess of Kent gave the New Look a royal sanction in Britain, much to the chagrin of the politicians. Within months British designers and manufacturers created modifications of the New Look using smaller amounts of fabric, as only non-Utility cloth could be used.

In 1948 the London Model House Group (LMHG) was founded to represent the interests of fourteen top-quality ready-to-wear fashion companies including Dorville, Matita, Brenner Sports and Frederick Starke, who were assuming an increasingly dominant role in the home fashion market. Like Inc. Soc., LMHG arranged synchronized showings of their collections and established and maintained standards within the industry. Chaired by Leslie Carr-Jones, the group did much to enhance the prestige of British ready-to-wear fashion at home and abroad.

Ready-to-wear was to become central to the survival of international couture houses. In the years that followed the war, many Parisian couturiers diversified into top-level ready-made fashions. This was a bid to extend their markets and suited the reduced financial circumstances of many existing customers. These departments, sited within the couture houses, were called boutiques and Hardy Amies was the first British designer to open one in 1950. While it was based on French lines, he stressed that, 'Throughout we made strenuous efforts to ensure that what we offered was unmistakably English and unlike the *frivolités* to be found in the French boutiques.'[6]

From 1951 Hardy Amies dressed the Queen and in 1955 he was awarded the much-coveted royal warrant. He expanded his export market and developed an extensive and highly lucrative network of licensing arrangements. Licensing involves creating designs for niche markets or endorsing merchandise on a royalty basis. Ideally, designers bene-

LEFT:
FIG. 4.
Coronation portrait of Her Majesty Queen Elizabeth II, 1953, by Cecil Beaton. Embroidered gown by Norman Hartnell. (P.H 3475-1953 x908A.)

fit financially without jeopardizing the exclusivity of their name. Norman Hartnell was also shrewd in business and, like Hardy Amies, enjoyed good public relations. He successfully designed for the British royal family and Britain's most affluent women, at the same time as operating high-profile licensing agreements.

In 1951 the Festival of Britain celebrations to assert post-war regeneration and national identity were staged on London's South Bank. This event would have provided an ideal platform to promote Britain's high-fashion industry, and initially fashion had been on the agenda. The reasons underlying its omission are worth considering, as they highlight significant issues that are still pertinent. Professor Jonathan Woodham (Director of Brighton University's Design History Research Centre, which houses the Festival of Britain archive) explains that designer-level fashion did not fit neatly into the COID's *Breakdown of Industries as Used by the Industrial Design Division*:

> This *Breakdown* only included one catch-all category that could straightforwardly accommodate it: 'Clothing and Personal Accessories'; dress textiles fell under the equally broad heading of 'Textiles, Soft Goods, Carpets'. There was also perhaps something of a hidden agenda in the Council's outlook insofar as it was ideologically opposed to ephemeral styling and notions of obsolescence...Fashion, in its very essence, was readily associated with a short lifespan and was an activity about which the male modernist of the COID felt distinctly uncomfortable.

Interestingly however, the Festival site was used as a photographic location by *Vogue* as a backdrop for images of fashions designed by British designers.

London's couturiers fared well during the early 1950s and were joined by talented newcomers John Cavanagh, Michael Sherard and Ronald Paterson. In 1953 the Coronation of Elizabeth II reinforced the role of the monarchy and peerage at the centre of British cultural life. Television transmitted this message directly into 25 million homes. The patriotism engendered by the Coronation encouraged a swift boost in patronage for the London couture houses.

From the mid-1950s British fashion experienced a radical new impetus in the form of young, iconoclastic designers, who were often trained in art schools. From the outset they existed alongside the more traditional *haute couture* and top-level ready-to-wear houses, presenting the dual identity that has characterized post-war high fashion in Britain. The unique and superlative fashion training provided by Britain's art schools was central to the rise of this new generation of fashion designers.

FASHION IN THE ART SCHOOLS

Practical skills had traditionally been learnt within the industry and at trade schools such as the Technical School of Dressmaking at Barrett Street in London's West End, which opened in 1915. From the late nineteenth century, trade schools were set up throughout the country to provide skilled workers for local industries. The first needle-trade school in London was opened in Shoreditch in 1906 to cater for the wholesale clothing trades, which were based in the East End of London. The Barrett Street school, in contrast, aimed to train young women for the more exclusive fashion houses and provided full-time, day release and evening classes. There were also private establishments, such as the Paris Academy of Dressmaking in Old Bond Street. By the 1930s courses on dress were also offered within many art colleges, but the emphasis remained upon teaching technical, rather than creative skills.

Commissioned by the Council for Art and Industry in 1939, *Design and the Designer in the Dress Trade* was an important report that was eventually published in 1945. It describes how the designer in the British fashion industry was not considered to have a creative role, but rather one that adapted and translated Paris models. The manufacturers interviewed were adamant that this role could only be filled by promotion from within the industry. Indeed, it states that 'the possibility of any Art School, as at present constituted, turning out designers was generally dismissed by the manufacturers as fantastic.'[7]

This attitude was not surprising. The majority of Britain's art schools were run by those with a pronounced bias towards the fine arts or traditional crafts. They were often contemptuous or dismissive of industry and, at the extreme, considered it a social evil. Manufacturers in turn retaliated by ignoring or mocking the naïvety of college-trained students.

While a fine art student at the Royal College of Art in the 1930s, Muriel Pemberton challenged the limitations of existing courses by arranging to work on a part-time basis at the London fashion house of Reville while continuing her fine art studies. In the late 1930s, when she was working as a fashion illustrator for the *Daily Herald*, she introduced evening classes in creative fashion at St Martin's School of Art, under the umbrella of the Graphics School.

As a result of the reorganization and expansion of further education in the post-war years, combined with the allocation of state-funded grants, students from all social classes now had access to higher education. Fashion departments were established in art schools throughout Britain. (In France and America there have always been far fewer schools, and most are private establishments.) After the war Muriel Pemberton's pioneering course was developed on a full-time basis and, under her inspired tutorage, St Martin's embarked upon a new approach to teaching fashion which included contextual studies in dress and art history. Throughout her career she actively campaigned to elevate the status of fashion within the art school system, and her work has been sustained by many notable figures, including Bobby Hillson (who introduced the fashion MA course in 1978) and fashion designer Wendy Dagworthy. By the late 1940s a number of colleges had started fashion schools, including Manchester, Leeds and Leicester.

In 1948 Madge Garland, ex-editor of British *Vogue*, was appointed to found a Fashion School at the Royal College of Art (RCA) to replace the existing Dress course. Her contacts provided the students with materials, sponsorship and, ultimately, good introductions into the industry. Early RCA graduates included Gina Fratini, Gerald McCann and Bernard Nevill who went on to become leading forces in British fashion. Garland was undoubtedly a seminal figure in fashion education, even though she was Paris-led and couture-orientated.

The school embarked upon a new direction when Madge Garland's assistant, Janey Ironside, took the helm in 1956. Ironside's aim was to promote a new look in British fashion that would be internationally accepted and in this she succeeded. Many of her students from working-class backgrounds felt that Parisian *haute couture* had little relevance to their lives. They wanted to design stylish, youthful fashions and Janey Ironside nurtured and developed their skills to this end. David Sassoon, Marion Foale, Sally Tuffin, Ossie Clark, Antony Price and Janice Wainwright were among the RCA students who went on to make a significant contribution to British fashion. In 1964 the RCA launched a menswear department within the Fashion School, which trained a new generation of menswear fashion designers.

In spite of her successes, Janey Ironside had to fight to gain fashion its due recognition. In 1967, the RCA was granted university status, which permitted it to award Bachelor of Arts degrees to replace the Diploma of Art and Design. However, the Academic Advisory Council singled out the Fashion School as unworthy of this higher qualification. They claimed that fashion was too intimately connected with industry; an irony, considering that the college had been founded to feed industry. Protesting vigorously, Ironside ultimately resigned. Two years later the decision was revoked, by which time the highly regarded Joanne Brogden had become head. Since 1989 both the Fashion and Textile Schools have been jointly headed by John Miles.

From 1972 all British art schools have been able to apply for degree status in fashion. This has done much to elevate the status of fashion as a professional qualification and career. Many other fashion schools – including Nottingham, Manchester, Ravensbourne, Liverpool, Middlesex and Harrow (now the University of Westminster) – have all made major contributions. The Barrett Street Trade School amalgamated with the London College of Fashion, and is the only state-funded entirely fashion-focused college in Britain. From 1952 to 1972 Mary Bromley headed the highly successful Fashion School at Newcastle, which became a leader in developing fashion-related courses such as business studies, marketing and promotion. Each of the colleges has a different emphasis, training designers, tailors and technicians to work in all levels of the industry. For example, the highly respected Fashion School at Kingston has prioritized the training of designers to work within the international manufacturing industry, a focus established by its first head Daphne Brooker.

British art schools now teach all areas of fashion and clothing, and offer a broad range of related subjects. Fashion graduates from art schools are employed in design studios throughout the world, as well as having high-profile own-label collections.

TIARAS, TWEEDS AND TWIGGY: TRADITION AND MODERNITY

From the mid-1950s conditions were ripe for a modernizing force in British fashion to flourish. An economic boom, profound social change and full employment gave rise to a relatively affluent teenage market, to whom fashion clothing was highly desirable. During this period the fashion press proliferated and fuelled the vogue for built-in obsolescence, by constantly redefining consumer tastes.

In 1955 Mary Quant, with her husband Alexander Plunket Greene and business partner Archie MacNair, opened their London boutique, Bazaar, in the King's Road. Quant had trained in fine art at Goldsmiths' College and attended evening classes in pattern-cutting. In a recent interview she explained, 'My parents didn't want me to go to fashion school, saying it was too dangerous, as I would not earn a living. With art, they thought I could teach or whatever.'[8]

Bazaar caused a fashion revolution. Its short production runs of youthful ready-to-wear clothes were a far cry from the established formula for formal, structured and highly accessorized styles. In comparison to *haute couture* prices, Mary Quant's clothes were considered cheap. Rejecting the conventional categories of day and evening wear and seasonal collections, she produced new designs all year round.

In 1955 Mary Quant introduced shorter skirts and began a trend that was to culminate in the ubiquitous mini-skirt of the 1960s. She also pioneered the use of new materials, such as PVC, for fashion clothing. Although Quant's aesthetic was modernistic, her sources were often rooted in British sartorial tradition. Edwardian children's clothing, pinstripe worsted of men's business suits and aristocratic country attire, such as Norfolk jackets, were among her sources of inspiration. Thus she achieved 'romantic modernity' by turning tradition on its head, a premise with which she agrees: 'Yes, that is always what I did, reversing or perversely looking at things.'[9]

This dualism has characterized the approach of many British designers. Even the most radical make overt reference to historical styles or traditional clothing in terms of cut, fabric or detailing. For example, that ephemeral fashion trend of about 1967 for disposable bonded-fibre 'paper' garments, such as those designed by Ossie Clarke, exploited early 1920s art deco patterning. In the 1990s Hussein Chalayan's paper fashions (in fact made of Tyvek) feature photographically printed meadow flowers (detailed in plate 2). In both instances the material and cut is utterly modern, but the surface pattern is not.

In 1958 the LMHG was reorganized to represent the larger Fashion House Group of London. Their first initiative was to launch the now well-established, bi-annual London Fashion Week, which was first staged in May 1959. By the early 1960s, many young designers had followed in Mary Quant's wake, selling up-to-the-minute, off-the-peg fashions for a fairly affluent, young clientele. While London remained the pre-eminent fashion centre – with the King's Road and Carnaby Street becoming meccas for boutiques – many innovative, youthful, clothing outlets emerged throughout Britain. The young and trendy headed for Lee Bender's Bus Stop, Jeff Banks's Clobber, John Stephen, Foale & Tuffin, Ossie Clark and Alice Pollock's Quorum, and the Fulham Road Clothes Shop run by Zandra Rhodes and Sylvia Ayton. Mexicana and Savita catered for the demand for authentic ethnic garments. The cheap and stylish fashions sold in Biba, which opened in 1963, were worn by working teenagers, high society and media stars alike. Biba sold an eclectic range of clothing and accessories which re-invented 1930s Hollywood glamour and pastoral styles in an utterly contemporary idiom.

Boutique culture launched the 1960s vogue for unisex garments, breaking down long-established codes of dressing based on gender. Designers also started to create ranges of informal and flamboyant menswear. In April 1966 *Time* magazine published its famous article on 'Swinging London', celebrating Britain's youth revolution and the new boutique culture.

For many fashion designers the patronage of discerning store owners and buyers is crucial. The fashion press is central in making and breaking fashion careers, but of paramount importance is the role of buyers who anticipate what will sell and put money behind their convictions. In 1961 Martin Moss revamped Woollands department store, which featured the 21 Shop. With Vanessa Denza appointed as buyer, it quickly became an important showcase for young British fashion talent. At various times, other top department stores including Fortnum & Mason, Simpson's of Piccadilly, Harvey Nichols and Liberty have promoted British designers in a major way. Exclusive shops such as Joan Burstein's Browns, Lucienne Phillips, and Rita Britton's shop Pollyanna have consistently supported domestic talents.

Fashion models are also critical to the marketing of high fashion and, since the 1950s, Britain has provided many top mannequins. Before the war fashion magazines featured society beauties, film stars and actresses, but professional models were anonymous. After the war, models were accorded celebrity status. Fiona Campbell Walter, Bronwyn Pugh, Barbara Goalen and Anne Gunning were among the most successful models who married into British high society. Their hauteur was ideally suited to the promotion of *haute couture*. By the 1960s a new generation of models, including Jean Shrimpton, Celia Hammond and the highly celebrated and remarkably thin Lesley Hornby, nicknamed 'Twiggy', modelled the fashions of Britain's new generation of designers. Celebrated as the *Daily Express* 'Face of 1966',

BELOW:
FIG. 5. Twiggy modelling a Foale & Tuffin fringed jersey dress. Photograph by Cecil Beaton for 'Young Ideas', *Vogue* (1 October 1967). (P.H 975-1975.)

Twiggy weighed just six-and-a-half stone and launched the cult for waif-like models, revived in the 1990s by Kate Moss. Today, international models Honor Fraser and Stella Tennant have British aristocratic backgrounds.

With little intention of addressing modernity, except in the sparing use of synthetic fibres, Britain's couturiers staged their high-profile fashion show 'From Tweeds to Tiaras' at Osterley House on 22 March 1960. This prestigious event was attended by the Queen Mother and Princess Margaret. Inc. Soc.'s members celebrated their own fashion strengths, which met the requirements of their refined clientele. The show was divided into six sections: town and country clothes in wool; full summer clothes in cotton and Irish linen; cocktail and short evening dresses in lace or silk; dance dresses in synthetics and synthetic-mixes; clothes to wear before and after lunch; and the grand finale featuring twenty ball gowns, which were modelled with priceless jewelled tiaras. *Country Life's* review of the show (7 April 1960) noted, with particular reference to Britain's speciality eveningwear, that 'International high fashion these may not have been, but traditional British they were – and very pretty.' In total 132 models were shown, 88 of which were made from British fabrics.

London's couture houses continued to operate on a relatively small scale throughout the 1960s, presenting around sixty models each season, while the Paris houses showed some 200. Other high-profile shows were staged at prestigious venues, including St James's Palace and Lancaster House, and inroads were made into the American market through touring fashion shows. In spite of these initiatives, the demand for *haute couture* clothing gradually declined and the clientele largely consisted of older women. Many wealthy young women were not prepared to undertake the lengthy fittings necessary for the creation of a perfectly fitted garment. Instead, they chose more ephemeral, ready-made, top-level fashion boutique clothing for its innovative styling.

The Parisian *haute couture* houses also witnessed a decline in private customers, although store buyers, who purchased *toiles* (patterns in calico) for authorized copying, became major clients. From the 1960s Parisian designers became more reliant upon the commercial feedback from their ready-to-wear collections and from the goods they designed under licence. The *haute couture* shows became glamorous but loss-making advertising platforms, from which top designers could gain publicity and market their more lucrative perfume and ready-to-wear spin-offs. As British fashion designers have never enjoyed the same degree of backing and rarely gained the international stature of the French, few have been in a position to set up similar large-scale operations.

In 1965 Norman Hartnell introduced his 'Special Collection', in response to the changing times. This was a mid-price range which bridged the gap between *haute couture* and ready-to-wear. Costing between twenty and sixty guineas, models were made to order to the client's nearest stock size. Initially the main seams were left unsewn, which was a cost-saving ploy, requiring just one fitting. John Cavanagh, who opened his London house in 1952, had introduced a similar collection which he called 'boutique-couture', in 1959. By the mid-1960s he was describing this range as, 'Too cool for kookie, too current for couture.'[10] In 1966 he ceased working in *haute couture*, in order to focus upon his boutique-couture and ready-to-wear lines.

The new 'swinging' force in British fashion greatly affected the top-level model houses. Fashion journalist Alison Adburgham recalled how,

> Even the long-established members of the London Fashion House Group were shaken by the kooky explosion. Indeed, one could say that the Group was fatally undermined, for in its London Fashion Week presentation to overseas buyers in May 1964, their collections fell between two styles: the one style stemming from the couture culture; the other influenced by the new kooky culture.[11]

In 1965 the group disbanded. Some members turned to the new fashions for the young, while others continued to cater for those still wanting establishment clothing. Inc. Soc., which had performed a valiant role in promoting domestic fashion, had gradually petered out during the early 1960s.

By the end of the decade many houses had closed or diversified into ready-to-wear, and ceased trading in *haute couture*. Those remaining continued to serve their established market and were largely uninfluenced by the youth revolution. In contrast, Parisian couturiers André Courrèges, Paco Rabanne and Pierre Cardin fully embraced modernity. Their sources of inspiration included the futuristic clothing and materials worn by astronauts, contemporary art and Left Bank influences.

Between 1955 and 1966 British high fashion had divided into two distinctive areas. The most exclusive *haute couturiers* catered for the continued demand for stylish but never *outré* tailored daywear and luxurious evening gowns. Meanwhile, the more iconoclastic designers, often trained in art schools, consolidated their role within British industry.

FASHION TEXTILES

With industrialization textiles became Britain's largest industry and a major source of export revenue, but by the 1890s it was clearly in decline. Reluctance to progress from traditional designs and invest in creative skills partly accounted for this, as did the failure to keep up with technological developments and recessionary factors. Relations between British textile manufacturers – sited in the industrial North, Midlands and Scotland – and London-based fashion designers have often been strained. Many British fashion designers have sourced their fabrics abroad because the home textile manufacturers have focused their efforts on producing a traditional product, paying little attention to the vicissitudes of international fashion. These high-quality fabrics – in weaves such as classic tartans, pinstripes and checks – do come to fashion's forefront periodically, however.

In France, and in Italy since the mid-1970s, textile manufacturers have entered into productive relationships with fashion designers, which bring glamorous showcases for their product and lucrative business arrangements. This has been the exception rather than the rule in Britain. Since the late 1980s domestic designers have bought just 35 per cent of their fabrics and 55 per cent of yarns from British manufacturers, importing 20 per cent of their fabrics in France and 25 per cent from Italy.[12] The small-scale nature of the domestic industry means that designers are not in a strong position to specify design requirements and negotiate advantageous deals with textile manufacturers.

With few exceptions, it is in the field of classic fabrics and colourings, rather than high fashion, that British textile manufacturers have excelled. The finest wools, from worsted suitings through to tweeds, are central to the revered products of Britain's most exclusive tailoring establishments, as well as serving international fashion demands. Although traditional high-quality British wools remain highly desirable, many mills have struggled to survive in the post-war period. While the International Wool Secretariat, founded in 1937, did much to elevate the status of woollen fabrics in a high-fashion con-

text, British textile manufacturers have remained notoriously reluctant to produce small runs of high-fashion fabrics.

Linton Tweeds, based in Cumberland, stand out for their responsive approach to the constantly changing demands of high-fashion designers. Since the late 1920s they have sustained a fruitful relationship with the House of Chanel and helped fund the launch of Hardy Amies' couture house. They continue to be innovative in their use of colour, yarn and weight of cloth.

Harris Tweed, which is produced in the western isles of Lewis and Harris in Scotland, has successfully exploited tradition and modernity in order to retain their existing client base and attract the more extreme end of the fashion market. In 1982 they pledged support to Vivienne Westwood, who incorporates their name into her innovative garments. Harris Tweed have thus acquired a 'double-edged' international market appeal. None the less in 1996 only two Harris Tweed producers remain: Donald MacLeod and Kenneth MacLeod.

Small mills, such as the one opened in Galashiels by Yugoslavian emigré Bernat Klein in 1951, were exceptional. Klein studied textile technology at Leeds University, and worked in a Lancashire cotton mill and then as designer for a top Scottish woollen mill before setting up on his own. Inspired by the Impressionist and Cubist schools of painting, Klein took nature as the inspiration for his own paintings. They were the starting-point for his distinctive woven textiles in rich jewel colours which were made for the couture market. Klein's geometric velvet tweed, introduced in 1964 with its velvet ribbon warp crossed with wool or mohair wefts, and his textured multi-coloured tweeds found favour with top designers (plate 3).

While domestic wools have been used extensively, Britain's couture houses have traditionally found it difficult to source UK textiles for their luxurious, romantic evening wear. Britain's once-thriving silk industry was no longer in the vanguard. France and Italy took the lead in the production of top-quality silks with fashionable designs. However, two British companies stand out for their influential couture-level fashion textiles in the early post-war period: Sekers and Ascher.

With government aid, Hungarian emigré Nicholas 'Miki' Sekers founded his West Cumberland Silk Mills in 1938. Sekers became renowned for their exquisite woven silks, which were used extensively by British couturiers as well as by top French and Italian houses including Dior, Balenciaga and Capucci. In July 1959 Sekers held an exhibition in London of their acclaimed range of textiles, designed by artists and designers including Graham Sutherland, Cecil Beaton and Oliver Messel. Public relations for Sekers and for Bernat Klein were ably managed by Peter Hope-Lumley, who had direct links with the London couture houses since he, then as now, managed public relations for Hardy Amies.

Ascher Ltd was established by Zika and Lida Ascher in 1942. In their first year of trading Lida's designs were spotted by Molyneux, who subsequently became a loyal client. In 1943 Zika Ascher commissioned British sculptor Henry Moore to design a range of textiles. In 1946 he extended his repertoire to include international artists, theatrical designers, sculptors and graphic designers, including such prestigious figures as Henri Matisse, Ben Nicholson and Feliks Topolski, to design limited editions of screen-printed silk headscarves as well as dress prints (plate 4). Ascher also excelled in woven fabrics. The shaggy mohair textiles so central to fashion during the 1950s and '60s were an Ascher speciality. When Ascher instructed Scottish weavers to combine mohair with nylon for strength, and dyed it in neon colours, it became a top international fashion fabric. This trio of emigré textile entrepreneurs with a broad artistic awareness established new standards for British fashion textiles.

It is significant that Ascher and Sekers commissioned artists and 'non-textile' designers to create textile designs. In spite of endeavours by government bodies to unite art and industry, the British textile industry was blighted by the emphasis on encouraging designers to copy rather than create and this approach was paralleled in the fashion industry. Art schools were to play a major role in training professional textile designers to work in a truly creative capacity. However, it was not until the early 1960s that textile courses, which had traditionally focused upon furnishing fabrics, also started to embrace fashion textiles. Since this period Britain has experienced a flowering of printed fashion textile talents, with celebrated designers and teams including Bernard Nevill, Celia Birtwell, Zandra Rhodes, Susan Collier and Sarah Campbell, The Cloth, English Eccentrics, Timney Fowler and Georgina von Etzdorf.

In the post-war period the British Cotton Board continued to promote cotton with enormous panache, though it had to cope with an industry suffering from an influx of cheap imports. Attempts had been made to elevate the status of cotton in the 1930s but it was not until the 1950s that it fully shed its prosaic 'washtub' image and entered the repertoire of high fashion. Horrockses Fashions' top-quality printed cotton frocks, with overblown floral designs, were quintessential British fashion statements.

From the 1950s Irish fashion designers started to gain an international reputation for the cut of their clothes, which often exploited linen fabrics. Based in the Republic of

Ireland, Sybil Connolly, who opened in 1957, was particularly successful in this respect, reviving pleated handkerchief linen and other traditional Irish fabrics. Through the 1960s and '70s crease-resistant linen-mix fabrics were developed. In the early 1980s the Italian-led vogue for softly tailored, crumpled linens resulted in an international demand for 100 per cent natural linen. Today, there is a worldwide fashion demand for Irish linen and Irish designer Paul Costelloe consistently promotes this fabric.

In spite of the massive strides made in the development of synthetic fibres since 1945, top-level fashion designers have continued to use natural silks, wools, linens and cottons. Fabrics such as Orlon, Dacron and Terylene predominantly fed the mass market. Though manufacturers have employed top designers to endorse their products in lavish campaigns, only rarely do these fabrics dominate collections. In the 1960s plastics, including PVC and synthetic suitings, enjoyed a brief vogue among leading British fashion designers including Mary Quant, Clive and John Bates. Since the heightened awareness of ecological issues, however, synthetics made from irreplaceable fossil fuels have been blighted for not being 'green'.

Lycra, developed in the USA by Du Pont in 1959 but not extensively used until the late 1970s, has been exploited at all market levels on an international basis.

LEFT:
PLATE 4. Ascher dress fabric, designed by Cecil Beaton, 1945-48. Screen printed black flowers on white silk crêpe. (T.145-1988.) Reproduced courtesy of Ascher Studio, ©Peter Ascher.

Combined with natural fibres to provide greater elasticity for fashion clothing, it has facilitated the introduction of stretch tailoring as well as providing a great boon to sportswear. The marketing of recent synthetic fibres stresses their similarity to natural fibres, and significant strides have been made. Fibres such Supplex and Tactel (both nylon) and Coolmax (polyester), all manufactured by Du Pont, are now hydrophilic, enabling them to 'breathe'. The innovative Tencel, manufactured by Courtaulds, replicates the feel and appearance of natural silk. Helen Storey and Katharine Hamnett have recognized its high-fashion appeal, and it has revolutionized middle-level ready-to-wear.

TRADITIONS REVISITED

By 1967 the optimism engendered by the 'Swinging Sixties' was beginning to evaporate. The following decade was characterized by social fragmentation, economic decline and general disenchantment. Social inequalities and the marginalization of large sections of soci-

ABOVE:
PLATE 6. Detail of Ossie Clark coat and dress, 1970-71. Cream rayon crêpe with red-and-black flower print, chiffon inserts. Print by Celia Birtwell. Worn and given by Miss Pauline Vogelpoel. (T.148 & A-1983.)

ety resulted in the higher profile of feminism, gay politics and black pride. Many areas of production were enriched by designers who reflected, rebelled against and retreated from these circumstances.

Critics argued that obsolescence, which had fuelled the boom, was morally reprehensible and that consumerism and big business were to blame for the state of the economy and damage to the environment. Among the fashion casualties of the recession were many boutiques and young designers, who lacked the necessary backing and survival skills. A return to the values of traditional crafts was presented as desirable. Many fashion designers looked to the past and to non-industrial cultures for inspiration and there was a revived interest in hand-decorated textiles.

London's position as a world fashion leader was again eclipsed by Paris and, from the late 1970s, by Milan. During the 1950s Florence and Rome became leading forces in high fashion, aided by a weak currency, government support and a highly sophisticated textile industry. By the late 1970s Milan was all-important. With admirable organization and speed, Italian designers became major international players, carving for themselves a niche for overtly glamorous eveningwear, understated and relaxed tailoring and use of innovative Italian textiles.

In the early 1970s the role of international *haute couture* was much debated within fashion circles. In London the long-standing and highly successful houses of Norman Hartnell, Lachasse and Hardy Amies continued to serve their established clientele. But Clive and Michael closed in 1971 (plate 5), Mattli and Worth (London) closed during the early 1970s and John Cavanagh ceased trading in 1974. However, a new school of couturiers had become established. Starting her business in 1953, Belinda Bellville had become, with partner David Sassoon, highly successful. Murray Arbeid, Franka and Victor Edelstein had also established significant roles in British *haute couture*. Some designers, including Zandra Rhodes, also offered a couture service alongside their ready-to-wear line.

During the late 1960s and early '70s, British ready-to-wear fashion was led by a few top names, notably Gina Fratini, Bill Gibb, Thea Porter, John Bates, Ossie Clark and Zandra Rhodes. Their work was united by an emphasis on decorative textiles and a penchant for fantasy and escapism. Ossie Clark addressed modernity as well as nostalgia. In 1965 he had utilized bold monochrome op art printed textiles. By the later 1960s, his fashion mood was decidedly romantic. Ossie Clark's evening dresses, in slinky as well as fluid designs made from the printed, stylized floral crêpe and chiffon textiles designed by his wife Celia Birtwell, received great acclaim (plate 6).

Unlike many designers working at this time, Yuki, who became celebrated for his fluid draped jersey garments, embraced developments in synthetic fibres and assiduously avoided period revival styles.

In 1970 the British Knitting and Clothing Export Council (BKCEC) became the umbrella organization for the British fashion and clothing industry. In 1973 Princess Anne bypassed the couture houses and went to Susan Small, a top-level model house, for her wedding dress. Chief designer Maureen Baker designed an understated dress for the Princess in a special silk commissioned from Stephen Walters & Sons. The focus of the British collections, which had traditionally been dominated by the couture shows each January and July, shifted to the ready-to-wear collections, staged in March and October.

The London Designer Collections Association (LDC) was founded by Annette Worsley-Taylor in 1974, and was run on a co-operative basis. With funding from the BKCEC, the group staged an exhibition, 'New Wave', at the Ritz Hotel. The following year, as a cost-saving measure due to the withdrawal of this funding, the designer level of the industry proposed showing its work alongside that of the mass-market sector. This prompted Worsley-Taylor to organize a breakaway group of the designer members of the LDC, to show their work in a more exclusive hotel setting. The London Designer Collections became a powerful force in British fashion, providing an information service for members, hosting receptions and producing a bi-annual catalogue.

Jean Muir was an articulate and vocal supporter of the British fashion industry and, indeed, she became its unofficial spokeswoman. She described herself as a dressmaker and was emphatic that her profession was a trade and a craft, rather than art. Jean Muir was self-trained, a natural technician and creator, who combined a rare talent for tailoring and draping fabrics. She worked within the industry before establishing her own company, with her husband Harry Leuckert, in 1966. Jean Muir's clothes were instantly recognizable. They were precision-cut, always elegant, eminently wearable and at the same time authoritative. Hallmark fabrics were jerseys, crêpes, supple suedes and leathers. These were dyed into subtle colourings and, her standard issue, navy blue and black. Rows of top stitching, decorative cut-work and exquisite trimmings, often especially commissioned from craftspeople, accented immaculately executed garments (plate 7).

Britain's staple classic clothing companies, such as Burberry (founded 1856), Aquascutum (founded 1851), Jaeger (founded early 1880s) and Pringle

BELOW:
FIG. 8. Jean Muir ink-drawing of a dress with fabric swatch for her spring 1975 collection. (E134-1978.)

JEAN MUIR
LONDON

ABOVE:
PLATE 7. Detail
of Jean Muir
suit, autumn/
winter 1995.
Midnight-
blue wool
barathea.
Given by Mr
H. Leuckert
on behalf of
Jean Muir
Ltd. (T.217:
1&2-1996.)

(founded 1815) had long enjoyed international success. They attracted an even wider clientele with shrewd marketing campaigns, which emphasized the traditional qualities and fashionable validity of their products. In so doing, they appealed to a much broader age group. The uncertainty of recession encouraged the investment in reliable, time-honoured clothes. In high-quality fabrics with excellent finish, such garments provide good value for money and embody British understatement.

Many young British designers re-worked traditional country and sporting classics for the fashion market. Margaret Howell, Arabella Pollen and Sheridan Barnett were among those who excelled in this field. At high-street level, Laura Ashley exploited the British love of country life, designing garments in floral sprigged cottons, based on Edwardian summer dresses, and gardening smocks.

Many hand-crafted textile techniques, knitting especially, were revived and brought to the forefront of fashion. Scottish knitwear led the world with perennial designs such as Fair Isle and argyll. Pringle introduced the twinset in the 1930s. These designs have been widely used in classic and more unconventional fashions in the post-war period. From the late 1960s a new generation of hand knitwear designers, such as Edina & Lena, Kaffe Fassett and Patricia Roberts, introduced exciting new approaches to colour, pattern and texture. Machine and hand knitwear became a staple of the British collections and designers, including Bill Gibb, introduced their own ranges. Martin Kidman's hand knits decorated with cherubs for Joseph in spring/summer 1986 were highly influential (plate 8). In the 1990s designers with as diverse an output as Bella Freud, renowned for her saucy, tailored knits, and Shirin Guild, who produces enveloping square garments in luxurious yarns, continue this tradition.

Since the late 1970s New York has become a leading international fashion force. In the years following the war, American designers established their pre-eminence in the field of sportswear and this was brought to the fore with the vogue for health and fitness. American designers have also excelled in the design of professional workwear and leisure clothes, which sometimes derive inspiration from British aristocratic country life and classic garments. American designers quickly adapted from being individual designers to commercial directors of massive diffusion organizations. New York now boasts the highest international sales of designer and diffusion lines.

Punk emerged on the streets of London in the mid-1970s and did much to revive Britain's reputation as a leader of youth style. It also exerted a profound influence upon many areas of cultural production. In terms of high fashion, a number of young fashion designers exploited confrontational Punk devices, but it had little influence upon the very top end of the British fashion market. In complete contrast, the late 1960s and '70s was a period in which Britain fully exploited the romantic and classic *style anglaise* and this was picked up by designers working abroad.

BRITISH FASHION TODAY

During the boom years of the mid-1980s the international couture industry enjoyed a revival, largely due to the strength of the American dollar and the advent of a new, oil-rich Middle Eastern clientele. For a wealthy coterie, social life was global and, as always, high fashion clothing announced social standing. The vogue for lavish charity galas provided a platform for unabashed conspicuous consumption. *Haute couture* clients numbered some 3,000 worldwide – in the late 1940s there had been around 15,000 – but none the less this was a significant upturn in fortunes for the industry.

London's most exclusive fashion houses received a fillip from the patronage of Lady Diana Spencer, who chose David and Elizabeth Emmanuel to design the wedding dress for her marriage to Prince Charles in 1981. As the Princess of Wales, she became a high-profile international fashion icon, wearing clothes by Jasper Conran, Bruce Oldfield, Arabella Pollen, Amanda Wakeley, Bellville Sassoon and Catherine Walker. At a time when the other fashion capitals were specializing in overt glamour, Britain's top-level designers focused upon their speciality, that is classic, understated tailoring and fairy-tale eveningwear.

In complete contrast to European and American output, a second generation of Japanese fashion designers shocked audiences with their dramatic new fashion vision. Oversize, often asymmetric, black and ink-blue garments were sometimes creased and slashed, with irregularly placed necks and sleeves. The Japanese did not propose Tokyo as a new fashion centre, instead they went to Paris, the traditional fashion capital, where they combined their flair for design with great showmanship.

Since the early 1980s London has also enjoyed a burgeoning of young fashion talents. Georgina Godley, Scott Crolla and John Galliano have played a key role in regenerating London's reputation for innovative and challenging collections. Many young designers obtained massive, although sometimes short-lived, media coverage, and did much to put London at the very centre of the fashion map. A number of these designers were successful, but many have foundered because they were naïve in business or failed to obtain financial backing. Stevie Stewart and David Hollah, the design duo behind the Body Map label, enjoyed early acclaim for their unstructured, layered monochrome and day-glo-coloured printed jersey garments. For a time they went out of business because they could not obtain funding, in spite of full order books. It is often said that the British have great affection for highly creative 'amateurism'. In the case of fashion, it rarely stretches to financing ideas and turning them into viable businesses.

RIGHT:
PLATE 8. Detail of Martin Kidman for Joseph Tricot jumper, autumn/winter 1987. Cherub design, hand-knitted wool with metallic yarns. Given by Mr Martin Kidman on behalf of Joseph Tricot. (T.210A-1990.)

Many art school trained designers felt disillusioned and betrayed by a government that had paid to train them, but then failed to sustain them during their fledgling years. Some criticized the art schools for developing skills inappropriate to the requirements of the domestic industry, for stressing creativity and intellectualism over technique and commercial reality. Unable to find work in Britain, fashion graduates have often taken their talents abroad. Those that remain have been condemned for setting up in business straight from college. The fact is that the small scale of the domestic, designer-level industry has rendered it unable to absorb the ever-escalating number of fashion graduates.

In a culture that prizes creative skills more highly than technical expertise, it is not surprising that the larger-scale clothing industry holds little appeal for budding designers. However, it is this sector that dominates the British market. In 1989 clothing bought from chain stores accounted for some 75 per cent of British expenditure on clothes, compared with 50 per cent in Germany and France and just 25 per cent in Italy.[13] While the British spend only marginally less on clothing than other Europeans, their expenditure on designer-level clothing is significantly lower.

Naturally, UK manufacturing industry has become geared towards these conditions and is reluctant to accommodate demands for small-scale high-quality fashion clothing. Some designers have been compelled to manufacture in-house, which in the light of the industry's peaks and troughs significantly increases overheads. Others have gone abroad to have their clothes made up. Since the early 1980s, some of Britain's most successful designers have shown their collections in Paris and Milan, where they benefit from a sophisticated media and communications network.

Vivienne Westwood has possibly exploited Britishness more than any other designer, combining traditional techniques and materials with modernity and wit. She started her career as a teacher and was self-trained as a designer. From 1971, with partner Malcolm McLaren, she created top-level subcultural and streetstyle clothing and was central in determining the hard-edged iconography of Punk. Subsequently her collections became softer and more romantic. In 1983 she started to work under her own name and established a more exclusive fashion identity, based on re-working historical styles in a contemporary idiom. She shows her women's collections in Paris and her menswear in Milan. Vivienne Westwood has consistently embraced concepts of the British monarchy, aristocratic and popular culture in the design and presentation of her work. She deliberately makes reference to that which is quintessentially British, such as public school uniforms (plate 9), tartan fabrics and teatime. She has revolutionized traditional areas of British expertise in tailoring and romantic eveningwear.

In 1983 the British Fashion Council (BFC) was formed as the umbrella organization for the designer-level industry and took responsibility for London Fashion Week. A year later they inaugurated the British Designer of the Year Awards, won by Katharine Hamnett in 1984, Betty Jackson (1985), Jasper Conran (1986), John Galliano (1987, 1994 and 1995), Rifat Ozbek (1988 and 1992), Workers for Freedom (1989), Vivienne Westwood (1990 and 1991), John Rocha in 1993 and Alexander McQueen in 1996.

In 1990 the BFC, with financial assistance from the Department of Trade and Industry, invited Kurt Salmon Associates to undertake the most detailed analysis of the industry to date. The BFC kindly granted permission for the findings of this report, *A Survey of the UK Designer Fashion Industry*, to be cited here and has confirmed that with the exception of export figures, which have improved during the mid-1990s, the statistics accumulated in 1989 were also representative in spring 1996.

The survey revealed that the designer-level trade represents just 2.6 per cent of the value of the UK clothing industry output at wholesale and provides employment for 1 per cent (some 200,000 people) of the UK clothing industry workforce, with 80 per cent of garments made in the UK and 35 per cent of fabrics bought from the UK. In 1989, direct sales of British designer clothes amounted to £60 million, in comparison to France (£200m), Italy (£550m) and America (£200m). Total sales of designer and diffusion ranges in Britain came to £265 million. In contrast, France had sales of £1,400m,

RIGHT:
PLATE 9.
Vivienne
Westwood
blazer, 1986.
Striped wool,
Crini
Collection.
Tie, striped,
designer
unknown.
Given by Mr
David Barber
and worn by
Rupert
Michael
Dolan. (T.247-
1991; T.248-
1991.)

Italy £1,850m and the USA £3,500m. The newly expanding German market had sales of £50m and £880m respectively. In Britain the domestic market accounted for 35 per cent of sales, with major export markets being Italy (14 per cent), Japan (16 per cent), USA (12 per cent) and Germany (9 per cent).[14]

In other fashion capitals the designer industry is heavily capitalized and has developed a highly sophisticated network of licensing and retail opportunities. Bruce Oldfield stated in 1991 that in Paris, Milan and New York 'you know perfectly well the designer is making his real money from diffusion clothes, perfume or whatever. But when you see the clothes of a British designer on the catwalk you know that it is probably all he has to sell'.[15]

The innate fragmentation of the British fashion industry has led to the formation of a series of effective though short-lived professional organizations. For some reason the British fashion industry has not benefited from the development of an all-encompassing body like the Chambre Syndicale. Such an organization imposes regulations, but it is also empowering.

JOHN **G**ALLIANO

ABOVE:

FIG. 9.
Fashion poster
advertising
John Galliano's
1990 collection.
(E238-1991
Y66C.)

In 1989 the British Couture Collections was formed by a group of top-level designers, including Charles and Patricia Lester, Ian & Marcel, and Yuki, who were disillusioned by their marginalization from the London Designer Collections. They organized their own shows, and other members included Lindka Cierach and Tomasz Starzewski. In 1990 another group, the British Couture Federation, was brought together to represent *haute couture* by Manny Silverman (former Chief Executive of Moss Bros. who had become Executive Chairman of Norman Hartnell in 1987). The first united showing for the British Couture Federation presented collections by Anouska Hempel, Hardy Amies, Norman Hartnell, Lachasse, Victor Edelstein and Franka. In 1991 a group of young, innovative menswear designers – Nick Coleman, John Richmond, Joe Casely Hayford, The Duffer of St George and the Destroy label – formed the Fifth Circle. The designers organized their own exhibitions and bi-annual fashion shows as they felt that other events were not reflecting their direction and image.

British fashion is served by regional organizations as well as national bodies. The Welsh Development Agency provides a pro-active support network for designers born, working or living in Wales. In 1990 it inaugurated the Welsh Fashion Awards as a showcase for local talent and supported winner Lezley George to show, and milliner Alison Tod to exhibit, as part of London Fashion Week in March 1996. The clothing and textile industries in Britain, including designer-level fashion, come under the wing of the Department of Trade and Industry, while craft is represented by the Department of Heritage. The Crafts Council has provided funding for some accessory designers and has occasionally helped fashion designers when the textile element fits their remit.

In recent years the commercial potential of design talents has been increasingly addressed by all levels of the British fashion industry. London Fashion Week and the Graduate Fashion Awards have been supported by a number of laudable key companies, including Vidal Sassoon, Lloyds Bank, Marks & Spencer and British Home Stores, but this needs to be underpinned by a forward-thinking long-term policy for the industry. Documents have been submitted to government ministers outlining possible ways forward.[16]

To survive in today's competitive markets it is necessary for companies to carve themselves a distinctive niche. The employment of highly talented designers achieves this. In the 1990s classic brand-name fashions have successfully re-launched their products within the fashion arena. High-street multiples, such as British Home Stores, have also significantly revamped their image. Marks & Spencer have a long-established tradition of commissioning fashion designers. In 1961 they engaged the talents of leading British fashion designer Michael as a consultant, and have continued this practice with recent liaisons including Tanya Sarne of Ghost and Paul Smith.

In the mid-1990s, British fashion stands alone. In spite of the plurality of contemporary fashion, each season Paris, Milan and New York present identifiable seasonal trends. In contrast, the London collections flaunt individuality. In 1996 the Parisian fashion house, Givenchy, appointed Alexander McQueen to succeed fellow British designer John Galliano to design their collections. The mid-1990s has seen a new wave of highly directional designers trained in art schools: Antonio Berardi, Owen Gaster, Alexander McQueen, Hussein Chalayan, Clements Ribeiro and Pearce Fionda. Established names, who have shown abroad for many seasons, are also starting to return to London. The future for British fashion looks optimistic.

POSTSCRIPT

The end of a century is a time for reflection on the past and preparation for the future. As the twenty-first century approaches, British fashion is enjoying a peak. In the 1920s designers were struggling to establish their role as creators, whereas in recent years Britain's fashion strength has been celebrated for the diverse creative drives of its designers. The combination of modernity and tradition has facilitated the development of an iconography that is peculiar to British fashion. If the industry is to advance into the next century with confidence, it needs to continue to develop the infrastructure that other nations enjoy. Can the brilliance of individuals endlessly sustain an entire industry and art form?

Acknowledgements

I am most grateful for the insights, information and support given by Valerie Mendes, Paul Greenhalgh, Manny Silverman, Tony Glenville, Marion Hume, Bobby Hillson, Professor Lou Taylor, Clinton Silver, Professor Jonathan Woodham, Annette Worsley-Taylor, Mary Bromley, Charles Lester, Peter Hope-Lumley, John Cavanagh, Nikki Rowntree, Ian Griffiths and Mary Bates.

Footnotes

1 Pevsner 1988, p.18. This text is equally applicable to the British people.
2 For example, Coleman, E.A. *The Opulent Era: Fashions of Worth, Doucet and Pingat* (Brooklyn Museum / Thames & Hudson 1990); de Marly, D. *Worth, Father of Haute Couture* (London: Batsford 1980).
3 Hartnell, N. *Silver and Gold* (London: Evans Brothers 1955), p.14.
4 'First Annual Report of the Incorporated Society of London Fashion Designers' (1942), p.8.
5 Becket, M. *Picture Post* (27 September 1947).
6 Amies, H. *Still Here* (London: Weidenfeld & Nicolson 1984), p.64.
7 Council for Art and Industry (1945), p.7.
8 Mary Quant, interview with the author, April 1996.
9 See note 8.
10 *Herald and Express* (26 January 1967).
11 Adburgham, A. '1953 to 1973: A Journalist's View', *Costume* (no.8, 1974), p.5.
12 British Fashion Council (1991), p.24.
13 Pagano, M., Thomson, R. 'How Britain Can Design Rags For Riches', *Independent on Sunday* (10 March 1991).
14 British Fashion Council (1991).
15 See note 13.

16 There have been at least two reports in recent years: *Report on the British Fashion Designer Industry* presented to Mr Eric Forth MP, Parliamentary Under-Secretary of State, by Charles Lester in March 1989, and Annette Worsley-Taylor's *Strategy for the British Fashion Designer Industry* presented to the Department of Trade and Industry in October 1992.

Selected Bibliography

British Fashion Council/Kurt Salmon Associates *Survey of the UK Fashion Designer Industry* (London 1991).
Cannadine, D. *The Decline and Fall of the British Aristocracy* (London: Papermac 1996; first published by Yale University Press 1990).
Colls, R., Dodd, P. *Englishness: Politics and Culture 1880-1920* (London: Croom Helm 1986).
Cook, M., Duncan, P. *The British Social Season* (London: Little Brown & Co./ Royal Mail 1994).
Council for Art and Industry *Design and the Designer in Industry* (London: HMSO 1937).
Council for Art and Industry *Design and the Designer in the Dress Trade* (London: HMSO 1945).
Ewing, E. *History of 20th-Century Fashion* (London: Batsford 1974).
Gloag, J. *The English Tradition in Design* (London: Penguin 1947).
Greenhalgh, P. 'The English Compromise: Modern Design and National Consciousness 1870-1940', from W. Kaplin, ed. *Designing Modernity: The Arts of Reform and Persuasion* (London: Thames & Hudson 1995).
Hewison, R. *Culture and Consensus* (London: Methuen 1995).
Huygen, F. *British Design: Image and Identity* (London: Thames & Hudson 1989).
Pevsner, N. *The Englishness of English Art* (London: Penguin 1988; first published 1956).

Tailoring

MARION HUME

If my shops didn't exist, I would get things made on Savile Row. It is very important, that sense of the hand in something.

(Vivienne Westwood, interview with the author, July 1994)

PREVIOUS
PAGES:
Detail of Tommy
Nutter suit,
1983. Grey wool
chalk-stripe;
shirt, pale grey
cotton; tie,
black-and-white
spot silk. Given
by Mr Tommy
Nutter. (T.10:A-B-
1983. T.11-1983,
T.12-1983.)

Signs of Britain's rich tailoring tradition turn up today in the most unlikely places. A Vivienne Westwood cunningly cut curvy jacket scooped down over corseted breasts; a pair of Alexander McQueen rear-cleavage 'bumpster' trousers; a John Galliano sugar-pink jacket worn over nothing but visible knickers and a suspender belt – all are informed by a heritage which includes Savile Row and one of the earliest tailors of women's daywear, John Redfern. The latest British fashion sensation, Alexander McQueen, served a two-year apprenticeship at Anderson & Sheppard of Savile Row. As a student, John Galliano worked for six months with Row 'revolutionary', Tommy Nutter.

Savile Row is not just a West End street (Savile Row tailors have always had 'sittings' in the streets surrounding it): the term also denotes a level of hand-craftsmanship that has existed for considerably more than 100 years. Despite tailors being situated in the area since the Regency days of renowned dandy Beau Brummel, 'The Row' really started in earnest when the tailor Henry Poole decided he was grand enough to require architect-designed premises to show off his high-class wares. As Richard Walker explores in *The Savile Row Story*, Poole's showroom, decorated with mirrors and sculptures from the Great Exhibition of 1851, soon became the place for gentlemen to while away the time. The very dapper Bertie, Prince of Wales (son of Queen Victoria and Prince Albert), was a dedicated Poole customer.[1] Over the years Henry Poole changed premises, and the original building no longer exists, but there is still a direct family line to the current 'Guv'nor' Angus Cundey, which will be continued by his son Simon.

Other smart tailors soon colonized the area and, despite all manner of threats from rising rents to the frailties of the fashion trade, the heartland of bespoke tailoring remains intact to this day. Its 'brother' street (for it is predominantly, though not exclusively, a male bastion), is Jermyn Street, home of bespoke shirts and of ties.

A parallel tradition in women's tailoring stretches back to John Redfern, who first opened a draper's on the Isle of Wight in the 1850s and has gone down in history as one of the first to tailor daywear, rather than purely equestrian clothes, to the female body. The Redfern business in its heyday had branches in New York, Chicago, London and

LEFT:
PLATE 10. Utility
suit by Digby
Morton, 1942.
Grey herring-
bone wool.
Given by the
Board of Trade.
(T.45:A-B-1942.)

ABOVE:
PLATE 11. Detail
of Utility suit,
1940s. Brown
flecked wool.
Utility shirt/col-
lar, 1941. Blue
stripe cotton.
Tootal tie,
1940s. Printed
cotton. Shirt
and collar given
by Mrs J.
Anderson.
(T.242:A-1981,
T.77-1981, T.77:
B-1981.)

Paris, which customers visited for tailoring 'à l'Anglaise'. But most important was London, where Queen Victoria and Queen Alexandra were customers.

Today the traditions are not only being revisited by the British. American designer Ralph Lauren, who hails from Brooklyn, offered Savile-Row-style pinstripe suits worn over Jermyn-Street-style crisp shirts and ties in his autumn/winter 1996 collection. His twist: the strict, skinny suits, the collars and the ties were worn by women. Tailoring – whether for a man, bespoke and in gaudy bright tweed, from Savile Row's most light-hearted player, Richard James; or for a woman, factory manufactured and in a vanilla crêpe by the young duo, Pearce Fionda – is central to British fashion identity in the late twentieth century. Nowadays tailoring could mean a trouser suit, it could mean a tweed skirt and a jacket, or it could mean a strange siren suit by Alexander McQueen that is missing one sleeve. The choices are legion.

In the 1940s, both hand-crafted and mass-produced tailoring were every bit as important to the British wardrobe as they remain today. But, despite the best efforts of fashion designers to be inventive without wasting precious yardage, choice was extremely limited. Utility tailoring involved a thrifty use of cloth: selvages used as hems, the position of every seam plotted with military precision. The V&A collection houses Utility prototypes from The Incorporated Society of London Fashion Designers (Inc. Soc.), including a woman's three-piece suit of slim wool skirt, neat herringbone jacket and matching blouse (plate 10); and a man's wool suit (plate 11). The woman's suit is a fine response to the government's call for stylish Utility clothing. By utilizing the herringbone stripes vertically and horizontally, pattern is created and wastage minimized.

The man's suit is a more humble piece, and helps to explain the desperation people felt for a change of clothes. But that could not happen until Utility was abolished, rationing lifted, and government-issue 'Demob' suits, which men wore to re-enter civilian life, could at last be relegated to second best. Every feature of this suit has been honed down; there is no waistcoat, no drape. It has an economically made breast pocket and the trousers have no turn-ups, for these were forbidden. The fabric, the interior pockets and waistband of cheapest cotton, all mark this out as Utility. By 1945 Utility clothes embodied a frustration and stagnation in the face of the desire to move on to new lives, in new clothes.

Fashion's spring came not in London but in Paris, with Dior's sensational New Look. Ailsa Garland, editor of *Vogue* from 1960-64, 'started in fashion in the year of the New Look' and recalls, 'I bought my version of the New Look from Dereta, for spring 1948, one year after its introduction in Paris. When I wore it in Regent Street never in my life have I caused more heads to turn. It aroused as much interest as the first mini-skirts'.[2] But in the main, the British fashion silhouette remained that of a tightly furled umbrella. When the effect of the abundant New Look did cross the Channel (other than in parliamentary discussion or music-hall jokes), it was more frequently in romantic eveningwear than in tailored daytime styles.

Not that the effect of Dior could be ignored. British designers drew on it to create clothes which gave the effect of shapely hips and fulsome skirts without all the fabric. A Lachasse suit (plate 12) is a clever riposte to Dior by a nation still under rationing. The front flaps were added on top to exaggerate the effect, and the skirt is cut in five panels, with the back panel formed into six knife pleats to give the effect of fullness. Pleats and peplums were the British solution to change: 'Pleats in every form and for all clothes' said *Vogue* in March 1948. British designer clothes were relying heavily on optical illusion rather than cloth.

From the late 1940s, female fashion was being moved forward principally by Dior and Balenciaga. But in a Britain that was 'gung-ho' with the rather forced optimism engendered by the Festival of Britain, home-grown designers were on good form. In 1951 an optimistic Hardy Amies, who had built his own fashion house from the bombed-out shell of a Savile Row townhouse, offered angular, slender tailoring exaggerated by big pocket flaps and lapels. A year later the New Look influence was clearly represented in a pho-

tograph by Henry Clarke from *Vogue* (March 1952), showing a softly tailored dress by Amies in which an immense gored skirt falls from a deep-pointed bodice yoke and a nipped waist. By this point the 'furled umbrella' and the New Look silhouettes existed simultaneously.

Womenswear had its nostalgic New Look. Menswear found nostalgia in Neo-Edwardian clothes, an upper-class trend which, ironically, was to detonate the first British post-war subculture: that of the Teddy Boys. Before the war young men – whatever their class – dressed like their fathers. Afterwards, some of those with money wanted to hark back to a time when their class really meant something, and so they dressed like their grandfathers in dark suits and white shirts of a pre-1914 formality. They went to Savile Row for elongated single-breasted jackets[3] with narrow sleeves and velvet collars, for slender trousers and frivolous waistcoats. 'Back to Formality' was how *Vogue* captioned Norman Parkinson's well-known backview photograph of three besuited gentlemen in its issue of April 1950.

The look spread from West End to East End and up through the harsher elements of north London. Dubbed the 'Toff's Look', this working-class version became the 'Ted' style (which also absorbed elements of the American zoot suit and cowboy-and-western styling). As Nik Cohn describes in *Today There Are No Gentlemen*, the Teddy Boys were 'the start of…the whole concept of a private teen life style separate from the adult world'.[4]

The Neo-Edwardians of the 1950s soon wanted no part in a look that had shifted so radically in meaning. But what the Teddy Boys added to the look was sex, which in turn would inform the clothes 'posh toffs' wore in the sixties. As Cohn explains:

After one hundred and fifty years of concealment, the Teds brought back flamboyance and preening…the tightness in the thigh and crotch and their rituals of attraction, like the hair-combing in front of women – all of this was in the peacock tradition: direct sexual display…The other great breakthrough was in establishing the working class as the new arbiter of style…the old order was turned upside down.[5]

Savile Row dropped the look like a hot brick, shocked to discover that 'the proletariat could now adopt – and adapt – the styles of their superiors overnight'.[6] It needed, but could not find, an icon, a post-war equivalent of Edward VII or the Duke of Windsor who would encourage gentlemen to wear sartorially suitable attire. Savile Row faced rising labour costs and recruitment difficulties – few lads of apprenticeable age wanted to spend their post-war lives sitting cramped and cross-legged, wielding a needle. Demand was also shrinking as customers were turning to ready-to-wear clothes, their standards raised both by the stringent demands of Utility and the influence of American factory quality.

Plate 13 shows a Neo-Edwardian-style bespoke jacket, single-breasted and in cavalry twill, made 'off the Row' in 1956 by André Cann (pictured as later worn by its owner, Geoffrey Squires, combined with slim-line trousers from the early 1960s). The slightly shaped jacket has broad lapels and flapped pockets set low on the hips, plus a smaller ticket pocket. The back of the jacket flares out to give fullness over the hips with the long vent at the centre adding to this effect.

As the 1950s progressed, the survival of Savile Row's supremacy was not helped by traditional core customers deciding they would rather dress in the Italian style. By the second half of the decade, Brioni of Rome had considerable influence on top-level menswear, while Cecil Gee, responsible for importing American suits just post-war, filled his middle-market shops with Italian styles. The short boxy jacket, which became known as 'the bum-freezer', went with tight, shorter, undeniably sexy trousers (which to the trained eye, Savile

LEFT:
PLATE 13. André Cann jacket, 1954. Brown wool cavalry twill. Jaeger trousers, early 1960s. Grey wool. Tie, early 1960s. Green Terylene. Woollands of Knightsbridge shirt, early 1960s. Pale blue-and-white striped cotton. Worn and given by Mr Geoffrey Squires. (T.897:A-C-1974.)

Row style, looked unspeakably vulgar).

American customers were vitally important to Savile Row. During the war it owed its survival mainly to transatlantic clients who would also help weather the lean 1970s, the fraught 1980s and the 1990s. In the 1950s American clothing exerted a big influence on how British people wanted to dress, but some of the most 'American' of suits, their images preserved today on celluloid, were in fact British. In the Hollywood film *North by Northwest* (1959), Cary Grant's roomy suit was made by Kilgour, French & Stanbury – then, as now, at 8 Savile Row. Deliberately designed to disguise Grant's disproportionately large head, the suit was built out a full inch over each shoulder, making him look the perfect matinée idol. Clark Gable, Gregory Peck, Fred Astaire, Gary Cooper, Douglas Fairbanks, as well as lesser-known Americans charmed by its history and (more particularly) its old-world prices, kept Savile Row alive.

RIGHT:
PLATE 14.
Ronald
Paterson suit,
late 1950s.
Beige-and-brown wool
tweed. Given
by Mrs C.
Nattey and
worn by her
mother.
(T.312:A-1987.)

High-fashion womenswear was not immune to the growing threat of better quality ready-to-wear either. 1954 saw the summer of the flower print suit: 'Big news, closely printed, closely cut', said *Vogue* in March, featuring a version by Hartnell 'where lilies of the valley grow thickly [over the] unusually large stand-up collar, and the high moulded bust and smooth waist'. In the following month's issue, a similarly slim suit in a floral emblazoned cotton piqué appeared, this time by the top-level ready-to-wear manufacturer, Matita. Plate 14 shows a resolutely winter season couture outfit by Ronald Paterson: the chunky two-piece, with its shawl collar, reveals a more boxy silhouette.

It was in the mid-1950s that Mary Quant began to cause a stir by advocating that designer-level fashion could be less élite, and specifically aimed at the youth market. By the 1960s this had made her world-famous.

In 1954 Chanel had returned to the Paris fashion scene. In 1956 Balenciaga unveiled the sack dress (probably more influential than the New Look in real, rather than publicity, terms) and *ingénue* sensation Audrey Hepburn's appearance in the film *Funny Face* in 1957 increased the desire amongst the young to dress like her. By 1958 British tailoring was looking more cosmopolitan. The 'jet age' had begun, and customers of British couture were boarding planes in suits of finer weight cloth and in lighter colours.

The first seeds of the 1960s were being sewn in younger, girlish styles. The silhouette of the carefree 1920s began to return to favour with belts on the hips and hemlines inching up. The barrel silhouette, with its skirt shaped out over the hips and its short

jacket, loose and curving over the back, was also popular. In 1956 a Glasgwegian by the name of John Stephen opened the shop that would lead to the phenomenon of Carnaby Street. Others, including Bill Green of Vince of Newburgh Street, were already playing a part in moving menswear away from the traditional tailor, and indeed from tailoring altogether. A new breed of men were becoming braver in their clothing choices and, as Cohn states, 'narcissism and flirtation and cattiness – all these had become acceptable as male components…skintight pants expressed the change.'[7]

It did not happen in an instant. In 1959, Cecil Beaton took delivery of a navy, single-breasted, two-piece Savile Row suit (now in the V&A collection) made by Sullivan, Williams & Co. of Conduit Street. Conservative of cut, with generous lapels to the jacket and a loose cut to the trousers, it has a silk lining

and a three-button cuff (two of the buttonholes are open, the third 'blind'). Under the right lapel there is a corded silk loop for holding the stem of a rose. But six years later Beaton was tired of Savile Row acting like an ostrich with its head in the sand: 'It is ridiculous that they go on turning out clothes that make men look like characters from P.G. Wodehouse. I'm terribly bored with their styling…Savile Row has got to reorganize itself and…get with it.'[8] By this stage, Beaton was dressed by the modernist Parisian designer Pierre Cardin.

Cardin's most influential design, a collarless boxy jacket, would become famous under another name: as 'the Beatles jacket', worn of course by the 'Fab Four'. In fact, the style reached the group via its fifth member, Stuart Sutcliffe, who died in 1962. While performing in Hamburg in August 1960 Sutcliffe met young photographer Astrid Kirscherr who, having made her own versions of the Cardin jacket for herself and her boyfriend, soon made one for Stuart, her new lover. The other group members, who went to Germany dressed like art school beatniks, ordered similar jackets from showbiz tailor Dougie Millings of Great Pulteney Street soon after their return to England. One of the key looks of 1960s Britain had been born.

This was the time of groovy gear, not just in throw-away Carnaby Street clothes but in tailoring which no longer signalled 'I am a gentleman', but rather 'I am a man', through its emphasis on a tight silhouette and its focus on the crotch. Anthony Corbett's narrow, charcoal-grey wool man's three-piece suit (plate 15) features a high, single-breasted button stance, a waistcoat so skinny it has darts in the back, and low-cut trousers which conceal a curious inner truss (presumably to keep one's shirt inside one's hipsters).

As London was just starting to swing, *Vogue*, in September 1960, pondered the question: 'Couture clothes: Are they worth the money?'. Concluding that they were, Hartnell's fairy-tale ball gowns were recommended, as were Charles Creed for 'the best I ever had' kind of suit, with 'probably the most flawless tailoring in London'; Ronald Paterson and Hardy Amies, respectively, for tweeds and 'having a finger in innumerable pies'; Michael, who *Vogue* notes 'has been called the Balenciaga of London', and John Cavanagh because 'the woman who dresses at Cavanagh buys clothes that stand competition with the best that Paris can produce'. Today, Cavanagh's clothes still stand up to the competition. A flawlessly constructed, cream zibeline single-breasted semi-fitted jacket, with slightly

flared skirt (plate 16) dates from 1963, but labelled Prada or Isaac Mizrahi, it could pass convincingly for *c*.1994.

Mary Quant's grey flannel suit with pie-crust trim (plate 17) is not flawless in construction. But that was not her point. Her clothes sought a new customer, the independent working girl for whom couture was old-fashioned and irrelevant. Fashion in Britain now meant ready-to-wear, although the most steely of the couturiers carried on regardless. Hardy Amies, while he did persuade the Queen into slightly shorter skirts, largely ignored what he described as matchbox shapes from Courrèges and Mary Quant. He and his customers waited for fashion to regain its senses – it was to take about thirty years before high fashion embraced arch elegance again.

While the Beatles were singing 'Love Me Do', not everyone under thirty was aspiring to dress in throwaway clothing. Men's increasing narcissism was bringing about a new mode of dress at street level which would, in turn, 'bubble up' to affect Savile Row tailoring. Nik Cohn described Mod as 'the notion of dressing out of self love rather than rebellion', and in 1964 its own pop icon, Pete Townshend of The Who, was spending £100 a week on clothes.[9] Mod was about pristine and stylistically puritanical dressing (Parka-clad fights with Rockers came later). Its sartorial influences were old Savile Row and America's Ivy League, fused with the boxiness and the narrow trousers of the Italian look.

Television shows like 'Ready, Steady Go' featured movers and shakers in Mod silhouette suits. To be young was to be fashionable, as natty dressers like Beatles manager Brian Epstein, Andrew Loog Lodham, the first manager and record producer of the Rolling Stones, and Ronan O'Rahilly, organizer of Radio Caroline, were to prove. And, to some, tailoring began to spell career possibilities. In the 1960s a lad from the East End could be his own 'Guv'nor'. Doug Hayward built a West End business on clothing ambitious lads who, like him, were migrating from East London. Terence Stamp, Tommy Steele and Michael Caine – the last still a customer – were among his early showbiz clientele, as were younger members of the aristocracy who thought it trendy to go to a tailor who didn't behave like Uriah Heep in the face of a man with an inheritance.

Rupert Lycett Green set up Blades, a business catering for men like himself, public-school educated but who neither wanted to look like their fathers nor dress in the tatty clothes of Carnaby Street. He poached some of Savile Row's customers too, including the Marquess of Londonderry and John Betjeman. New from Blades were tailored suits in fresh, pale colours, which Lycett Green attributed not just to his own grooviness but to

LEFT:
PLATE 16. John Cavanagh suit, 1963. Cream silk zibeline. Worn and given by the Hon. Mrs J.J. Astor. (T.84:A-1974.)

RIGHT:
PLATE 17. Mary Quant suit, design 1962 (re-made 1973). Grey wool flannel. Blouse: white synthetic crêpe. Given by Miss Mary Quant. (T.104:A-B-1976.)

'the clean air act…Only three or four years ago, the air was so dirty you had to change your collar twice a day. But now you can wear a cream coloured suit without worrying about it getting dirty almost at once'. [10] Despite years of searching by Savile Row for a smart royal ambassador, it was Blades who secured the patronage of Patrick, Earl of Lichfield, the Queen's cousin. In the 1960s he was a high-profile peacock who, in his own words was, 'dress[ing] to attract the girls…to be sexy like [a] cock pheasant in the mating season'. [11] Later, however, he did become a Savile Row customer.

Denis Hallbery, then a cutter at Anderson & Sheppard, was generally unimpressed. His work attire was a single-breasted, three-piece suit in Glen Urquhart check (commonly but mistakenly known as Prince of Wales check), made to his precise measurements. Reflecting the fact that Savile Row did not like change at this point, this 1964 suit (plate 18) is more typical of the 1950s. Hallbery cut it out himself, and it was worked on by three specialist tailors for the jacket, trousers and waistcoat. It is highly likely that these specialists also worked on clothes for Hollywood stars. But while the new breed of men's outfitters boasted of their customers, Anderson & Sheppard maintained (and still adheres to) the Savile Row code of client confidentiality and a discreet avoidance of all publicity.

Leslie Charteris, author of *The Saint*, suited his protagonist at Anderson & Sheppard. The first James Bond, Sean Connery, went to Antony Sinclair. The Cold War sixties was the decade of the secret agent, from *The Man from U.N.C.L.E.* and Steed in *The Avengers* to gritty Harry Palmer in *The Ipcress File* (the last more John Collier or Dunn & Co. in his dress than Savile Row). Lethally sharp spy dressing had something to offer, and still does – the current James Bond, Pierce Brosnan, is the most traditionally Savile Row of all the Bonds. Ironically, the production capacity necessitated by the multi-million dollar *Goldeneye*, with all its stunt doubles, walk-on doubles and so on, resulted in costume designer Lindy Hemming having Savile Row style made by Brioni of Rome – the very firm that had shaken up Savile Row in the 1950s. The cloth, however, came from Yorkshire.

As Mick Jagger sneered his way through the hit song 'Satisfaction', the London youthquake was hot news: 'Scarcely a day went by without news of the opening of a new boutique, without a feature on Terence Stamp or Michael Caine or Carnaby Street, without a picture of Jean Shrimpton or a mention of Mick Jagger or decoration hints from David Hicks', writes Christopher Booker in his critique of swinging London, *The Neophiliacs*.[12] Even the traditionalists could no longer ignore the sea change. In September 1965 Austin Reed opened Cue, to attract the young man of the 1960s. Cue offered suitably groovy lower waist bands and tighter arm holes. Jermyn Street was feeling groovy too. In 1962 Turnbull & Asser refused to make a cream-coloured shirt in slubbed silk for David Mlinaric, interior decorator and gentleman of style – yet three years later, the facade of their building had been repainted in the bright gaudy colours of the 1960s.

Eric Lucking, store-display director and man about town, ordered a single-breasted two-piece suit from Bernard Weatherill of Savile Row in 1966. Featuring a slightly shaped waist, covered buttons and curved edges, its highly stylized character is completely in tune with the mid-1960s (plate 19). The stylistic changes that occurred over the next four years are clearly seen in a charcoal wool twill, single-breasted Nehru jacket and trousers by Moss Bros. (plate 20). The suit has a flashy purple lining, a concealed five-button front fastening, fishtail cuffs and trousers so low-slung that they need the feminine detail of darts to stay on.

In 1966 Twiggy was declared 'The Face of the Year' and the shell dress with a 1920s-style low belt, the androgynous trouser suit, and the sporty, skinny zip-front tunic were the things to wear. Much of the influence was French, embracing elements from Courrèges and Chanel. British versions of Courrèges style came in tweeds and checks, and so looked rather different. Jeffrey Wallis's versions of Chanel were already established and sought after. They looked almost identical to the Paris originals. Like Chanel, Wallis used British cloth, and he bought the Paris patterns legitimately.[13]

By 1967 Vern Lambert and Adrian Emmerton's hippie shop in the Chelsea Antiques Market was at last finding men willing to pay for Demob suits, now second-hand, taken in and sold alongside bangles and beads. Michael Fish was very successfully selling fab gear to clients such as David Bailey and Lord Snowdon, while in Portobello Road Ian Fisk flogged off military uniforms (also part of the Savile Row tradition) at his boutique 'I was Lord Kitchener's Valet'.

The late 1960s was not a high point for tailoring, although there has always been a sustained demand for tailored clothes. The V&A houses a slim, hip-length jacket and dress by Michael of Carlos Place, dating from 1968 (see plate 5) with a graphic black-and-white printed silk scarf, which has a smart, rather stark appeal.

On 22 June 1968 the Beatles' record company, Apple, acquired premises at 3 Savile Row and 'Let It Be' was recorded on the roof. Cilla Black announced that she was going into business with 'a very snob tailor's': opening at 35a Savile Row, Tommy Nutter added a plate glass window to the premises.[14] Both his wildly broad lapels (plate 21) and the appearances in the shop of neighbours John, Paul and Ringo (George preferring to wear blue jeans on the cover of the Abbey Road album) drew gasps. John and Yoko got their white wedding suits from Tommy Nutter, where Bianca Jagger also shopped. Suddenly, Savile Row was all the rage, in spite of itself.

In later years Tommy Nutter designed Jack Nicholson's wardrobe for his role in *Batman*, and Bill Wyman's suit for his wedding to Mandy Smith. A suit from 1983 (plate 22) shows both his traditional tailoring skills and his inventiveness; a chalk stripe runs horizontally over jacket, tapered trousers and waistcoat. There is no doubt that Tommy Nutter woke up Savile Row, but nothing could disguise the fact that its supremacy was from another age. Apart from the high-profile trendy customers who caught the headlines the customer base was, literally, dying off, as were the skilled workers. Without the business to go round tailors started merging, or 'sharing sittings'. Perhaps the most successful merger was that of military tailor Gieves teaming up with Hawkes in 1974. Located at 1 Savile Row they combined to make great play of the best address in menswear, and to conquer international markets with everything from ready-to-wear suits to socks.

At the end of the 1960s the archetypal image of the British businessman in a suit was

LEFT:
PLATE 21. Detail of Tommy Nutter suit, c.1969. Mid-blue checked wool. Yves Saint Laurent blouse, c.1969. Cream silk, French. Worn and given by Jill Ritblat. (T.75:1-3-1996, T.76-1996.)

RIGHT:
PLATE 22. Tommy Nutter suit, 1983. Grey wool chalk-stripe. Shirt, pale grey cotton. Tie, black-and-white spot silk. Given by Mr Tommy Nutter. (T.10:A-B-1983, T.11-1983, T.12-1983.)

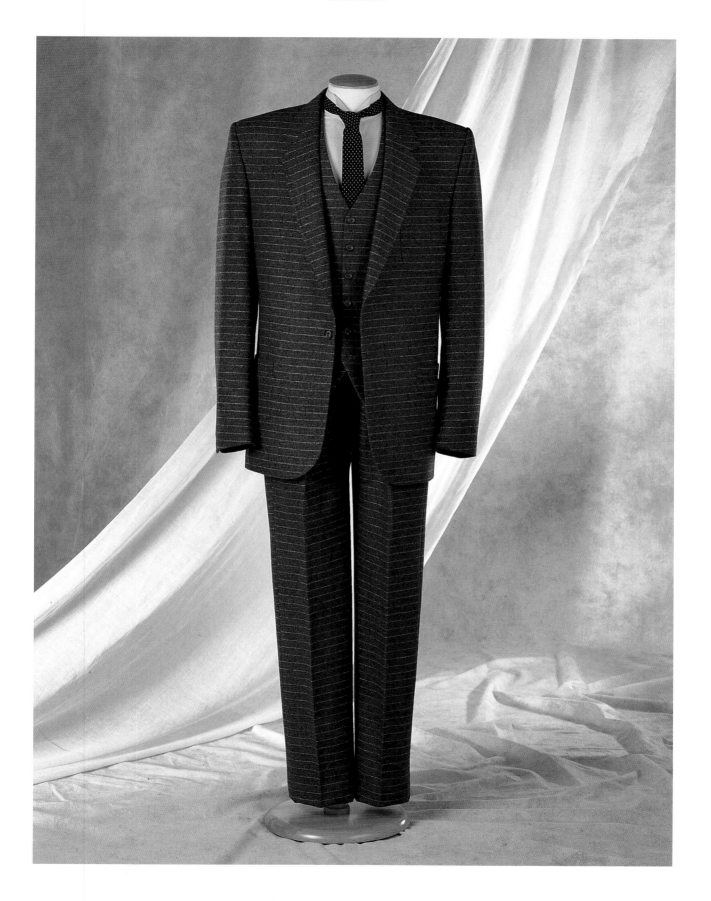

RIGHT:
PLATE 23.
Hardy Amies
suit, 1970s.
Wool tweed
by Bernat
Klein. Given
by
Mrs Gould.
(T.82:1-2-
1992.)

John Cleese, as Monty Python's Minister for Silly Walks. But for Savile Row, faced with terrifying inflation and rent rises that would threaten its historic street, the 1970s saw a fight for survival that was no laughing matter.

The early 1970s witnessed a contrast between traditional elegance and resolutely trendy tailored outfits imbued with nostalgia and appealing to the young and the slim. By now, Hardy Amies had been a designer for almost forty years. His heathery slub two-piece tweed suit (plate 23) features the illusion of a blouse and skirt to minimalize bulk. There is no bulk whatsoever in Biba's black double-breasted pant suit, which is reminis-

cent of the 1940s in its curved shoulder pads (plate 24). The huge lapels, high, long vents, wide trouser waistband and large turn-ups are, however, pure early seventies. By this time Biba was phenomenally popular and had expanded its headquarters on Kensington High Street, where everything was painted purple or black. Customers (and shoplifters) got used to communal fitting rooms and helping themselves from the racks in semi-darkness.

For women on fashion's front line, the tailored items of the 1970s were the tight pant suit and the narrow coat. By the middle of the decade, if fashion had to be summed up in one word, it would be 'jersey'; its shape coming from the stretch of the cloth and rarely involving anything so complicated as a bust dart. The notable exception was Jean Muir, who rather than draping the material tailored it, thus taking the softest of cloth and giving it an almost imperceptible structure and an evident authority. Bella Freud in the 1990s follows a similar idea, making a play of 'soft' tailoring by taking knitwear and moulding it in tight, saucy shapes.

In the second half of the 1970s, when Paris-based Montana & Mugler were embarking on inter-galactic adventures in shoulder pads, Britain was feeling comfy in slacks, shifts, jersey dresses and even ponchos. Meanwhile in Milan, Giorgio Armani was gaining attention for the menswear firm of Cerruti, before going out on his own.

RIGHT:
PLATE 24.
Left: Biba, c.1968-72. Black synthetic gaberdine (jacket only shown; suit has matching flared trousers). Right: Antony Price, 1977-78. Black wool. Biba suit given by Mr Roger Baresel. (T.133:1-1991.) Antony Price suit worn and given by Ms Janine du Plessis. (T.149: 1-2-1996.)

As Savile Row limped on, the excitement (barring what was going on through the plate-glass windows at Tommy Nutter) was elsewhere. John Stephen for one had retained his edge in the 1970s. A suit from this time (plate 25) belonged to the flamboyant hatter David Shilling, who was in his late teens when he sported the low-waisted flared trousers under a navy pinstripe double-breasted jacket with patch pockets, looking curiously androgynous. Also worn by Shilling was the Bugatti suit detailed in plate 26.

Making clothes for men and women, Antony Price was not interested in androgyny: his hallmark in the mid-70s was raw sexiness (as it is today), in clothes that emphasized anatomical differences. In 1972 he had dressed Roxy Music's Bryan Ferry, and his female backing singers, in second-skin, GI-inspired military shirts and trousers – but the boys and girls did not look a bit alike. Similarly, Price's 'bell-boy' suit of tight spencer jacket and multi-pleated trousers was designed for women, and was worn by Janine du Plessis. Price was fusing fashion and music. Meanwhile Vivienne Westwood and Malcolm McLaren were fusing fashion and rebellion, and by 1977 they had been through all manner of guises to

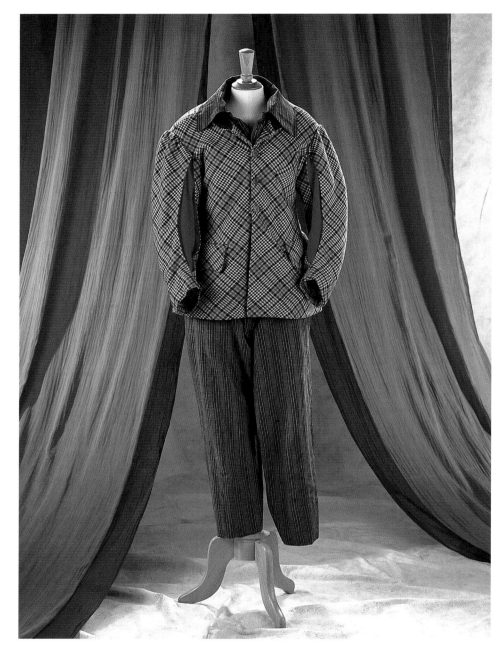

become the official clothiers to punk. Westwood would go on to become perhaps the most significant innovative fashion designer in the tailoring tradition of this half-century.

A fine example of Westwood's tailoring is the brown tweed buccaneer's jacket (plate 27), which features slashed sleeves revealing a red embroidered silk lining. The slashed effect, influenced by 17th-century clothing, shows Westwood's fascination with historical dress as well as with modern design. Looking backwards as well as forwards, pieces like her slash-and-burn anti-establishment punk repertoire, as well as her latest and much more prim collections for men and women (for she has always done both), represent her work. She is imbued with British tradition and its techniques. As she herself explains, 'the technique comes first. That's why I never dry up for ideas, because when you master a technique, self expression is automatic'.[15]

LEFT:
PLATE 28.
Pearce Fionda
suit, autumn/
winter 1996.
Vanilla acetate,
rayon crêpe.
Given by Mr
Reynold Pearce
and Mr Andrew
Fionda. (T.431:
1-2-1996.)

Second-hand baggy, tweedy clothes such as hacking jackets, trousers with braces, and flat caps were adapted in the 1970s to form unstructured, roomy pieces in designer collections. In America, the look was paralleled by the movie *Annie Hall* (1977) in which Diane Keaton wore her own mix of Ralph Lauren's American-meets-old-English inspired clothes. Britain found its home-grown versions in the town-and-country clothes of Margaret Howell, Sheridan Barnett, Paul Costelloe and Betty Jackson. Also notable at the end of the 1970s were the clothes of Adrian Cartmell, whose crisp, clean lines are mirrored in Pearce Fionda's tailoring today. The latter duo's work, represented by a vanilla crêpe shirt jacket and boot trousers (plate 28), display an international sophistication.

In 1974 Paul Smith had opened his first, windowless, shop in Nottingham; five years later he came to London's Covent Garden. According to Dylan Jones in *True Brit, Paul*

Smith, 'He wasn't Savile Row and he wasn't Camden Market; he wasn't Kings Road and he certainly wasn't Oxford Street…it didn't take long before the rest of London took notice'. Describing Smith's creation of the Paul Smith man, Jones continues:

> Classic with a twist – the words were to creep into every Paul Smith profile for the next decade. In 1982 Suzy Menkes was to write of his first Paris show, 'Paul Smith has the foresight and the dogged determination to make what I have always longed to see: the great classics of British menswear reinterpreted in a modern idiom'.[16]

1980s Britain is typified as the decade of desire and gratification, of Dockland apartments, of filofaxes, and of Armani suits. From their floral boxer shorts to their wide City suits, Paul Smith clothed managing directors and advertising art directors. The Smith suit shown in plate 29 is a powerful carapace for a 'corporate raider'. However, many of the stylistic innovations pushing menswear forward were coming from Milan. In 1988 the Federation of Merchant Tailors (since disbanded) celebrated its centenary on Savile Row: the event was marked by an open day on which many in the Row shut their doors and the public was largely uninterested.

One media view of British fashion at the time was the necessarily sharp and 'camera-ready' look epitomized by Diana, Princess of Wales. Despite her title she somehow seemed less remote than high fashion, and so brought the clothes of designers to the masses. Although many 1980s clothes were loose and fluid – the most radical of these coming from Japanese designers such as Rei Kawakubo of Comme des Garçons and Yohji Yamamoto – 1980s women tend to be thought of in 'executive dress'. The British players were Alistair Blair, Jasper Conran, Roland Klein and Caroline Charles (plate 30). Arabella Pollen's success (lamentably followed by a 1990s decline) was based on her knowledge of clothes for Britain's social season combined with her desire to pep things up a bit. The Princess of Wales was a fan. Eveningwear was tailored too, thanks in particular to Jasper Conran and Catherine Walker. The Princess also wore a jewel-bright turquoise tailored suit by Rifat Ozbek.

Ending with women worshipping the ease of black and navy, the 1980s was a decade with great moments of high colour. In a memorable sequence of photographs in *Vogue* (August 1986), the model Yasmin Le Bon stops traffic in a pumpkin-coloured seamed, full-skirted coat of wool jersey. The surprise is that it is by the high priestess of black and navy, Jean Muir. The quietly elegant midnight-blue barathea, eight button, double-breasted jacket and straight skirt finishing just above the knee (plate 31) is from Jean

LEFT:
PLATE 29. Paul Smith suit, 1988. Navy wool pinstripe. Shirt, white cotton. Belt, black leather, as before. (T.3:A-C-1988.)

RIGHT:
PLATE 30. Caroline Charles ensemble, 1989. Jacket, orange wool crêpe. Trousers, black wool crêpe. Scarf, orange-and-black stripe wool crêpe. Given by Miss Caroline Charles. (T.249:A-B-1989.)

ABOVE:
PLATE 31. Jean
Muir suit,
autumn/
winter 1995.
Midnight-blue
wool barathea.
Given by Mr
H. Leuckert on
behalf of Jean
Muir Ltd.
(T.217:1-2-1996.)

Muir's autumn/winter 1995 collection. This was to be her final collection, although the company she founded still continues in her name.

In 1985 a new force in British tailoring emerged, turning sleeves into trousers and jackets into coats that trailed to the knees. John Galliano's first commercial collection merged the traditional dress of western gentlemen with striped Berber trousers. Subsequent pieces have had similar ethnically mixed messages, or have been reworkings of historical pieces; one of Galliano's most successful designs to date is the 1995 dogtooth suit with a slim below-the-knee skirt and padded hips. It would not have been out of place forty years earlier. Galliano's tailoring is informed by international inspiration, although he makes a point of coming home to London on research trips which often include the V&A.

By the beginning of the 1990s fashion had become utterly international. Yet by drawing on its strong tailoring tradition British womenswear continues to retain its own identity. With menswear, the Savile Row tradition is dominant once more now that the fashion pendulum has swung back in favour of British styles. Richard James's suit for the shoemaker Patrick Cox (plate 32) is slender of fit and jaunty of cloth, in bright contrast to Italian offerings.

ABOVE:
PLATE 32.
Richard James
suit, 1994. Blue
overcheck
wool. Shirt,
blue-and-white
cotton. Tie,
blue, white and
black check
silk. Worn and
given by Mr
Patrick Cox.
(T.434:1-4-
1996.)

Today, Savile Row style has in part migrated away from the West End (where rents are too high for most newcomers), to Spitalfields and Soho and beyond. Here, tailors including Ozwald Boateng, Mark Powell, John Pearce, Charlie Allen and Timothy Everest are wooing clients out of their Armani, Comme des Garçons and, indeed, Paul Smith ready-to-wear clothing. Many customers have never experienced bespoke before. There is a renewed interest in the slim suit, as once worn by James Bond and Bianca Jagger. Today's tailors attract women as well as men. As Timothy Everest explains, 'We are men's tailors, but women seek us out as a viable alternative to *haute couture*. The price of a British bespoke trouser suit is much less'.[17]

Yet long after the hubs of other trades have been moved out of the capital's centre, there are still tailors (some of them young) in London's West End. Fashion designers such as Calvin Klein, Ralph Lauren and Isaac Mizrahi, even though they design or have designed their own menswear collections, are attracted by the magic and mystique of Savile Row. Lured by clothing (created with layers of invisible interlinings and canvases and moulded into shape by steaming and pad-stitching) that cannot be replicated by ready-to-wear, clients are also attracted by the historical appeal of the Row. The sight of tailors sitting up on their benches (these days, chairs are provided) used to signal how out-of-touch the establishments were, but is now seen as reassuring and romantic. The rich traditions of Savile Row have now become a marketing tool with which it can try to ensure a future. This future rests in the careful exploitation of a working theme park, while maintaining the privacy that makes it unique.

Acknowledgements

I would like to thank Fiona Anderson for providing me with detailed descriptions and contextual information about items in the V&A collection.

Footnotes

1 Walker (1988), p.46-55.
2 Garland (1970), p.39.
3 Savile Row calls a jacket a 'coat' and a coat an 'over-coat' or 'top coat', but because it does not imply a coat when referring to womenswear, jacket has been used for both sexes here to avoid confusion.
4 Cohn (1971), p.27.
5 Cohn (1971), p.269.
6 Walker (1988), p.109.
7 Cohn (1971), p.282.
8 Walker (1988), p.117.
9 Cohn (1971), p.291 and 294.
10 Fairley (1969), p.120.
11 de Marly (1985), p.135.
12 Booker (1969), p.275.
13 *Vogue*, September 1964.
14 Fairley (1969), p.121.
15 Vivienne Westwood, interview with author, quoted in the US edition of *Vogue*, September 1994.
16 Jones (1996), p.35.
17 Timothy Everest, interview with author, quoted in the US edition of *Vogue*, March 1995.

Bibliography

Amies, Hardy. *Just So Far* (London: Collins 1954).
Amies, Hardy. *The Englishman's Suit* (London: Quartet Books 1994).
Amies, Hardy. *Still Here* (London: Weidenfeld and Nicolson 1984).
Beaton, Cecil. *The Parting Years: Diaries 1963-74* (London: Weidenfeld and Nicolson 1978).
Billson, Anne. *My Name is Michael Caine: A Life in Film*. (London: Muller 1991).
Booker, Christopher. *The Neophiliacs: The Revolution in English life...* (London, Pimlico 1969, 1992).
Byrde, Penelope. *The Male Image: Men's Fashion in Britain 1300-1970* (London, Batsford 1979).
Carter, Ernestine. *With Tongue in Chic* (London: Michael Joseph 1974).
Cohn, Nik. *Today There Are No Gentlemen: The Changes in Englishmen's Dress Since The War* (London: Weidenfeld and Nicolson, 1971).
Creed, Charles. *Maid to Measure* (Norwich: Jarrolds 1961).
Fairley, Roma. *A Bomb in the Collection* (Brighton: Clifton Books 1969).
Garland, Ailsa. *Lion's Share* (London: Michael Joseph 1970).
Giorgetti, Cristina. *Brioni: Fifty Years of Style* (Florence: Octavo 1995).
Jones, Dylan. *Paul Smith, True Brit.* (London: The Design Museum 1996).
de Marly, Diana. *Fashion for Men: An Illustrated History* (London, Batsford 1985).
Scott-James, Anne. *In the Mink* (London: Michael Joseph 1952).
Walker, Richard. *The Savile Row Story: An Illustrated History* (London, Prion 1988).

Romantic

LOU TAYLOR

Yes, tiaras *and*
sparklers…I am absolutely
sure *that* is the dress.

(Hardy Amies, 1960)

After the end of the Second World War London's couture houses continued to provide clothes that met the sartorial requirements of their traditional clients, the upper and upper middle class who made up the top echelon of British society. The couture garments that emerged from the discreet world of Mayfair salons were created in specific response to the demands of the Season and associated events. The social and etiquette systems were still functioning in the 1950s as they had in the days of Queens Victoria, Alexandra and Mary, albeit not as rigorously. The purpose of traditional systems of etiquette had been to erect a protective social barrier around the court, aristocracy and circles of political power in Britain. From the late nineteenth century these circles had merged increasingly with those of industry and business, to form a socially more extensive ruling class that adopted the social and dress etiquette patterns of the old aristocracy.

A woman who moved within Society circles dressed according to a set of complex formalized rules. Recent research has identified such garments as 'both a professional and social uniform' and indicates that wearers had 'to be initiated into the exclusive circle of couture connoisseurship', through introductions to the couture salons and to the etiquette of selecting and wearing the clothes.[1] As the couturier Lucile (Lady Duff-Gordon) explained in her autobiography *Discretions and Indiscretions* (Jarrolds 1932), socially élite Edwardian women changed their ensembles 'five or six times a day'. In the 1940s and '50s, the dress codes that covered every occasion and every time of day were still followed by couture designers, who understood them as well as, if not better than, some of their clientele.

Men too were obliged to dress according to an established sartorial code, although this was free of the seasonal ephemerality of the woman's wardrobe. Equipped with a basic wardrobe consisting of, for example, formal 'white tie' dinner suit, with matching braid-trimmed trousers; a grey frock coat and top hat for garden parties (see plate 35), Ascot and formal weddings; more informal 'black tie' dinner jackets (see plate 36); dark cloth town suits and coats; and a range of brown and lovat-toned country walking and shooting tweeds, a man could, and did, wear the same clothes over many Seasons (provided he kept his figure under control).

The apex of British feminine fashion production was the very specific formalized court dress required for royal and state occasions and made by the best couture houses of Paris and London. The style worn by royalty can be traced back at least to Queen Victoria's Coronation dress of 1837, if not to the symbol-bestrewn state robes of Elizabeth I. Typified by rich embroidery on a cream-coloured satin ground, such dresses feature imperial, colonial, national and royal symbolic motifs in heavy gold and brightly coloured three-dimensional embroidery.

Elizabeth II's Coronation in 1953 created a demand for this type of state dress and focused attention on a traditional Britain of title, rank and privilege apparently untouched by two world wars. The design produced by Norman Hartnell for the Queen's Coronation

dress has been described as the couturier's finest hour. Colin McDowell has commented in the *Daily Mail* (5 November 1992) that this dress 'symbolized the strength of the Commonwealth in its rich sweeping motifs and, even more, symbolized the freshness, youth and hope of the new reign in its ravishingly blended pastel embroidery and precious stones. There is no dress in existence that can compare with it'.[2]

The cultural significance of these garments as examples of a distinctive and unique royal 'social uniform' are clear. No other woman in Britain would dare to wear a dress such as that worn by Elizabeth II in 1957 (plates 33 and 34). This state evening gown is embellished with embroidery representing 'the flowers of France' interspersed with large gold bees, the emblem of Napoleon. The dress, as these designs indicate, was intended as a compliment to the French nation. It was worn in April 1957 during the Queen's state visit to France, for a banquet at the Elysée Palace which was followed by a visit to the Paris Opera. Such a garment is at once recognizably and uniquely 'queenly' attire.

However, while these splendid garments conferred high status and provided much publicity for London couture, the postwar social and economic stresses that were impacting on the old way of life and leisure also began to influence British couture fashion. As historian David Cannadine has said, 'this display of noble pre-eminence was in retrospect more a requiem than a renewal.'[3]

The ramifications of these changes though were not immediately obvious when débutante presentations restarted in 1947 and the Season picked up again. The London Season, which had stopped for the duration of the war, survived the Second World War and a new Labour Government surprisingly well. *Picture Post* commented on 6 August 1955, 'It is over again – the London Season! The Socialists attack it and the debs defend it; the papers religiously report it.' Since Queen Victoria's day the function of the Season was to launch the 17-year-old daughters of the wealthiest five per cent of British society on to an engineered marriage market. *Picture Post* remarked that, 'it takes England and

Débutante at the Photographer's

ABOVE:
FIG.11.
Débutante
at the photo-
grapher's.
Illustration
by Francis
Marshall
from 'London
West', Studio,
1944.

the Summer Season to produce the kind of party called the coming-out ball. Through June and most of July these functions occur nightly (and sometimes clash)…There can be months of planning, weeks of manual labour, nights without sleep…' Many of the private and public events that made up the social round of the Season demanded special occasion evening clothes.

The cost of launching a deb in the 1950s ran from £2,000 to £10,000.[4] Many families were operating the Season on the edge of their incomes. The Duchess of Argyll was reported by Venetia Murray in *Picture Post* as saying: 'If a mother can only afford a small dance, she treats it as a business proposition', sending out restrictive invitations from within her 'own set'.[5] In 1955 she herself, by contrast, gave dinner to 100 guests at Claridge's before the coming-out ball for her daughter, who later became the Duchess of Rutland.[6]

By the late 1950s the final remnants of exclusivity that were left within the system were threatened by the social and cultural changes taking place in Britain. Richard Berens, editor of Hickey's gossip column in the *Daily Express*, believed that the Season 'was becoming overwhelmingly middle class.' By 1957 it was estimated that the numbers participating in the Season had swelled to 1,000,[7] all of whom needed special 'social uniform' clothing. Wearers were still expected to manifest a certain degree of exclusivity in their grandest dinner, cocktail and evening dresses. Above all, ball dresses were an absolute requirement for both mothers and daughters for coming-out balls, the Queen Charlotte's Ball and a range of country weekend, hunt and May balls.

At least three distinctive types of evening dress were produced by the couture and top model houses. The first was the formal, elegant and romantic evening dress for mature women – the deb's mother and her friends. Often strapless, or with narrow shoulder straps, this style usually featured slimmer, or softly flared, full-length skirts. The second style was that of the fresh *ingénue*, for the 17-year-old débutante. The third was the short evening or cocktail dress worn by debs and younger married women. The first two of these styles were based on pre-war sartorial codes; and between them these three distinctive styles of eveningwear provided lucrative and staple orders for London couturiers.

The elegant, mature and romantic type of evening dress, an international style, was made up in plain, clear, brightly coloured or black fabrics, often extravagantly embroidered satins or glinting

BELOW:
PLATE 37. Norman
Hartnell evening
dress, 1953.
Cream satin with
pink beaded flo-
ral motifs. Given
by Mrs Hilde J.
Ross. (T.253-1981.)

ABOVE:

PLATE 38. John Cavanagh evening dress, 1950s. Ivory silk with gold brocade orchid design. Worn and given by Lady Cornwallis. (T.294-1984.)

brocades. In 1937 the new queen's wardrobe included a range of slim and sophisticated embroidered Hartnell evening designs. In May 1938 *Vogue* was already emphasizing the glamour: 'Hartnell signs his name with jewels and sequins'. Post-war examples of this type of British design are in the V&A's collection. Hartnell's cream-coloured satin, strapless evening dress, made in Coronation year, is covered in heavy deep-pink beaded embroidery on the bodice with a finer scattering of beads all over its flared skirt (plate 37). John Cavanagh's late 1950s full-length brocaded evening dress (plate 38) is a perfect, understated model of this type. The chartreuse satin ball dress made in London by Worth in 1967 (plate 39) is a later, full-skirted example. Hardy Amies's slim-skirted pink, grey and black 1961 version of this adultly sexual style, also in the V&A collection, has a dramatic flying side panel of matching pink silk. This elegant look flourishes in the 1990s and has been worn by Princess Diana with much *éclat* over the past ten years. Catherine Walker's long, slim design in black velvet with its pearl-beaded collar (plate 40) is a successful reworking of this style from 1994-95.

A débutante's ball dress could be central to her success in the Season. Formal codes of etiquette required that designs had to be reasonably modest and simple and worn with 'good' but delicate jewellery, usually a necklet of fine pearls. Débutantes' dresses were strapless or held up with shoe-string straps. Bodices were always neatly fitted and skirts full, gathered into layer upon layer of frothy tulle, organdie or fine silk. Coded colours were 'young' sugared almond tones. Dresses were trimmed with delicate *ingénue* embroidery or pale, artificial flowers. The style dated to the nineteenth century, when 'A Member of the Aristocracy' advised that 'the white dresses worn by débutantes...may be trimmed with either coloured or white flowers, according to individual taste.'[8]

ABOVE:

PLATE 39. Worth evening dress, about 1960. Chartreuse silk satin, embroidered bodice of gold thread and pastes. Worn and given by Mrs Roy Hudson. (T.215 & A-1973.)

ABOVE:
FIG. 12.
Débutante
Miss Raine
McCorquodale,
photographed
by Cecil
Beaton for
Vogue (June
1947).

LEFT:
PLATE 40.
Back view of
Catherine
Walker evening
dress, autumn/
winter 1994-5.
Black silk-velvet
with pearl collar
and diamanté
pendant.
Given by Mrs
Catherine
Walker.
(T.49-1995.)

L'Art et la Mode in the August/ September 1947 edition described the toast of the Season, Raine McCorquodale, daughter of the romantic novelist Barbara Cartland, as 'a lovely girl…with the most charming manners, who has been lucky in having three dances given for her. Miss Raine wore the exquisite white crinoline evening dress threaded with pale blue ribbon and trimmed with pale pink roses which is a Worth creation dress designed for the Empress Eugénie.' Lady Diana Herbert, in 1955, wore a pretty Victor Stiebel strapless, flared, full-length ball dress (plate 41) for her much-reported ball at Wilton House. This dress was in classic *ingénue* style with the suggestion of an 1870s bustle.

This British reworking of styles from the 1850s to '70s in the twentieth century owes its origins to the work of royal couturier Norman Hartnell. The popularity and longevity of this style of full-skirted *ingénue* evening dress deserves to be examined carefully because it has been an internationally recognized British fashion classic since Hartnell first launched it in 1938 for the Queen Mother. Colin McDowell's *Daily Mail* article of 5 November 1992 commented that Hartnell was asked by George VI to create a specifically 'picturesque' appearance for the new queen, who was not renowned for her elegance. She needed to have 'a modern image but one recognizably in the grand tradition of royal dress, an image that was her own but which would become instantly recognized throughout the world as the style of the House of Windsor.'

Hartnell achieved exactly that with his full-skirted all-white collection, designed specifically for the royal post-Coronation visit to Paris in July 1938. The clothes were based, at the King's request, on the 1860s Winterhalter royal portraits in Buckingham Palace. Hartnell's collection was made up in white because the new queen's mother had recently died, and she could not go to France draped in funereal black. White was the only etiquette-correct alternative.

In spring 1938 Hartnell launched his own full-blown crinoline collection. 'Make no mistake', declared *Vogue* in October 1938, 'you'll be wearing, as a matter of course, clothes that a year ago would have seemed pure fancy dress, notably crinolines, authentic hoops, strapless bodices, bustle backs…You may have one *à la Eugénie* or a Victorian – but have one you must; they are truly contemporary.'

This style remained constant throughout the post-war period and was especially favoured by debs. Alison Settle, in her fashion column in the *Observer* of 28 July

BELOW:
PLATE 41. Victor
Stiebel evening
dress, 1955.
Blue-and-white
striped silk.
Worn and given
by Lady Diana
Herbert.
(T6-1977.)

ABOVE:

PLATE 42. Hardy
Amies evening
dress, 1955.
Dark-red
flocked tulle,
with ribboned
bodice. Given
by Mrs McPeake
and worn by
her mother.
(T.259-1976.)

1957, described Victor Stiebel's designs as 'a series of enchanting Winterhalter-inspired wide-skirted silks, satins and chiffons, with minutely small bodices.' Plate 42 is a version by Amies of 1955 made with an extravagantly full dark-red tulle skirt.

Nearly 25 years later Princess Diana was famously married in a version of this style designed by David and Elizabeth Emanuel. Her dress, which eschewed heavy satin and symbolic embroidery, broke with the conventional royal wedding dress codes that her mother-in-law's own Hartnell bridal dress of 1947 had so carefully reflected. Diana's crinoline wedding dress was similar to the Emanuels' 1979 wedding dress now in the V&A (plate 43). This is also crinolined, trained and trimmed with frills, bows and artificial flowers. The Museum records clarify that this essentially romantic design was specifically inspired by the looped-up styles of the 1860s – the Winterhalter period.

Dior's autumn/winter 1949-50 Paris collections witnessed the launch of the third type of post-war couture eveningwear: short evening and cocktail dresses. Styles could be slim or full-skirted, strapless or short-sleeved. By the early 1950s, this new and modern alternative to formal eveningwear was widely popular both with débutantes and the more progressive young married set. *Vogue* commented in March 1954 that 'many young and pretty women…say they now never wear long dresses'. By September of the same year, the magazine noted that 'unless it's a formal ball, dresses are short and full and rely for glamour on exquisite fabrics'. The House of Worth designed just such styles, including the pretty 1955 pink princess-line evening dress (plate 44) with bands of paillette embroidery on bodice and skirt.

These dresses are all beautifully made classic examples of the skill of couturiers. Examination of the inside of the garments reveals hours of careful handwork, not only on the hemming and beading, but also on individually fitted boning and judicious padding designed to flatter the flattest chest. A number of the dresses in the V&A show signs of

ABOVE:

PLATE 44. Worth
evening dress,
1955. Pink
beaded silk
satin with floral
appliqué
embroidery.
Worn and
given by Mrs
Roy Hudson.
(T.217 & A-1973.)

RIGHT:

PLATE 43. David
and Elizabeth
Emanuel wed-
ding ensemble,
1979. Ivory silk
taffeta dress
with pink bows,
taffeta under-
skirt, tulle
sequinned veil,
wreath of flow-
ers headband.
Given by Mr
David and
Mrs Elizabeth
Emanuel.
(T.181:A-D-1980.)

wear and alteration. Recent research has confirmed that couture dresses were worn over a period of several, if not many, years. Not a few were returned to the original couture house for repairs and most were seen by purchasers as a necessary social investment.[9]

However, by the late 1950s London couturiers faced problems on three fronts. First, how to survive the evident and inexorable decline in private clientele; second, how to tackle increasing rivalry from flourishing model houses; and third, how to deal with the powerful revival of Paris couture occasioned by the triumph of the New Look in 1947.

The Incorporated Society of London Fashion Designers mounted a strong export campaign both during and immediately after the war. The dramatic yet charming bustle-backed Victor Stiebel dress, made up in green-and yellow silk grosgrain with narrow horizontal stripes, dates from this period (plate 45).

London had faced competition from Paris since the establishment of court dressmaking in eighteenth-century London, but by 1947 it posed a severe threat. The bad odour caused by the continuaton of couture activities under Nazi occupation had been so skilfully dispelled that the Paris industry was able to reassert its manufacturing strength and overwhelming dominance of international style only two years after the end of the Second World War.[10] By the early 1950s Paris couture was once again on the scale of a major national industry. Dior employed 1,200 staff in 1955 and by 1959 the Paris couture industry had 5,000 full-time workers, with a further 3,000 employed on a part-time basis.[11] In comparison, in July 1952 Hardy Amies, who along with Hartnell ran the most successful London establishments, employed 120 sewing hands and engaged 180 others in workshops.[12]

A number of stylish and well-off British women deliberately opted for the higher cachet carried by the purchase of Paris couture. Lady Tavistock, only daughter of a rich banker, recalled her mother giving her 'some very pretty clothes from Paris. We went over and got them from Balmain.'[13] But to see or buy French couture it was not even necessary to go to Paris. Dior put on his first fashion show in London at the Savoy Hotel in April 1950; Balmain put on his first London show in August of the same year. These events were part of the aggressive international marketing policy of the French *haute couture* industry, which from 1947 regularly toured collections all over the world. Paris couture clothes were also sold at London branch houses and, by the mid-1950s, even manufactured in London under licence. Fortunately for London couturiers, British audiences admired the glamour of Paris evening dresses but often the pure sense of modern ele-

LEFT:
PLATE 45. Back view of Victor Stiebel dress, autumn/winter 1947. Green-and-yellow striped silk grosgrain with self-fabric bow. Worn and given by Lady Cornwallis. (T.292-1984.)

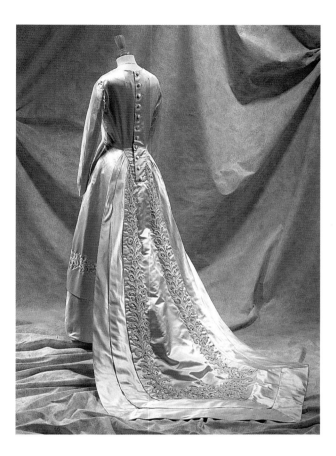

gance combined with the prices (a Givenchy could cost £900) were too much for them, as *Picture Post* reported on 19 November 1955.

Wedding dresses provided London's couture houses with an opportunity to counter Paris competition. For the design of Princess Margaret's wedding dress in 1961 Norman Hartnell was allowed a great deal of creative freedom, an occasion he seems to have relished. He produced a perfectly simple white dress, an archetypal romantic revival style, with a very full crinoline skirt; watchers gasped at its beauty. In the same year, a Miss Hewison's wedding dress, now in the V&A (plate 46) was made at the London salon of Worth in the more formal style, with delicate embroidery in *fleur-de-lis* motifs. Hartnell's wedding dress for Mrs H.S. Ball was more formally trained and beaded, in 1957 (plate 47). The very last wedding dress that Victor Stiebel designed, the farewell dress for his retirement collection in spring/summer 1963 (plate 48), was made in splendid moiré silk.

As the older designers faded, new stars rose. In 1970 Jean Muir produced one of her characteristically simple and supremely elegant designs for the wedding dress of Pamela, Lady Harlech, in cream-coloured linen featuring appliquéd Celtic motifs (plate 49).

A series of major cultural, political and economic shifts had been taking place in British society. The late 1950s have been described as 'a moment marking a profound shift in the cultural life of the nation, a watershed around which a series of significant "before and after" contrasts can be drawn'.[14] One such watershed took place on 17 November 1957 when the Lord Chamberlain announced that the Queen would no longer be receiving débutantes individually at court.

Some notes of dissidence had already been heard. A deb of 1952 described her presentation dress as 'the sort of thing a grandmother might wear...I must have looked about 100', and when actress Anna Massey found that her commitment to a West End theatre role was threatened by her Season in 1955, she simply cancelled it: 'It all seemed

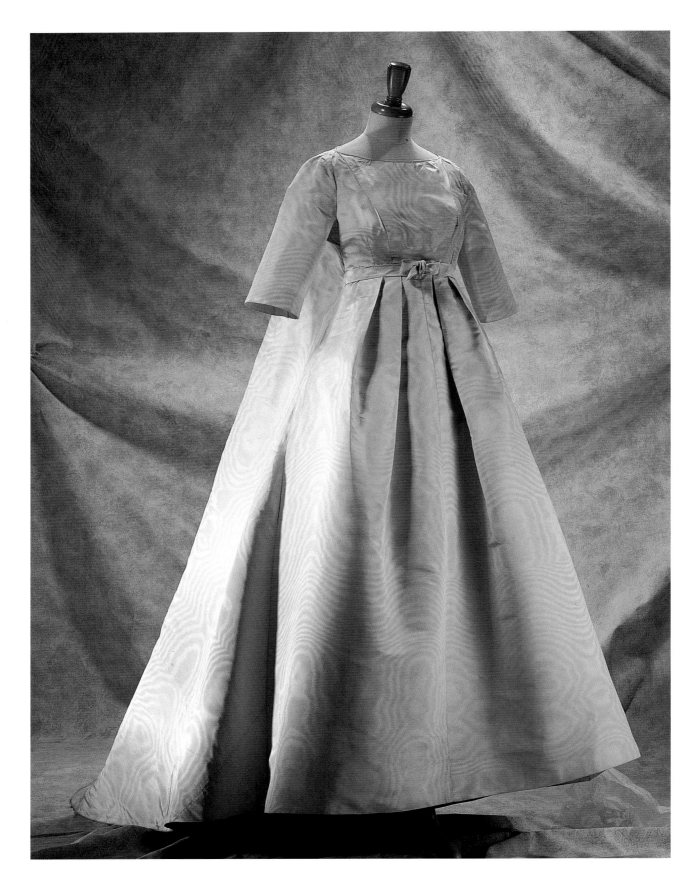

so pointless compared to interesting work and intelligent people. The Season's alright for people with nothing to do'.[15] The financial viability of London *haute couture* began slowly to unravel, with fatal consequences for many British salons.

The pressures within establishment and Society circles cracked open in the 1960s. Harold Wilson won the 1964 election for the Labour Party, fiercely attacking the aristocratic lifestyle of his rival, the fourteenth Earl of Home. Beard comments that 'in 1953, in the glory of the Coronation year, such a bitter attack would have been entirely out of place. By 1963 times had changed.'[16] Alison Adburgham declared firmly in the *Guardian* that British fashion had 'reached the point of no departure...Something once so alive is now dead, quite dead'.[17] In 1966 Alison Settle agreed that 'today one is against the dressed-up look, which does not seem to go with the life of today...the clothes the couturiers were making were over-formal for the lives being led.'[18] In 1964 the House of

Molyneux, closed since 1950, reopened for a brief last fling. The simpler, younger designs produced included a slim pink dress in silk satin with matching ostrich-feather halter neckband (plate 50).

Amies and Hartnell apart, the old guard was retiring or dying. Victor Stiebel retired through ill health in 1963, Peter Russell died and Michael Sherard closed in 1965. The London House of Worth, which had been bought by Sydney Massin, closed in 1967, the same year as Ronald Paterson. The V&A's chartreuse evening dress (see plate 39) was made in the last year of the salon. Clive, seen as a young, modern hope when he opened in 1962, closed in 1971.

RIGHT:
PLATE 50.
Edward
Molyneux
evening
dress, mid-
1960s. Pink
silk gazar
with ostrich
feather trim.
Worn and
given by
Margaret,
Duchess of
Argyll. (T.31-
1977.)

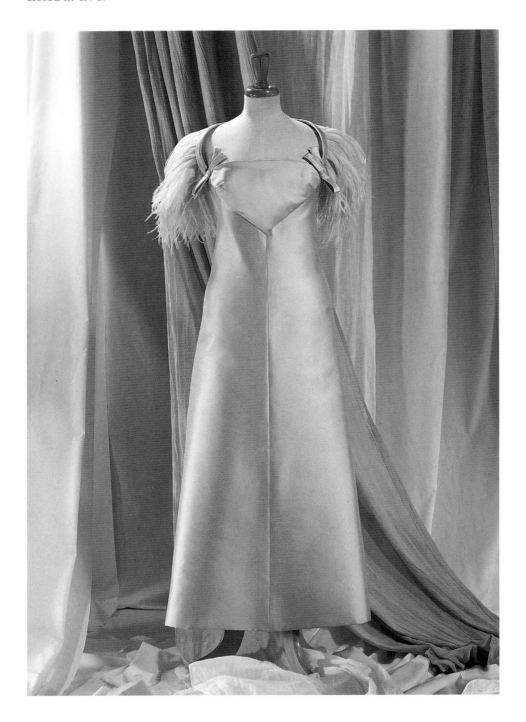

ABOVE:
PLATE 51.
Mary Quant
evening
dress, 1967-8.
Black crêpe.
Given by Mrs
A. Walford.
(T.52-1985.)

The Season drifted into decline and with it establishment dress requirements that increasingly meant little to the younger generation. High-profile young Londoners were the young women emerging from the energetic, alternative pop music and fashion scene, such as Twiggy, Lulu and Jean Shrimpton. Raine McCorquodale's brother Ian believed that 'the whole thing started to deteriorate when we stopped wearing white ties and began to shuffle around in dinner jackets…then suddenly it was the pop age and long hair, and everything was different.'[19] Indeed, young men soon abandoned dinner jackets altogether.

For a while it seemed as if pop culture might have a fatal impact on grand occasion dressing in London, as clients aged with couturiers and the new generation of young designers simply rejected the old sartorial codes as irrelevant. The work of Mary Quant and Bellville Sassoon, two favourite designers of this period, was typical of the vibrant challenge exerted against classic couture design. Quant's plain and simple black crêpe evening mini-dress (plate 51) is a good example. Less controversial in design, Sassoon's pink full-length dress (plate 52) nevertheless exudes the new power of this simple, very young, minimalist style.

ABOVE:
PLATE 52. Bellville
Sassoon evening
dress, 1964. Pink
beaded organdie
with silk satin bow.
Worn and given
by Jill Ritblat.
(T.77-1996.)

Although the headline in the fashion report of *The Times* on 18 January 1972 was 'The Life and Hard Times of British Couture', Hartnell was putting up a fight. The vivacity and pure psychedelic play with lime green and citrus yellow, used in a 1970 dress and coat now in the V&A Collection, scarcely indicates the work of a defeated designer.

English couture eveningwear just survived the difficult period of the 1960s and '70s, but by the time of Hartnell's death in 1979 the good times had flown. Although still loyally patronized by the Queen Mother, in November 1992 the salon finally closed. On 5 November Colin McDowell's tribute to the salon in the *Daily Mail* identified a peculiarly Hartnell couture characteristic, the ability 'to create clothes which had glamour but were never glacial; clothes that had dignity but never made their wearers appear remote and too grand for human contact; clothes that could be surprisingly cosy, despite their perfection'.

Younger designers had moved on and were producing the creatively free styles of new

London, Romantic dressing. Many of these designers were more interested in top-quality ready-to-wear production than in any notions of *haute couture* craft. Besides Quant and Sassoon, Ossie Clark, Gina Fratini and Zandra Rhodes were all stars of this new London style. The work of Bill Gibb, a farmer's son from the north of Scotland and a 1966 graduate from St Martin's School of Art, was typical. Gibb opened a fashion house in 1972 but was always at the mercy of financial problems. Tragically, he died at the age of only forty-four. The *Guardian* (4 January 1988) described Gibb's work as 'beautiful fantasy...rooted in medievalism, Celtic romance and the lavish grandeur of the court dress of many periods, mated with a traditional, theatrical-peasant love of layers of contrasting textures and patterns, matched [to] the exoticism of the mid-Seventies young.' The *Independent* obituary on the same day acknowledged his 'extraordinary and inventive evening and wedding dresses.' The late 1970s pink silk taffeta jacket with its full-length embroidered tulle skirt (plate 53) is typical of the quality and fantasy of Gibb's work. Gina Fratini's 1970 smocked organza wedding ensemble is also typical of this period (plate 54).

The re-election of a Conservative government in 1979 might have raised hopes that the lifestyle of the landed gentry and their codes of genteel establishment dressing would be revived, but during the Thatcher years, as Cannadine points out, 'the decline of the old order on the right in politics has been almost as complete as on the left'.[20] It was the advent of Diana Spencer, rather than Mrs Thatcher, who ensured the continuation and revitalization of romantic British evening and wedding wear. From the early 1980s her massive international and media popularity, coupled with her specific and deliberate support of London evening couture, boosted the international fame of a new generation of British eveningwear designers.

The dearth of private clients has none the less remained a problem. This is reflected

in the fact that the 1994 official programme for Queen Charlotte's Birthday Ball listed only 31 'débutantes' participating in the London Season, compared to 1,000 some thirty years earlier. Even worse was the reality that many of the debs wore hired or borrowed clothes for the Ball. Libby Spurrier commented in the *Independent* on 2 April 1996 that girls who would formerly have been 'coming out' have 'flown the coop – most probably not into matrimony at all, but to go back-packing in Nepal, share a flat in Fulham or even to live in unwedded bliss with some quite unsuitable fellow.' Even in Paris, the problem facing the industry clearly was 'whether it could afford to employ 2,000 to dress 2,000 women.'[21] In 1991, according to the *Nouvel Observateur* (24-30 January 1991), it took 800 hours of work to produce a couture wedding dress at the House of St Laurent and an embroidered Paris couture evening dress could cost 500,000 francs (£55,500).

The difference between the two industries in Paris and London was that the top Paris (and Milan and New York) couture and fashion companies had already dealt with this problem. In Paris from the mid-1950s couture had become the engine that pulled along overflowing carriages of mass-marketed perfumes, cosmetics, diffusion lines and fashion accessories. G.Y. Dryansky verified in *Women's Wear Daily* on 3 February 1972 that the '$40 million yearly volume done by 20 couture houses in Paris is far and away a deficit operation…a small price to pay for the reputation couture makes for a name'. Although Yves St Laurent lost $700,000 a year on its couture operation it was, after less than six years of production, selling ready-to-wear worth $24 million worldwide. The exploitation of images of exotic and romantic couture eveningwear still plays a central role in this whole process and ensures the continued production of couture.

London designers, while long aware that the days of the discreet couturier had largely died out, have been so under-capitalized that they have never been able seriously to join in this powerful international franchise market. The survival of crafted couture dressing for the grand occasion has been continuously under threat since the 1970s. None the less, and importantly, the rundown of the Season may have proved to be a blessing in disguise. Freed from the shackles of the old dress codes, generation after generation of British fashion designers have since wittily and lovingly re-worked the style and image of romantic London-made evening and wedding wear, with very real success. In a late twentieth-century mix of gentle nostalgia, parody and even subversion, they have recently built upon, rather than rejected, its traditions.

Thus the classic Worth/Hartnell style of crinoline dress has bloomed again in the hands of designers of the 1980s and '90s, as the V&A's Emanuel wedding dress shows. More interestingly still, the style has caught the imagination of Britain's two most famous once-dissident women designers: Zandra Rhodes and Vivienne Westwood. In 1981 Zandra Rhodes reworked eighteenth-century garments she had studied in the V&A for her exotic 'Renaissance Cloth of Gold Crinoline' (plate 55).

LEFT:
PLATE 55.
Zandra Rhodes 'Renaissance' evening ensemble, autumn/ winter 1981. Black quilted satin bodice, gold pleated polyamide, polyester and lamé skirt and paniers over black silk tulle. From the Elizabethan Collection. Given by Miss Zandra Rhodes. (T.124-C-1983.)

Vivienne Westwood too has created glorious yet simple versions of the hooped skirt over recent years for both the mature and the *ingénue* markets. She also drew on mid-eighteenth-century Rococo styles, though with more literal interpretations. She dramatically subverted the *sacque*-back style of Watteau, making it sexily strapless and exaggerating the tightness of the bodice and the flamboyance of the *echelles* bows that trim the corset-bodice (plate 56). An *ingénue* version of this style was designed in white organdie as a débutante ball dress for Lady Bianca Job-Tyoran to wear to the Queen Charlotte's Ball of 1994. The dramatic impact of these dresses shows that the crinoline style can still be, to paraphrase 1938 *Vogue*, 'truly contemporary'.

RIGHT:

PLATE 57. Back view of Joe Casely Hayford wedding dress, 'Farewell Sweet Liberty', 1992/1993. Ivory raw silk, decorated with pearls, metal rivets, chains and studs. Given by Liberty plc. (T.323-1993)

RIGHT:

PLATE 58. Victor Edelstein wedding dress, 1987. White lace and satin. Frederick Fox veil: white tulle with cream satin rose headpiece. Worn and given by Miss Marilyn Watts. (T.100 & A-1993.)

Joe Casely Hayford and John Galliano have subverted the virginal white bridal dress into designs immediately recognizable as lively, fresh and British. Both John Galliano's sculptured, bridal dress of 1987 (see detail beginning this chapter) and Joe Casely Hayford's post-Punk 1992-93 bridal dress trimmed with pearls, rivets, chains and studs (plate 57) epitomize the skill, fun and pure beauty of this style. Victor Edelstein's more classic 1987 white lace wedding dress was worn with a tulle and rose headpiece (plate 58).

Galliano's sense of romantic modernity is exemplified too in his wedding and evening dresses, such as his 1988 short, green-and-white 'Seashell' evening dress (plate 59). It is this that drew Arnault, the financial support behind the House of Givenchy, to take the risk of launching Galliano as designer-supreme at Givenchy. There is no doubt of the

LEFT:
PLATE 59. John Galliano evening dress, 'Seashell', 1988. White organza with green-and-white striped cotton sash. Given by Mr John Galliano. (T.389-1988.)

RIGHT:
PLATE 60. Antony Price evening dress, 'Bird's Wing', autumn/winter 1986. White rayon taffeta. Given by Mr Antony Price. (T.345-1989.)

FAR RIGHT:
PLATE 61. Bruce Oldfield evening coat, 1986. White silk-velvet with white fur collar. Given by Mr Bruce Oldfield. (T.6-1987.)

accolade that this appointment gave to British fashion. 'All Paris awaits the coming of the plumber's son from Streatham', declared Marion Hume in the *Independent* on 29 January 1996, adding that Galliano was already producing day dresses that retail at about £8,000 and wedding dresses priced at least at £25,000.

His sense of challenging sartorial wit is shared by other British eveningwear designers. Antony Price, with his 1986 'Bird's Wing' dress in taffeta, and Bruce Oldfield, in his design for a full-length evening coat in white velvet and fur dating from 1986-87, both enjoy developing the impact of pure white (plates 60 and 61). Anouska Hempel's 1991-

LEFT:
PLATE 62. Anouska
Hempel evening
ensemble,
'Enamelling',
autumn/winter
1991-2. Black vel-
vet and white silk
satin bustier with
white silk satin
skirt. Given by
Lady Weinberg.
(T.110:1&2-1992.)

RIGHT:
PLATE 63. Detail
of Cathryn
Avison ensemble,
1996. Pink
embroidered
floral silk dress,
tunic, underskirt
and stole. Given
by Miss Cathryn
Avison. (T.127:1-
4-1996.)

92 white-and-black evening dress plays elegant games with colour contrast (plate 62). The mid-1990s generation is typified by Cathryn Avison, who graduated from the Royal College of Art in 1994. Her organically dyed pink chiffon and silk dress and shawl, delicately handworked with daisy motifs, is a perfect contemporary reworking of the long-established *ingénue* style (plate 63).

Although the secretive world of the discreet private dressmaker still exists in London, the past thirty years have seen the end of couture evening clothes as the élitist social uniform of the British ruling class. Hindsight shows us that the decade immediately fol-

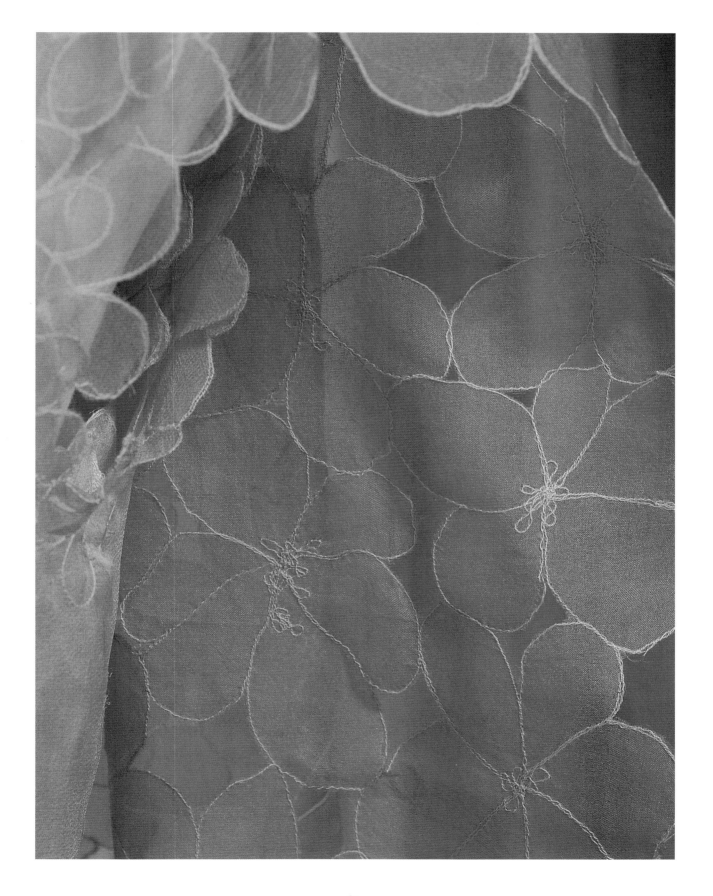

ABOVE:

PLATE 64. Norman Hartnell evening ensemble, about 1955. Light pink and mid-green satin embroidered dress and pink velvet embroidered jacket. Given by Mrs Lee Landau. (T.432 & A-1985.)

lowing the end of the Second World War witnessed the last flowering of the craft of classic, formal British court/couture evening dressing, a style exemplified by Hartnell's 1955 pink evening dress and jacket, so beautifully and delicately decorated with elaborate pink and green floral embroidery (plate 64).

The function of such confident 'dressing up' was always clearly acknowledged. At its flamboyant best, both clients and couturiers relished the coded etiquette whereby the glitter of heirloom tiaras and beaded silks manifested so confidently their social and cultural dominance of British society. An article in the *Daily Mail* of 5 September 1960 describes Hardy Amies reassuring a nervous client in 1960 who was anxious that her new ball dress gave out 'too much of a Christmas tree effect'. 'No, No,' he assured her, 'I think it looks absolutely splendid. Absolutely right for the occasion. Yes, tiaras *and* sparklers…I am absolutely sure *that* is the dress. There must be something of the theatre about it. You will look so distinguished. It will be absolutely marvellous'. Thirty years later Cannadine was writing that 'in the Britain of the 1990s, it is not altogether clear whether there exists anything that can be called a ruling class. In a society so complex in its structure and so multinational in its ramifications, it may well be that such a notion is too simplistic and too outmoded to be of any value'.[22]

However, as the designs of Westwood and Galliano show, the same confident relishing of the elegant and theatrical still survives in British fashion in the 1990s. What has changed is that it now carries different meanings, interpreted through entirely contemporary styling, to consumers with very different tastes and interests from those of the 1950s. These come from the wider circles of successful business, music, film, stage, fashion as well as 'Society' worlds. Some clients buy, others borrow, but what unites them is their ability to wear with real aplomb a great range of evening and wedding wear, from the most informal through to the most glamorous and progressive.

The designing and wearing of such clothes in Britain today reveals a refreshingly eclectic sense of modernity which has, with parody and post-modern subversion, been built upon a dynamic juxtaposition of nostalgia and tradition.

Footnotes

1 Palmer (1994), p.160 and 210.
2 McDowell, Colin (1992).
3 Cannadine (1990), p.678.
4 Pringle (1977), p.75.
5 *Picture Post*, Venetia Murray, Report on the London Season (6 August 1955, p.41).
6 Beard (1989), p.113, quoting *The Times* (1 November 1955).
7 Pringle (1977), p.77 and p.95, quoting Nancy Banks Smith, *The Daily Herald* (April 1957).
8 *Manners and Tone of Good Society...* (1880).
9 Palmer (1994), p.166.
10 Taylor (1992), pp.126-144.
11 Vincent (1987), p.61.
12 'Notes on an interview with Hardy Amies: July 23 1952', Alison Settle Archive.
13 Pringle (1977), p.111.
14 Waites, Bennett and Martin (1982), p.7.
15 Pringle (1977), pp 87-125.
16 Beard (1990), p.101.
17 *The Times*, Prudence Glyn, The Life and Hard Times of British Couture (18 January 1972, p.18) quoting Alison Adburgham in the *Guardian* (1963).
18 'Talk Back' lecture to the Costume Society (1966), Alison Settle Archive.
19 Pringle (1977), p.160.
20 Cannadine (1990), p.675.
21 Vincent (1987), p.61.
22 Cannadine (1990), p.677.

Selected Bibliography

Alison Settle Archive, University of Brighton
Beard, M. *English Society in the Twentieth Century* (London: Routledge 1989).
Cannadine, David *The Decline and Fall of the British Aristocracy* (New Haven and London: Yale University Press 1990).
Manners and Tone of Good Society, or Solecisms to Be Avoided (London: Frederick Warne; 11th edn 1880).
McDowell, Colin 'The Rise and Fall of the House of Hartnell', *Daily Mail* (5 November 1992).
Palmer, Alexandra 'The Myth and Reality of Haute Couture: Consumption, Social Function and Taste in Toronto 1945-63', PhD thesis (University of Brighton 1994).
Pringle, Margaret *Dance Little Ladies, the Days of the Débutante* (London: Orbis 1977).
Settle, Alison 'Notes on an interview with Hardy Amies, July 23 1952' (University of Brighton, Alison Settle Archive, BN 16.1).
Settle, Alison 'Talk Back' lecture to the Costume Society, 1966 (University of Brighton, Alison Settle Archive, AS.L.60.5.)
Taylor, Lou, 'Paris Couture 1940-44' *Chic Thrills: A Fashion Reader* (London: Pandora Press 1992).
Vincent, Ricard *La Mode* (Paris: Segliers 1987).
Waites, B., Bennett, T. and Martin, G., eds *Popular Culture: Past and Present* (London: Croom Helm 1982).

Bohemian

TONY GLENVILLE & AMY DE LA HAYE

At its truest the taste exhibited by the Englishwoman
has a certain 'literary' quality: almost, one might say, a Virginia Woolf
appreciation for clothes that possess the association of
ideas…Old things have a certain romantic charm about them, and
English women of sensibility appreciate this. Far from preferring
a trim, neat look, they incline more towards the picturesque.

(Cecil Beaton, 1954.) [1]

Before the Second World War the flagrant flouting of fashion conventions was often a means of expressing dissent. In the late nineteenth century the Dress Reform Movement, which found its most vocal expression in Britain, condemned clothing that constricted the body. Instead, members favoured loose, lightweight garments, such as pantaloons. From the early 1900s Roger Fry, Quaker, painter and art critic, wore shapeless Jaeger homespuns, with brilliantly coloured, shantung silk ties, open sandals and a broad brimmed hat. Famous Bloomsbury hostess, Lady Ottoline Morrell, dyed her hair violet and swathed herself in Turkish robes; poet Edith Sitwell donned flowing, medieval-style, brocaded gowns and bizarre hats, and Dorelia John, wife of the painter Augustus, wore Russian peasant and gypsy styles. Politics, aesthetics and health issues motivated this unconventional, and peculiarly British, stance.

In the post-war period this idiosyncratic, Bohemian approach to dressing up (rather than the Bohemian penchant for dressing down) has become assimilated within the British fashion psyche. While fashion's interest is primarily stylistic, this appropriation continues to signify an element of non-conformism. The phrase 'Bohemian fashion' is used to describe the work of designers which draws upon certain historical revival styles and ethnicity. Bohemian fashions are seen in abundance at arts-related social events, such as exhibition openings, book launches, the theatre, opera and ballet.

Bohemian fashions for women often transcend seasonal design changes and can thus eschew fashion's limelight. Many garments are based on the simple T-shape, which exploits the non-western clothing tradition of using fabric without the cutting and shaping intricacies of tailoring. Loosely draped and fluid styles form a distinct, but related,

strand. These clothes are comfortable, take shape on the body, and many are full length. As a result, they are flattering for a variety of figure types and age groups. Natural fabrics predominate, and there is much emphasis upon hand-worked surface decoration and a bold use of colour.

While ethnicity is omnipresent within fashion, it has enjoyed certain peaks in the last fifty years. Norman Hartnell's turquoise, silk-velvet, jewelled 'Chinese jacket', featured in *Vogue* in November 1949, represents an early post-war example. Throughout the 1950s, there were a limited number of fashion looks inspired by the ethnic, but then editors started to use exotic (to western eyes) locations for fashion shoots. From the mid- to the late 1960s, fashion designers fully embraced the silhouette, construction and textiles of a variety of non-western clothing traditions. This trend was international and found eloquent expression in Britain.

At the same time, British society was becoming increasingly multicultural. Fashion has been much enriched by designers who have imbued collections with references to their own non-British clothing traditions. Sophisticated technological developments and competitive pricing have brought speedy foreign travel within the reach of many. India, Turkey, China, Japan and North Africa are not only exciting places to visit, but have also become a series of vast bazaars to plunder for decoration and dress.

The London department store Liberty, founded in 1875, was among the first of many emporia to import and retail ethnic clothing in Britain. Museum collections and published works – in particular those by Max Tilke – with detailed illustrations of ethnic clothing patterns have been potent sources of inspiration to fashion designers. Art school trained and textile orientated, Gina Fratini, Thea Porter, Bill Gibb and Zandra Rhodes were particularly successful in their ability to incorporate ethnic clothing traditions within their own distinctive fashion idiom. Developing their shapes from non-western garment construction, they skilfully manipulated large expanses of fabric to create innovative fashion trends. This late 1960s shift to flowing, longer lines was a reaction to the reign of the angular mini.

Zandra Rhodes graduated from the textiles course at the Royal College of Art in 1966 and launched her own fashion label in 1969. She has consistently reflected the visual experiences of her travels and historical research in the textile patterns, embellishments and silhouettes of her garments. The V&A includes a screen-printed, silk chiffon, hooded, djellabah-style dress, from 1969 (plate 65). The printed design is called 'knitted circle' and was inspired by examples of historical knitting in the V&A Textiles Collection.

While Zandra Rhodes used her sources to inspire her, Syrian-born Thea Porter patch-worked genuine ethnic textiles into her fashion garments. In the early 1960s she opened a London shop to sell antique Turkish and Arabian carpets. She started to design clothes in 1964, drawing upon her extensive travel experiences and historical knowledge. Her caftans, made in brilliantly coloured printed, woven and embroidered silks, attracted an affluent clientele with a hippie sensibility. An example from the late 1960s can be seen in plate 66. Thea Porter also designed ethereal chiffon garments and shawls, crewel-worked in gold thread, with sequinned decoration.

From 1972 Bill Gibb regularly exploited ethnic cut and construction techniques in his collections. He often employed the Moroccan clothing tradition of using coloured braids to conceal seams decoratively. The asymmetry and drape of the Indian sari was another source of inspiration, which dominated his spring/summer 1976 collection.

ABOVE:
PLATE 67. Gina
Fratini ensemble,
autumn/winter
1970. Skirt,
Liberty print
wool; petticoat,
red cotton;
petticoat, yellow
cotton; blouse,
red wool crêpe;
waistcoat,
printed wool
crêpe. Given
by Miss Gina
Fratini. (T.276:A-
D-1990.)

While these designers lean towards the exotic, Gina Fratini, who was born in Japan, utilized a melange of ethnic sources which she combined with her own particular romantic look. An ensemble for autumn/winter 1970 (plate 67) is Slav inspired, with its dramatic red-and-black colouring and combination of layered garments. It was featured in *Vogue* magazine, styled with bright red stockings and shoes, and was described as a 'Frogged wallpaper print surcoat opening on a tucked strawberry wool crêpe tunic and magnificent Liberty wool skirt, full and braided'.[2]

John Bates designed modernistic, body-revealing garments, as well as Bohemian fashions. His full-length, zipped black worsted crêpe evening dress, with mandarin collar, embroidered with an ornamental bird and diamond design, dates from autumn/winter 1974 (plate 68). The embroidery around the pockets is reminiscent of nineteenth-century Turkish and Greek couched decoration. It was worn and given to the V&A by Pamela, Lady Harlech, and originally had a matching black embroidered tassel hat, made by Frederick Fox for John Bates.

Ethnic clothing came to the forefront again in the early 1980s when top designer-level and subcultural styles co-incided to create an environment where 'The New Orientalists' could don original and fashion-inspired Rajah coats, Turkish embroideries and Chinese tunics.

ABOVE:
PLATE 68. John
Bates dress,
autumn/
winter 1974.
Embroidered
black worsted
crêpe. Worn and
given by Pamela,
Lady Harlech.
(T.206-1987.)

Turkish-born St Martin's graduate Rifat Ozbek often uses the fez hat, harem trousers, the star and crescent moon of the Turkish flag and coin decoration in his work. His autumn/winter 1992 collection was inspired by indigenous Americans, featuring silk-velvet tunics, with clusters of coloured feathers at the hips. Also from this collection is the luxurious, full-length, white wool coat shown in plate 69. This takes elements from Russian military clothing and illustrations from fairy-tales. It is trimmed with ikat braiding, which is widely used on Central Asian clothing.

Shirin Guild, who presented her first collection in 1993, was born in Iran and is a self-taught designer. Her cut is derived from Iranian and Japanese clothing traditions, while fabrics and yarns are sourced exclusively from British mills. Capaciously cut Kurdish trousers, and sweaters that enfold the body, have become Shirin Guild signatures. For spring/summer 1996 she designed the layered, linen ensemble seen in plate 70. Two striped linen kimono jackets are combined with a linen vest and trousers. The distinctive front panel on the trousers was inspired by the dress of Iranian peasant women, who wear skirts over their trousers for warmth.

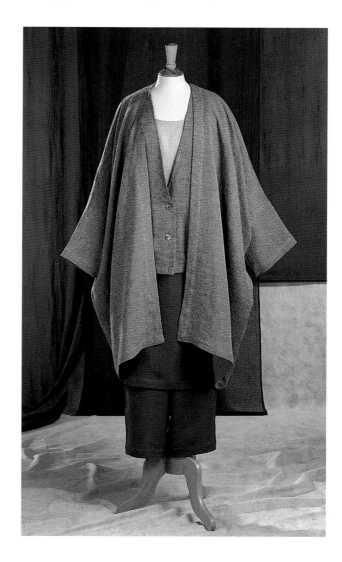

Fashion's appropriation of ethnicity and historical styles is selective, often romanticized and irreverent in its application. Original garments, as well as paintings, engravings, sculpture and decorative ceramics are frequently used by designers as reference sources. Pleated garments, originally part of classical antiquity, have consistently inspired artists, dress reformers and bohemian fashion designers. Painters and sculptors have long-exploited classical drapery, which accentuates the contours of the body and is timeless in its appeal. To members of the Dress Reform Movement, it presented a healthy alternative to the prevailing corsetted and cumbersome fashions. The classically inspired clothes of Venetian designer, Mariano Fortuny (1871-1949), attracted clients who were both unconventional and fashionable. Fortuny's name has become synonymous with intricate, pleated, silk garments. In 1907 he introduced his columnic, delphos dresses, named after the world-famous classical statue of a charioteer, found in Delphi. These dresses were painted in subtle colourings, hand-pleated according to his secret method, and weighted at the hem with tiny glass beads.

Ian Cooper and Marcel Aucoin, working as fashion designers Ian & Marcel, acknowledged their debt to Fortuny, having seen an exhibition of his work at Brighton Museum and Art Gallery in 1980. For ten years, Ian & Marcel created exquisite hand-crafted special occasion wear, and bequeathed a significant collection of their work to the V&A. This included one of their very finest ensembles, dating from 1985 – a silk caftan evening coat, with a painted, classical vine design, teamed with a pleated, delphos-style dress, in hues of purple and blue. Lady Holly Rumbold remembers, 'Ian & Marcel reminded us of medieval knights, whose quest was for beauty's perfection. They consecrated their lives to their art and the realisation of their ideals, with the same single-mindedness and fervour of Parsifal in pursuit of the Holy Grail.'[3] A close inspection of their outstanding artistry can be seen in the photographic detail at the beginning of this chapter.

The appeal and universality of pleats is manifest in the work of Charles and Patricia Lester, who are based in Abergavenny, Wales. Charles trained as a textile physicist and Patricia is self-taught. The creation of their garments involves meticulous craft skills and is highly labour intensive: each metre length of silk takes eight hours to pleat before being baked and hand-dyed. Their exquisite colourings reflect the drama of the Welsh countryside, faded Renaissance textiles and exotic jewels. Charles and Patricia Lester's 'poison apple' pleated silk lauder dress, with a silk-velvet *devoré* (an acid burn-away technique) jacket can be seen in plate 71. In addition to pleating silk, the duo also create sumptuous, deep-pleated silk-velvet evening coats, as well as textile furnishings. Prestigious clients include HRH Princess Michael of Kent, Shakira Caine and Bette Midler.

Gnyuki Torimaru – who formerly worked as 'Yuki' and is still informally known as such – has been inspired by both Japanese clothing traditions and by classical pleating. Yuki works in an utterly modern idiom, using polyester fabrics and hoop structures to create flower-trumpet shapes at the sleeves and hems of his pleated garments. Many other British designers, including John Flett, Helen Storey and Lezley George, have also featured classically inspired pleats in their collections.

The textile-led fashion company, Helen David English Eccentrics (previously known as English Eccentrics), draws on a colourful pot-pourri of historical, artistic and multicultural imagery. Plate 72 reveals a detail from the front panel of a *devoré* velvet tunic, which formed part of their New Bohemians collection for autumn/winter 1996-97. The textile design, which dates from 1994, has bold heraldic lion and unicorn motifs, in a rich rust colour, inspired by the clothes worn by Tibetan monks.

The British are devoted to original period and ethnic clothing. These garments are valued for the individuality they accord the wearer and the quality of workmanship. Loving a bargain, the discerning can often discover an exquisitely made and elaborately decorated piece at a give-away price. This penchant reflects a distrust and disdain for

LEFT:
PLATE 71. Charles and Patricia Lester ensemble, 1994. Jacket with swirl border, 'brown oil slick' silk-velvet *devoré*; lauder dress, 'poison apple' pleated and beaded silk. Given by Mr Charles and Mrs Patricia Lester.
(T. 1000-1994, T. 1003-1994.)

RIGHT:
PLATE 72. Detail of Helen David English Eccentrics ensemble, autumn/winter 1996-97. Rust velvet *devoré* tunic, scarf and trousers with 'Tudor' motif. Given by Mrs Helen David.
(T. 143: 1-1996, T.143:2-1996, T. 143:3-1996.)

'the new' combined with a romantic notion of the past. In the last fifty years, a cornucopia of period dress shops, ethnic emporia and auction houses have fuelled and served this demand.

In 1966 *Vogue* interviewed Jane Ormsby-Gore, the 23-year-old daughter of Lord Harlech, who would 'wear a tiara of black and pink pearls to luncheon if she felt like it...and thinks there should be far less difference between day clothes and evening clothes'. She was widely admired for her daring and irreverent Bohemian fashion philosophy, which not only involved breaking the rules, but demanded high standards too:

> She would like all her clothes to be exquisitely made, their hems hand rolled, their stitching of the greatest delicacy, and their fabrics rare and beautiful. Since such perfection would cost a king's ransom, she scours the Portobello Road and antique shops and markets throughout the land, searching for handfuls of Venetian lace, rich embroideries, and beautifully made clothes.[4]

This approach exudes a nonchalant confidence, and is a deliberate fashion statement based upon current trends and a heightened historical awareness. While differently expressed, the rules and semiology are no less élite than those governing other areas of high fashion. Since the 1960s, the British fashion press has stood alone in consistently reflecting the British love of mixing historical and ethnic dress with high fashion.

When Cecil Beaton was collecting high-fashion clothing for a major retrospective exhibition at the V&A in 1971, he was disappointed to discover that none of Lady Diana Cooper's clothes had survived. Beaton had written in 1954 that, in addition to patronizing leading fashion designers, this author and society beauty had, over the years, dressed in a remarkable variety of outfits. Her attire could be that of an 'apotheosized cowboy, a highwayman, a sublimated peasant with dirndl skirt and sandals', and he marvelled how that 'with head tied in a chiffon scarf she is like a nun in a coif. In a yachting cap Lady Diana is a young naval commander in an operata, while oyster-coloured satin metamorphosises her into a court lady of Charles II.'[5]

LEFT:
PLATE 73. Foale & Tuffin ensembles, 1972. Left: Bolero and trousers. Cotton seersucker printed with polka dots. Worn and given by Jill Ritblat. Right: 'Carnival', bolero and dress. Cotton seersucker printed with polka dots. Worn and given by Mrs Bobi Bartlett. (T.78 1+2-1996, T. 228 & A-1984).

British fashion designers and their clients understand and celebrate this 'dressing-up box' approach. With roots in an Alice in Wonderland world of childhood, romance and fancy dress, this Bohemian fashion mood has a freshness and wit that is endlessly appealing and quintessentially British in its reference points. London collections can be relied upon for an inventive pageant knitwear that draws on rich Arthur Rackham-style colours, and often features medieval Guinevere-type figures, Kate Greenaway shepherdesses and Dorelia John gypsies. In 1972 Foale & Tuffin produced their circus-ring, primary coloured collection of spotted and striped seersucker garments, covered with cascades of ruffles

LEFT:
PLATE 74. Yuki evening cloak, 1977. White rayon jersey with pleated organdie collar and cuffs. Given by Mr Gunyuki Torimaru. (T. 1-1979.)

(plate 73). Yuki designed an elegant and ethereal white rayon jersey evening cloak, inspired by traditional pierrot costume with its pleated organdie frills, in 1977 (plate 74). Together with Margaret Howell's autumn/winter 1980-81 school gym-slip dresses, made in wool suitings, and Vivienne Westwood's milkmaid styles from the 1990s, these are all fine examples of the British predilection for fantasy and escapism.

Knitwear is a special area of British fashion expertise, and has a particular kind of significance in this context. Hand-knitted garments reflect Britain's preoccupation with craft practice and love of individuality. The cosy and comfortable familiarity of knitwear, its stretchy qualities which take shape on the body, and its potential for layering, are

ABOVE:

PLATE 75. Detail of Patricia Roberts cardigan, 1982. Hand-knitted angora and wool, 'Romany' design. Given by Mrs Patricia Roberts. (T. 210-1985.)

highly regarded by the British. Patricia Roberts's 'Romany' cardigan from 1982 (plate 75) glories in a landscape of primary coloured angora and woollen yarns, hand-knitted in stocking and decorative textural stitches. The design of this cardigan, along with Martin Kidman's cherubic jumper from 1984 (see plate 8), were inspired by decorative china plates.

Bohemian fashions for men embrace a *mélange* of interests: history, art, literature, gardens, romance and the exotic. The look is always decorative and theatrical. It is not only cut, materials and colouring which identify Bohemian fashions – it is also the time when, and manner in which, certain clothes are worn.

In the late 1940s there was no designer-led equivalent to the New Look for men. Instead, wealthy clients patronized Savile Row tailors, who worked to their specifications. The most extreme sartorial statement was made by a flamboyant group who became known as the New Edwardians. After some ten years of clothing and style restrictions, this revival look was exceptional for its stylishness, quality and precision cut. Ultimately, it re-established the male peacock. However, it was not until the 1960s that the prerogative of the self-created dandy extended beyond a small coterie and entered fashion's repertoire. By this date, London boasted the finest classic, as well as the most flamboyant, tailors.

Before the Second World War Cecil Beaton had enjoyed causing a sensation with his theatrical demeanour, exaggerated by dramatic hats and flowing neck scarves. By the 1960s, it became acceptable – and even rather expected – for those involved in the arts to assume an unconventional appearance. British photographers provide a good example of this: Angus McBean favoured tweed all-in-one suits; Lord Patrick Lichfield masqueraded as a Russian Cossack, attired in velvet tunics and heavy boots. Norman Parkinson was truly eclectic in his dress, embracing traditional tweed suits as well as Indian-style silk tunics, accessorized with headwear selected from his impressive collection of Kashmiri wedding hats.

The Bohemian centre of London had moved from Soho to Chelsea in the mid-1950s (it has moved back again to Soho in recent years). This transition – to the more fashion-orientated borough – was paralleled by an increased interest in style. Simon Hodgson, Robert Jacobs, and most notably Christopher Gibbs, were aristocratic and Bohemian style leaders. Gibbs wore elaborate double-breasted waistcoats, velvet ties, striped Turkish shirts and cravats. Jane Ormsby-Gore was very much part of this scene, working as Christopher Gibb's assistant in the Camden-based antique shop that he opened in 1959. This group spawned the much spotlighted 'Chelsea Set' of the 1960s, which included style leaders Michael Rainey, Tara Browne, Mark Palmer and David Mlinaric.

In the early 1960s the Parisian tailor Gilbert Féruch introduced jackets with Mao collars into fashionable western tailoring. In Britain, it became known as the Nehru (or Rajah) style – reflecting a pacifist rather than revolutionary image – and was to become a mainstay of male Bohemian fashion. This jacket is slim in cut and buttons at the neck with a neat, stand collar, thus negating the need for the formal, starched shirt and tie conventionally worn with a suit.

RIGHT:
PLATE 76. Blades suit, 1968. Cream silk jacquard; shirt, natural silk crêpe. Worn and given by Mr Rupert Lycett Green. (T. 702: A-B-1974.)

A new generation of extrovert tailors was emerging. Key figures such as Tommy Nutter led by example and commercialized their own distinctive styles. In 1968 a collarless suit, buttoning to the neck, was designed and worn by Rupert Lycett Green, the designer-owner of Blades (plate 76). It combines historical and ethnic references with traditional western tailoring. The cream silk jacquard, hand-loomed in a Lyon silk mill in 1953, resembles a mid-nineteenth-century design. Rupert Lycett Green also designed a cream silk crêpe shirt, with an eighteenth-century style stock, to wear with the suit.

LEFT:
PLATE 77. Scott Crolla jacket. 1990. Gold-and-black silk damask. Given by Mr E.J.S. Kulukundis in memory of Mr Steven J. Haycock. (T.183-1992.)

RIGHT:
PLATE 78. Richard James jacket, spring/summer 1990. Pink raw silk, green silk embroidery, yellow organza appliqué roses. Given by Mr Richard James. (T.183-1996.)

In the early 1980s Scott Crolla introduced a range of brightly coloured, patterned and decorative menswear, which challenged the prevailing vogue for matt black minimalism. He designed a number of Nehru styles, and in 1990 designed the dramatic gold-and-black damask jacket, based on an Italian Renaissance textile design, seen in plate 77.

Richard James has taken the Nehru style to a romantic extreme. His pink raw-silk jacket, embellished with appliquéd yellow organza roses protruding from embroidered green stalks (plate 78), dates from spring/summer 1990. This formed part of his 'Cecil Beaton Collection', which was shown in Paris at the Opera Comique. It was designed in homage to Cecil Beaton's fancy-dress jacket from 1937, also owned by the V&A. Designed in a pseudo eighteenth-century style, it is made from cream corduroy appliquéd with deep pink roses of butter muslin and net, green-and-brown woollen yarn, and white plastic cracked egg shells complete with plastic egg whites.

Liberty had avoided the ephemeral excesses of the 1960s youthquake, but came into its own by providing fabrics and trimmings for Bohemian fashions. In 1960 William

ABOVE:
PLATE 79.
1960s shirts.
Left: Liberty,
yellow-and-white
paisley cotton.
Centre: Deborah
Clare, multi-
colour print
synthetic chiffon.
Right: Cockell &
Johnson multi-
colour floral
cotton lawn.
Liberty shirt
worn and given
by Sir Roy
Strong. (T.196-
1979) Cockell
& Johnson and
Deborah Clare
shirts given
by Mr R. D.
Middleton.
(T.339-1989;
T.335-1989.)

Poole of Liberty introduced the Lotus Range of textiles, which was inspired by late nine-teenth and early twentieth-century swirling and naturalistic Art Nouveau designs. These were printed in authentic, and new, colourways. A series of exhibitions across Europe prompted this revival, which retained its original, rather decadent appeal and remained in vogue until about 1970. The menswear boutique Take Six utilized Art-Nouveau revival fabrics for a range of shirts from about 1970, including that worn by historian and for-mer V&A Director Sir Roy Strong with a Tommy Nutter suit (see plate 82). William Poole left Liberty's in 1962 and Bernard Nevill was then appointed as Liberty's Design and Colour Consultant. In 1965, Nevill's 'Jazz' range spearheaded the vogue for textiles inspired by Art Deco.

Colourful and patterned shirts have been a popular Bohemian fashion expression, since the early 1960s. Cockell & Johnson used Liberty's floral Tana Lawn (designed by William Haynes Dorell); Deborah Clare exploited bold Art Deco revival styles and Liberty utilized colourful paisleys (plate 79). In addition to regular cotton or silk, translucent chiffon shirts, with stiffened collars and cuffs to give form to these otherwise flimsy gar-ments, were fashionable. Ossie Clark produced a range of chiffon shirts, made in Celia Birtwell's floral printed fabrics. In 1962, the traditional shirtmakers Turnbull & Asser engaged the talents of Mr Fish as designer. He created a dazzling range of patterned shirts, sometimes with matching ties, which they sold alongside their more classic lines.

RIGHT:
PLATE 80.
Detail of Mr Fish
jacket, 1970.
Blue, black and
silver, woven
wool-synthetic-
lurex mix. Shirt,
black synthetic
crêpe. Worn
and given by
Mr Fish. (T.705:
A-B-1974.)

LEFT:
PLATE 81. Just Men suit, 1968. Brown cotton velvet / Hunting Campbell wool tartan; Turnbull & Asser tie, brown silk, c.1972; shirt, white cotton, c.1970. Worn and given by Sir Roy Strong. (T.244:A-B-1981, T.207-1979.)

RIGHT:
PLATE 82. Tommy Nutter suit, 1973. Cream wool; Take Six shirt, multicolour print, wool mix, c.1970. Suit given by Mr R.W. Webb. (T.152-1995, T.153-1995, T.154-1995.) Shirt worn and given by Sir Roy Strong. (T.107-1985.)

Since the 1980s Scott Crolla, Paul Smith and Vivienne Westwood are among those to have created bold and floral patterned shirts.

Mr Fish opened his own menswear boutique in 1966, which attracted an artistic, pop and aristocratic clientele. In 1970 he designed himself a suit, in a lurid fabric, which had art nouveau overtones. The semi-fitted, collarless jacket was made in a blue, black and silver synthetic wool mix, which was jacquard woven in a design of linear, fuschia-like flowers. It features a corded silk fastening, with a tassel and jet beads (plate 80). The hipster-style trousers are made in a matching blue fabric with a broad, 'dinner suit' black satin stripe. The shirt, in black synthetic crêpe, has a boned high collar, pleated front, fastens with jet beads and has a side zip. This 'showy' suit draws upon ethnic and historical styles, as well as conventional tailored evening wear.

Stylish and flamboyant dressers also create their own Bohemian fashions. Plate 81 features one of Sir Roy Strong's evening suits from 1968. He bought the Hunting Campbell tartan fabric in Beauly, near Inverness in Scotland, and the brown cotton velvet, the ribbon edging and the blue lining material, from Harrods. The three-piece suit

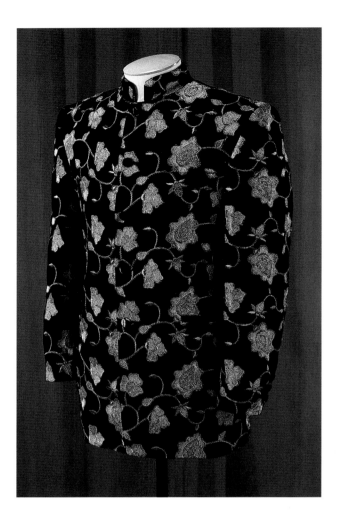

ABOVE:

PLATE 83.
Favourbrook
jacket, 1996.
Black cotton
velvet and silver
silk embroidery.
Given by
Favourbrook.
(T.160:1-1996.)

was tailor made by Just Men, in the up-to-the-minute style of wide lapels, pocket flaps and narrow trousers. A large brown silk tie, arranged with a double Windsor knot, was worn with a white shirt from Turnbull & Asser. Brown leather boots, with elastic sides, completed the ensemble. Sir Roy Strong ceased wearing this outfit in about 1974, when the vogue for decorative evening dressing petered out.

Beautifully laundered, white linen and pristine cream wool suits have long been the prerogative of the dandy. Traditionally, they had associations with colonial dress, picnics by the river and croquet. By the late 1960s, in exaggerated styling, they were much favoured by pop stars. This three-piece cream wool suit, with broad lapels and flared trousers by Tommy Nutter, reflects this latter mood (plate 82).

In the 1990s Favourbrook of Jermyn Street cater for men and women with Bohemian leanings. They specialise in Nehru jackets, decorative waistcoats, frock coats and velvet smoking jackets, with matching accessories. Many of the fabrics are inspired by historical designs. A Favourbrook black cotton velvet Nehru jacket from 1996 (plate 83) is embellished with silver silk embroidery, reminiscent of Iranian floral designs of a type seen on carpets and ceramics.

Men who are conservative in their dress occasionally indulge a Bohemian taste for the exotic at home. Opulent, brocaded silk dressing gowns, for example, have assumed an air of languid decadence since Noël Coward wore them with great panache, on stage, for his 1924 play *The Vortex*. Georgina von Etzdorf has perpetuated this trend in the 1990s with her deeply coloured, abstractly patterned, velvet dressing gown (plate 84).

ABOVE:

PLATE 84.
Georgina von
Etzdorf dressing
gown, autumn/
winter 1995.
Printed velvet
rayon. Given by
Miss Georgina
von Etzdorf.
(T. 185-1996.)

By looking both to the past and to distant horizons, designers of Bohemian fashions and their clients exploit a narrative which draws upon literature, ethnicity, artistic movements, historical revival styles and popular culture, which is read and understood by people with similar sensibilities.

Acknowledgements

We are grateful to Elizabeth Wilson for sharing her excellent manuscript about Bohemians with us, prior to publication. Also, thanks are due to Valerie Mendes, Fiona Anderson, Emma Damon and Jennifer Wearden.

Footnotes

1 Beaton 1954, p.244.
2 The outfit was modelled by Britt Ekland in *Vogue* (15 September 1970), p.82.
3 Cooper, Howard *Ian & Marcel* (catalogue produced to coincide with the V&A display of Ian and Marcel's clothes in 1993, with proceeds to the Terrence Higgins Trust), p.4.
4 *Vogue* (January 1966), pp. 48-49
5 Beaton (1954), p.326

Selected Bibliography

Baines, Barbara *Fashion Revivals* (London: Batsford 1981).
Beaton, Cecil *The Glass of Fashion* (London: Weidenfeld & Nicolson 1954).
Cohn, Nik *Today There Are No Gentlemen* (London: Weidenfeld & Nicolson 1971).
Eicher, Joanne *Fashion and Ethnicity* (Oxford: Berg 1995).
Newton, Stella Mary *Health, Art and Reason* (London: John Murray 1974).
Tilka, Max *Costume Patterns and Designs* (New York: Rizzoli 1990).

Country

AMY DE LA HAYE & TONY GLENVILLE

The Country Weekend is as much part of the British Way of Life as Cricket, Tea and the Weather. It is the bastion of leisure life, the linchpin of seduction, the focal point of sport.

(*British Style* magazine, 'Country Issue', vol.8, no.2, 1995, p.57)

PREVIOUS PAGES:
Detail of Joe Casely Hayford slipover, 1994. Brown wool knitted in alternating reverse stocking stitch (plate 100). Given by Mr Joe Casely Hayford. (T.120-1994.)

In spite of its pioneering industrial past, many determining images of Britishness in the twentieth century have been closely associated with the rural world. Re-invented as a pastoral arcadia, Britain becomes a clean, harmonious, honest, unpolluted land, free of political doctrine. The deep and abiding affection for the countryside is reflected in British literature, music and painting; landscapes by Constable and Stubbs' equine portraits continue to be national favourites. The land provides a reassuring haven, especially in times of crisis – during both world wars political propaganda fully exploited this. In the post-war period, fashion is among the many media to have reflected and reinforced this special relationship between the British and the countryside.

By the 1880s, the traditions of feudal ownership which had long underpinned the British establishment were crumbling. Rather than confront the new, many families retreated into their own private worlds. Historian David Cannadine describes a consequence of this shift: 'Dutiful recreation was gradually superseded by indulgent distraction...In many quarters the leisure class was becoming the pleasure class.'[1] Lavish hospitality had always been a central function of country house life and, with the advent of the motor car, the weekend party became ever more popular. In the early post-war period, the future of Britain's aristocracy and their country houses appeared to be in jeopardy. But by the 1950s, country houses had regained a certain degree of security, either in private ownership or under the paternalistic wing of the National Trust. Many country houses have been opened to the public, offering additional attractions to lure paying visitors. This accessibility, coupled with a number of highly successful television series and films, has helped sustain the idea of the country house within the popular consciousness.

Outdoor pursuits and sport have always played a central role in British country life. Aristocratic writer and gardener Vita Sackville-West, whose family home was the Knole estate in Kent, wrote in 1941: 'Outdoor life has always been more important to the English country gentleman than the indoor; the field more alluring than the hearth'.[2] During the

LEFT:
PLATE 85.
Left: Fair Isle sweater, 1920s. Multicolour hand-knitted wool. Right: Fair Isle slipover, c.1931. Multicolour hand-knitted wool. Sweater given by Mr R. A. Lamb. (T.146-1980.) Slipover given by Mr G. Nightingale. (T.363-1984.)

ABOVE:
PLATE 86.
Left: Sweater, Pringle, 1996. Grey, blue and cream cashmere argyle design. Right: Twinset, Pringle, 1996. Ivory cashmere, mother of pearl buttons (cardigan only shown). Given by Pringle of Scotland. (T.432:1-1996, T.433:1-2-1996.)

late nineteenth century, sporting activities had become increasingly organized, as well as socially exclusive. British specialist clothing, designed to provide warmth, protection and ease of movement for sporting and leisure wear, has long been internationally acclaimed, as are the British textiles and yarns from which the clothing is made. As a result, this has become a major part of Britain's sartorial identity and often becomes intermingled with British fashion.

The fashionable and fun-loving Edward, Prince of Wales, launched a number of menswear trends in the 1920s which soon became British staples. Fair Isle knitwear became internationally desirable when he was seen wearing it on the golf course at St Andrews in Scotland. Named after the Scottish Shetland isle from where it originated, it is made from local wool using a highly skilful stranded technique. Characterized by multicoloured, patterned bands, which are often subtly varied, Fair Isle retains an overall unity of design. Examples can be seen in plate 85. Distinctive diamond-patterned argyle sweaters and hose were also worn as stylish 1920s sportswear and, like Fair Isle, have subsequently been accorded British classic status. Examples of this distinctive knitwear, produced by Pringle (established in 1815), can be seen in plate 86.

Certain colourings, textiles and patterns are specific to the country wardrobe. Many textiles are designed to blend with the environment. The traditional rule of thumb is that black should be worn in the city and brown in the country. For sporting activities, such as shooting and stalking where stealth is required, camouflage greens and browns are essential.

Tweed is a mainstay for country clothes. In his portrayal of hunting society Simon Blow remembers that, during the early post-war period, his aunt and uncle's country house 'was always filled with ladies in tweedy coats-and-skirts and men in tweed, twill and large, brown brogue shoes'.[5] Woven from woollen yarns, which are carded but not combed, tweed is a sturdy, resilient fabric, suitable for outdoor life. Its bulkiness demands simplicity of cut, and its rich texture and harmonious colourings require little ornamentation. Moleskin, waxed cottons and corduroy also feature frequently in the country wardrobe.

The tweed or plain woollen Norfolk jacket was introduced in the 1860s, and subsequently became accepted as both everyday and sporting wear for men and women. Eminently practical, it is belted with deep, protective yokes, with box pleats facilitating ease of movement. Usually worn with plus fours, twos or sixes (the figure indicates, in inches, the width of fullness above the knee band of the breeches), the Norfolk jacket was popular right through the post-war period and its influence still prevails today.

Check patterned fabrics are intimately associated with Scottish textiles. Tartan, the woollen cloth originally worn by Scottish Highlanders, is made in various patterns, known as *setts*. These are popularly believed to signify clan membership. In 1747, one year after the Battle of Culloden, the wearing of tartan fabrics and Highland dress was banned. Severe penalties were imposed upon those who rebelled, and the law was not repealed until 1782. By this time, thousands of families had been cleared from their homes and the socio-economic organization of the Highlands had changed considerably. Lowlanders and English landlords replaced cattle-rearing with more profitable sheep farming, and commercialized estates for shooting and fishing. Estate tweeds, also known as district checks, were developed in the 1830s for those who lived and worked on these estates. They were based upon the predominantly black-and-white check

LEFT:

PLATE 87. Right: Bill Gibb suit, mid-1970s. Multicolour tartan-type check brushed wool. Left: Patti Searle ensemble, 1979. Jacket, mid-blue leather. Coat, brown, grey-and-blue checked brushed wool and mohair mix. Bill Gibb suit given by Mrs M. Wilson MacDonald. (T.444-A-1988.) Jacket and coat given by Miss Patti Searle. (T.298-1980, T.299-1980.)

plaids, worn by the new influx of Border shepherds. Perhaps the most famous district check is Glen Urquhart, commonly but mistakenly known as Prince of Wales check. Other designs include Shepherd, Altries and Kincardine Castle. Full Highland dress is now mainly worn for special occasions, such as weddings, ceilidhs or as military attire.

Shaggy wools and mohairs, as well as tartans and checks, are also British specialities, and a number of fashion designers have lifted them out of their traditional contexts. Bill Gibb had a particular talent for combining tradition with modernity: his 1970s tartan-type, brushed woollen, knickerbocker suit makes an elegant, yet entirely functional fashion statement, and Patti Searle's 'light as a feather' wool and mohair checked 'blanket' coat is a multi-purpose fashion garment, suited to both town and country (plate 87).

Vivienne Westwood has consistently featured tartan fabrics in her collections – from her subversive, punk, bondage trousers to exquisite silk ball gowns with overblown skirts, in shades of delphinium and cerise, in the 1990s. She has also made extensive use of

ABOVE:
FIG 15.
Drawing of a
man in hunt-
ing dress at
the Royal
Horse Show,
Olympia,
1940 by
Francis
Marshall,
1944.

of tweeds, and Harris Tweed in particular. For her autumn/winter 1988 collection, she designed a tweed Norfolk suit, complete with plus twos (plate 88).

The British aristocracy has often been lampooned for its rather down-at-heel appearance. The characters in P.G. Wodehouse's early twentieth-century novels, set in the ever-lasting, pastoral innocence of a fantasy rural England, are clearly identified by their clothing. Nancy Mitford set her novel, *The Pursuit of Love* (1945) in a mythical country house based on Faringdon House in Oxfordshire, and writes of the owner, Sir Leicester:

> He was potting in the garden as we drove up, in an old pair of corduroy trousers, so much designed as an old pair that it seemed improbable that they had ever been new, an old tweed coat on the same lines, secateurs in his hand, a depressed Corgi at his heels, and a mellow smile on his face.[4]

BELOW:
PLATE 89. Detail
of Cordings
covert coat,
1996. Mid-
brown wool,
green cotton
velvet trim.
Given by
Cordings.
(T.138-1996.)

Fashion sociologist Alison Lurie has observed that country fabrics 'are made into baggy, rumpled, rounded garments that echo the uneven rounded shapes of the landscape – of bush, tree and hill'.[5]

In complete contrast, however, great sartorial pride is taken in sporting events. From the eighteenth century onwards, hunting was Britain's premier country sport, and the prescribed 'uniform' has changed little since this time. Hunting dress for men traditionally consisted of a black silk top hat; a scarlet coat, with buttons embossed with the hunt crest; a white stock; white breeches and mahogany-top leather boots. In his description of the early post-war period, Simon Blow recalls 'the endless preparation of kit. You had to be spotless for the meet, only to be muddied five minutes later. The boning of boots, the polishing of spurs, the cleaning of coats, brushing and smoothing of hats and polishing of tack – all were important rituals'.[6]

LEFT:
PLATE 88. Detail
of Vivienne
Westwood
Norfolk-style
suit, 'Time
Machine
Collection'
autumn/winter
1988. Mid-pink
and grey wool
tweed. Given
by Mr David
Barber and
worn by
Mr Rupert
Michael Dolan.
(T.261:1-2-1991.)

The British are passionate about horses: racing is considered to be 'the sport of kings' and the British royal family has long set a standard in this respect, being accomplished riders and frequently seen at equestrian events. The tweed hacking jacket; the tailcoat, which evolved from the hunting coat; riding breeches; jodhpurs and riding boots, as well as the women's habit (hunting skirt and jacket) have all been incorporated into everyday dress and inspired high fashion. This is also true of the covert coat, introduced by Cordings, which is identified by its velvet collar, deep pocket flaps and rows of stitching on the cuffs and hem (plate 89).

The 'Glorious Twelfth' of August launches the grouse shooting season.

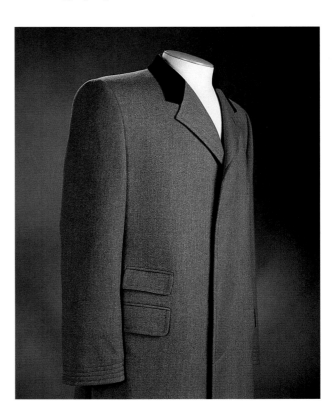

The London social season comes to a close, and wealthy families traditionally decamped from the town to their country estate. In mid-September duck and partridge shooting starts, and one month later it is the pheasant season. Shooting clothes must protect the wearers from the elements, be thorn-proof and blend with the environment. Hackett's luxurious shooting suit from 1996 is made in a heavy 22oz tweed, in a sage green herringbone, with a lavender window-pane over-check. Naming the design 'Country Life', *Country Life* magazine commissioned it from Hunter's of Brora for Hackett's exclusive use. Breeches accommodate long, thick wool socks, which are secured by knitted flashes (plate 90).

Salmon and trout fishing is another sport with aristocratic associations. Fishing can be a solitary as well as contemplative pastime, and the primary clothing requirements are for protection and warmth. Leading British brand names – Aquascutum (1851), Burberry (1856) and Barbour (1890) – all launched innovative, protective and waterproof clothing for sportsmen in the nineteenth century.

Thomas Burberry opened his clothing business in Hampshire to cater for farmers and sportsmen – two local rivers, the Itchen and the Test, were famous trout streams. Burberry set about developing a waterproof fabric, researching the resilience of local farmers' smocks. From 1888 he patented his specialist clothes, made from two layers of fabric – a twill of plain linen fabric over a waterproofed cloth tweed. By 1900, the company had become highly successful and opened its first London branch.

Cordings provide an exclusive range of stylish fishing clothes, and compiled an outfit for the V&A (plate 91). The wool and cotton mix shirt is in the popular Tattersall country check, which was derived from the design of blankets used at the famous Newmarket horse auctions. The rust wool sweater was hand-framed in Scotland; olive green moleskin plus twos and a Barbour towelling rain choker and fishing waistcoat complete the ensemble. The brown field boots were manufactured for Cordings by Hunter, makers of the original utilitarian green wellington. Lined in soft calf-leather, they feature a rubber sole for underfoot protection and to keep the feet warm.

In her satirical book of etiquette, *Say Please* published in 1949, Virginia Graham wrote a telling piece on rural convention in high society:

> There are two dates in the racing calendar to which ladies who dislike racing intensely should give particular attention. One is Ascot, the other their local Point-to-Point. Neither of these events can be avoided if a lady wishes to be well thought of, for if she fails to attend the former she shows a disrespect for both horseflesh and couture, for which lapses society will be slow to forgive, and if she ducks the latter her neighbours will brand her as the sort of woman who *only* goes to Ascot.[7]

LEFT
PLATE 90. Hackett shooting suit, 1996. Jacket, breeches and cap, green-and-purple check wool tweed. Shirt, checked cotton. Tie, silk paisley. Socks, knitted wool. Flashes, knitted wool. Boots, leather. Given by Mr Jeremy Hackett. (T.219:1-13-1996.)

RIGHT
PLATE 91. Cordings fishing outfit, 1996. Shirt, green-brown-and-cream checked cotton and wool. Sweater, brown knitted wool. Plus twos, green moleskin. Socks, yellow-and-brown Shetland wool, knitted. All Cordings. Waistcoat, green cotton. Rain-choker, green cotton towelling. Barbour. Wellington boots, brown rubber, leather lined. Hunter. Given by Cordings. (T.137:1-9-1996.)

ABOVE:
FIG 16. Harvey
Nichols chalk-
striped two-
piece suit,
with plumed
hat, 1950,
photographed
by John
French in a
rural setting
(F1536).

In March 1954, *Vogue* photographed Countess Beatty at home in Oxfordshire, at Astrop Park, Banbury. Wearing a Ronald Paterson tweed suit she is accompanied by Mrs John Wyndham, who is wearing a Charles Creed suit of Linton tweed. The editorial reiterated the oft-cited observation that 'English designers are world famous for their tweeds and ball dresses; English women have equal fame for their style in wearing them'. In the early post-war period, Lachasse, Peter Russell and Digby Morton also designed stylish tweed suits, and Hardy Amies has consistently featured them in his collections. Top-level ready-to-wear companies such as Hebe Sports, Dereta, Braemar, Harella and Brenner Sports, also specialized in this field.

The tweed suit, and the twinset and skirt, are traditional country clothes usually worn with thick stockings and stout shoes. The purchase of a top-quality tweed suit from a London designer always represented a considerable capital outlay. However, such an investment was seen to consolidate a woman's professional role and social standing within the community. High-quality, well-designed and tailored daytime clothes are often worn extensively over a period of years (and, as a result, rarely find their way into museum collections).

Trousers were worn by many women during the Second World War for utilitarian reasons. They presented country ladies with a comfortable option, but outside the stables and garden, the decision to wear them had to be taken with care. In her 1947 book of etiquette, Ira Morris advised country-based readers that 'trousers fall into two categories: slacks for relaxation, and working pants for the rough jobs about the house and garden. Trousers should never replace a skirt for everyday wear'.[8]

The relaxation of dress codes by the 1960s led to women's country dress styles becoming increasingly informal. In 1972 *Vogue* (15 September) interviewed Lady Lichfield at Shugborough, her Staffordshire country home: 'In the country Lady Lichfield wears jeans and denim shirts and skirts, silk scarves, fishing gear, loden coats and gumboots'. For the evening, she favoured romantic designs by Zandra Rhodes and Gina Fratini.

Summer textiles, like winter tweeds, fit perfectly into a pastoral environment. Britain has long excelled in the production of fabrics printed with floral patterns (plate 92). Liberty is renowned for its small-scale flowers which bloom on fine cottons, linens and supple silks, providing ideal materials for the garment known generically as the 'summer frock'. A myriad of British floral dress fabrics have been available in the post-war period. They represent a botanical feast, with flowers from herbaceous borders, meadows and woodlands as well as stylized, abstract designs, proving ideal both for everyday wear and special occasions such as garden parties, luncheons and summer fêtes, as well as for wear in town.

BELOW:
FIG 17. Tweed in town. John Cavanagh black-and-white tweed coat with high satin trimmed collar, autumn/winter 1954 . Hat by Simone Mirman. Photographed by John French.

In 1954 Hardy Amies stated that 'The English woman usually has some feel of the country about her clothes. I think that until six o'clock she likes to look like a woman who has come up from the country for the day and does not live in London. That is in contrast to the French woman who likes to look as though she were born and bred in Paris and would be awfully bored if she had to leave it'.[9] Alison Lurie described the early 1970s fashion for shepherdess styles as 'theatrical country clothes', because they were entirely unsuited to country life. 'When they are worn in town the message is "I don't really belong here, behind this desk or in this flat; my rightful place is in the garden of a rather large country house."'[10]

Deeply rooted in British class structures, this sartorial nuance acknowledges that the aristocracy are indelibly associated with the country, and that even today the wearing of top-quality country clothes retains vestiges of this élite association. As stated elsewhere, many British fashion designers strive to create a new look by juxtaposing tradition and modernity, by re-working traditional cutting techniques, decorative devices and textiles. London's post-war, youthful, fashion designers have predominantly catered for fashion-conscious urban clienteles. None the less, the styles and materials associated with upper-class country clothes have formed the basis of many collections.

RIGHT:
PLATE 93.
Detail of
Baccarat
ensemble,
1971. Jacket,
multicolour
butterfly print
glazed cotton,
with suede
collar and
belt. Skirt,
brown, black
suede. Given
by Mr Paul
Getty Junior.
(T.14-A-1974.)

RIGHT:
PLATE 94. Biba
trouser suit, 1970.
Pink-and-green
cabbage-rose
printed cotton.
Given by Miss
Petra Siniawski.
(T.265-A-1984.)

FAR RIGHT:
PLATE 95. Sally
Tuffin ensemble,
early 1970s. Coat,
multicolour wool
quilted with fox-
glove Liberty
print Varuna wool.
Blouse, foxglove
Liberty print
Varuna wool.
Trousers, multi-
colour wool, fox-
glove Liberty
print Varuna wool.
Given by Mrs
Valerie Lloyd.
(T.529:A-C-1985.)

In the early 1960s Pierre Cardin and his assistant, Robert Bruno, are credited with reviving the late eighteenth-century fashion term *'le style Anglais'*. Nik Cohn writes: 'This was a romantic version of the traditional English gentlemen: the squire. It involved a lot of tweeds and Prince of Wales checks, hacking jackets and deerstalkers, and even Bernard Shaw knickerbockers, and the garments were called things like "Lord" or "Sir", or mystifyingly "Perkins".[11]

The late 1960s witnessed the beginning of a vogue for dress fabrics printed with floral patterns on such an immense scale that they resembled furnishing textiles. Baccarat's two-piece ensemble (plate 93) has a refined design incorporating butterflies, based on a botanical engraving, and harks back to the glazed cottons printed with multicoloured flowers known as chintzes. The use of this term has now broadened, and is employed to embrace an enormous range of floral prints. The Biba trouser suit of the early 1970s, in cabbage-rose printed cretonne, draws on nineteenth-century British printed textiles, but is resolutely modern in its cut and its flared trousers (plate 94).

Sally Tuffin skilfully 'mixed and matched' throughout the 1960s and '70s. She was a keen advocate of Liberty prints. Unusually, she combined Liberty's Varuna wool, printed with a subdued pattern of foxgloves, with a rainbow-coloured wool, quilting them together for extra warmth in a trouser suit ensemble (plate 95). Gina Fratini, Mary Quant and John Bates for Jean Varon also made great use of floral prints in their collections. Laura Ashley came into her own during the early 1970s and made the country milkmaid look available to all. Sprigged cottons were her hallmark, and women swept the pavements in their full-length, *faux-naïf* flowing Laura Ashley frocks.

RIGHT:
PLATE 96.
Left: Sasha
Kagan sweater,
1981.
Multicolour
hand-knitted
wool. Above
right: Edina &
Lena sweater,
1979.
Multicolour
hand-knitted
cotton. Below
right: Kaffe
Fassett skirt,
early 1970s.
Multicolour
hand-knitted
Shetland wool.
Sasha Kagan
sweater given
by Mrs Sasha
Kagan (T.105-
1981.) Edina &
Lena sweater
given by Pamela
Dress Agency.
(T.154-1985),
(T.306-1985.)

Occupational knitwear, such as the heavy-duty Gansey sweaters worn by Channel Island fishermen since the eighteenth century, has been transferred into country and fashion wardrobes. Plate 96 shows three excellent examples of textural knits, in colours evoking heather, berries, soil and leaves, which have become British specialities. Sasha Kagan's sweater from 1981 reflects her love of the Welsh countryside from which she draws her inspiration. Kaffe Fassett has revolutionized approaches to colour and design. His hand-knitted fringed skirt from the early 1970s, in muted colourings, reflects his painterly approach to pattern. Edina & Lena perfectly captured the mood for nostalgic country styles, with patterns inspired by Fair Isle designs and 1930s knitwear fashions. Their 1979 summer sweater is hand-knitted in a fancy openwork stitch.

During the 1970s Sheridan Barnett, Stephen Marks and Wendy Dagworthy were skilfully interpreting country fabrics and styles. Margaret Howell's fashions are modern classics in natural fabrics. She has consistently used themes from countrywear as her

ABOVE:

PLATE 97.
Margaret Howell
ensemble,
spring/summer
1996. Dress,
grey, white,
green and red
floral print silk.
Cardigan, red
knitted cotton.
Neckerchief,
red-and-white
spot silk chif-
fon. Given by
Miss Margaret
Howell.
(T.159:1-3-1996.)

springboard, marrying traditional styles with modern appeal. For spring/summer 1996 she designed a demure summer frock in pale grey silk crêpe, strewn with flowers and teamed with a perky, short-sleeved cardigan and matching neckerchief. Like all her work it has a stylish timelessness (plate 97).

In the early days of the motor car, full-length, protective coats were required for open-top travel. Aquascutum, Burberry and Harrods provided their customers with practical and fashionable trench coats, made in Scottish tweed, Irish frieze, fur and leather. Bill Gibb's leather coat (plate 98) can be likened to these in terms of its mater-ial, colour, protective high collar and tight cuffs. It comes from his first collection, for autumn/winter 1972, when he designed a group of chestnut brown, leather garments, screen-printed in silver with bees (his signature motif, a play on 'B' for Bill) and trailing chrysanthemums. Nature was the theme of this collection: 'it was like a purification starting on my own and nature just matched my mood'.[12]

In the 1980s Peter York coined the term 'Sloane Ranger' in his memorable dig at the wealthy young men and women, living in fashionable Chelsea, who affected country clothes and accoutrements in town.[13] The archetypal female Sloane Ranger travelled on an old-fashioned bicycle, complete with a wicker basket on the front. She wore a Barbour jacket over a floral sprigged blouse, casual slacks or a gathered skirt, flat shoes or low-heeled courts and wore an Alice-band in her hair.

ABOVE:

PLATE 98. Bill Gibb
coat, 1972. Brown
leather screen-
printed with silver
bees and chrysan-
themum. Given
by Mr Clifford.
(T.171-1992.)

RIGHT:
PLATE 99.
Burberry
ensemble, 1988.
'Lawbry' rain-
coat, belt, beige
wool gaberdine.
'Ashwell' jacket,
green, brown,
navy and red
lambswool
tweed. Skirt,
beige wool
gaberdine.
'Watt' waistcoat,
mid-brown wool
flannel. Sweater,
yellow knitted
Geelong lambs-
wool. Given
by Burberry.
(T.22:A-D&F-
1988.)

Since the 1970s a number of clothing companies who had originally produced utilitarian country clothes have broadened their ranges to entice a fashion-conscious clientele. Burberry employed the talents of Lord Patrick Lichfield to photograph the advertisements they placed in glossy fashion magazines. Lord Lichfield and his friends also posed for some of the campaigns in the grounds of his family seat, Shugborough Hall. Burberry have continued to create distinguished, elegant clothes with a country theme. Their ensemble for 1988 features a beige wool gabardine, Burberry raincoat; a hacking-style, lambswool tweed jacket; a flannel waistcoat; yellow lambswool polo neck sweater and a beige wool gabardine skirt (plate 99).

Joe Casely Hayford's outfit from autumn/winter 1994 (plate 100) would appeal to the urban 'New Fogey' with a passion for country traditions. It comprises a check, collarless, brushed cotton shirt; a sleeveless pullover, in coarse wool, hand-knitted in alternating reverse stocking stitch bearing a resemblance to furrowed earth, and mid-brown moleskin trousers. The jacket, with practical patch pockets, is of dark brown corduroy. During the eighteenth century, this sturdy cut-pile cotton-velvet fabric was widely employed for utilitarian clothing worn by all levels of society, and by the nineteenth century was also used for hunting dress. In the post-war period, it has become widely popular for casual clothing.

ABOVE:
PLATE 100. Detail of Joe Casely Hayford ensemble, autumn/winter 1994. Jacket: brown cotton corduroy. Shirt, beige, brown and grey brushed cotton. Slipover, brown wool knitted in alternating reverse stocking stitch. Trousers (not shown), mid-brown moleskin. Given by Mr Joe Casely Hayford. (T.118-1994, T.119-1994, T.120-1994, T.121-1994.)

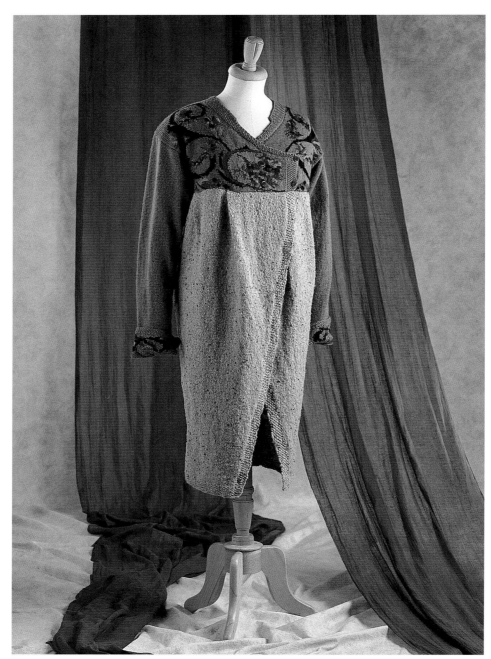

RIGHT:
PLATE 101. Muir & Osborne coat, autumn/winter 1996/7. Hand-knitted green, pink, black and purple wool and Irish flecked wool. Given by Ms Sally Muir and Ms Joanna Osborne. (T.141-1996.)

It is generally accepted that Otto Weisz, Pringle's Austrian designer, introduced the fine-knit jumper and cardigan twinset in the 1930s. Since this decade, the twinset has remained in the Pringle range and has been subtly re-styled to accommodate major fashion changes. It has two lives – as a classic look, and from time to time as a main fashion feature. In the mid-1990s, it acquired a new cachet among the young who favoured pastel colours. The twinset is a standard line for the leading knitwear companies, including N. Peal and Ballantyne, while Marks & Spencer makes twinsets accessible to the widest possible market. In 1996, Pringle donated the most luxurious of twinsets to the V&A, in ivory cashmere with mother-of-pearl buttons. It offers style and warmth without weight (see plate 86).

In a totally different vein, Muir & Osborne's 'Bennett coat' (plate 101), for autumn/winter 1996-97, illustrates their inventive approach to knitwear. Reflecting the current vogue for Jane Austen, the Bath-based design duo took Regency dress as the starting point for their hand-knitted empire-line coat. The ornate bodice in fine wool is juxtaposed with a chunky skirt in Irish flecked wool. Working under the name of Warm and Wonderful, their early 1980s black sheep sweater worn by Princess Diana displayed the same blend of fun and style.

In Britain, and in England in particular, many still yearn for a pastoral idyll which inevitably has alienating consequences in a modern, urban and multi-cultural society. This culturally conservative and nostalgic interpretation of what it means to be British is undoubtedly exclusive, but perhaps because of this it has an enduring appeal both in Britain and abroad. Indeed, in many ways it is this romanticized perception of the country and its clothing which signifies 'Britishness' worldwide. International fashion designers such as Chanel, Kenzo and Ralph Lauren have highly successfully appropriated and transformed clothes associated with British aristocratic country life, giving them a heightened chic and gloss.

Acknowledgements

We would like to thank Valerie Mendes, Fiona Anderson and Avril Hart.

Footnotes

1 Cannadine (1996), p.386.
2 Sackville-West (1941), p.27.
3 Blow (1983), p.8.
4 Mitford, Nancy. *The Pursuit of Love* (London: Hamish Hamilton, 1945), p.93.
5 Lurie (1982), p.104.
6 Blow (1983), p.8.
7 Graham (1949), p.23.
8 Morris (1947), pp.111-112.
9 Amies, Hardy. 'Wool in Fashion', lecture at the Royal Society of Arts in 1954. Published by the Department of the International Wool Secreteriat, excerpt from p.3.
10 Lurie (1982), p.104.
11 Cohn (1971), p.75.
12 *Vogue*, 15 September 1972, p.10.
13 York, Peter. *The Official Sloane Ranger Diary* (London: Ebury Press 1983).

Selected Bibliography

Blow, Simon. *Fields Elysian – a portrait of hunting society* (London: J M Dent and Sons Ltd 1983).
British Style magazine: 'Country Issue', vol. 8, no.2, 1995; 'A Salute to Scotland the Brave', vol. 8, no.4, 1995-6.
Cannadine, David. *The Decline and Fall of the British Aristocracy* (London: Papermac 1996).
Cohn, Nik. *Today There Are No Gentlemen* (London: Weidenfeld & Nicolson 1971).
Graham, Virginia (with illustrations by Osbert Lancaster) *Say Please* (London: Harvill Press 1949).
Lurie, Alison. *The Language of Clothes* (London: Hamlyn 1982).
Morris, Ira. *The Glass of Fashion* (London: The Pilot Press 1947).
Sackville-West, Vita. *English Country Houses* (London: HarperCollins 1941)

Hats

EMMA DAMON

ABOVE:

PLATE 102. John Boyd hat, 1996. White Sinamay crown and brim with black band, trimmed with black feathers. Given by Mr John Boyd. (T.135-1996.)

Darling, what is that?
That, angel, is a hat.
Are you positive? Are you certain?
Are you sure it's not a curtain?
Shall you really place your head in it?
How's for keeping cake or bread in it?
Do not wear it on your head;
Find some other use instead,
Say a cloth for drying dishes,
Or a net for catching fishes,
Or a veil by night to veto
The bill of the mosquito?
Darling, what is that?
Are you sure it is a hat?
And if so, what was the matter
With the hatter?
Was he troubled? Was he ill?
Was he laughing fit to kill?
Oh, what was on his mind
As he designed?

Ogden Nash, 'The Drop of a Hat', from
I'm A Stranger Here Myself (London: Gollancz 1938).

PREVIOUS PAGES: Detail of Philip Treacy hat, spring/summer 1995 (plate 117). Shocking pink goose feathers. Given by Mr Philip Treacy. (T.182-1996.)

Underlying their often ephemeral quality, fashion writer Alison Adburgham once described hats as 'the dragonflies of the dressworld'.[1] Yet traditional and designer British hats have found a permanent home in the nation's wardrobe. Traditional hats are worn as part of an immovable social uniform, whilst the British social season provides a saviour to couture millinery.

The rich diversity of British headwear ranges from the bowler hat of the city gentleman to the flamboyant millinery worn at Ascot, and to the crowns and tiaras paraded on state occasions. Hats belong to the tradition of class-related British dress codes: the straw boater and the deerstalker are defining badges of social status and purpose. The British also value the functional nature of hats as shelter from the notorious unpredictability of their island's climate. As Anne Edwards and Drusilla Beyfus wrote in 1956, 'A woman with a wonderful picture hat will forever be at odds with the weather, and if she has an expensive one, she will be hard pushed to get the wear out of it'.[2]

ABOVE:
PLATE 103.
Right: Lachasse turban, 1948-9. Maroon-and-black jersey. Worn by Mrs Ralph Dent and given by Mrs M. Webster. (T.186-1990.) Left: Lachasse snood, 1940s. Maroon felt with brown net snood. Given by Mr Peter Lewis-Crown. (T.186-1990.)

Ascot's reputation as one of the most prestigious events in the racing year is ensured by its close links with the royal family. Ladies' Day at Ascot is the most important daytime event in the social calendar and entry to the Royal Enclosure is highly selective. The flamboyant display is governed by strict etiquette, and the wearing of hats is obligatory for women. Inevitably, this dress code is emulated by other visitors to Ascot. The milliner Frederick Fox attributes the survival of hat-wearing in Britain to royal patronage and the institution of race meetings.[3] A stylish racegoer would never risk wearing the same hat on more than one occasion. Edwards and Beyfus's etiquette manual observed in 1956, 'Well-to-do people have been seen to wear the same dress twice, but they still wear different hats.' A couture hat for such occasions (plate 102) may require up to three fittings, a time-consuming procedure involving expert craftsmanship that contributes substantially to the cost. Some Ascot hats are nostalgic parodies, a celebration of traditional styles; others are designed to catch the eye and amuse. Mrs Gertrude Shilling, mother of milliner David Shilling, is renowned for the extravagant hats that she wears at Ascot. Her son says that these are less about couture and 'more about theatre'.[4]

The Royal Enclosure, Ascot

ABOVE:
FIG. 18. Illustration of the Royal Enclosure at Ascot, by Francis Marshall, in 'London West', *Studio*, 1944.

RIGHT:
PLATE 104. Alice Camus hat, 1940s. Black straw hat with multicoloured fabric flowers. Given by Mrs P. Pepper and worn by her mother, Mrs Bessie Love. (T. 33-1985.)

Each of the Season's sporting occasions demands specific headwear. For men, the top hat is *de rigueur* at Ascot, while panamas and boaters dominate at the Henley Regatta. Some prefer the panama because of its light, easy-to-wear soft structure. Originally made in Equador from Torquilla straw, the panama comes in two styles: ridged, which can be conveniently rolled up, or with a wide brim in an elegant trilby style (see plate 114). British hat firms in Luton and Christy's in Cheshire are famous for the top-quality panamas which are sold to the finest British hat shops and men's outfitters.

Although wartime shortages resulted in the standardization of clothing design, hats remained both unrationed and unrestricted, thus permitting women to make a small fashion statement. However, for reasons of practicality and safety many women wore snoods, scarves and turbans (plate 103). For the limited number of special events small fitted hats adorned with fabric flowers were popular, like Alice Camus's elegant black straw design decorated with pretty artificial flowers (plate 104).

Pillboxes with veils, miniature hats and neatly twisted turbans enabled fashionable long hair to be pinned and shown off to full advantage. These small hats were often worn tipped at an angle of 45 degrees and fastened with a small chin-strap. Veiling was another way to keep long hair neat. The V&A's miniature brown felt hat decorated with bird of paradise feathers illustrates this popular style (plate 105). It was fashionable at this time to incorporate a small comb to replace hat pins. Costs of materials, however, began to prove prohibitive, with an increase of up to 400 per cent according to a wartime survey.[5] As supplies of trimmings, decorative motifs and materials dwindled, it became necessary to make hats from only tiny pieces of fabric.

ABOVE:
PLATE 105. Miniature hats. Left: Hat, designer unknown, early 1940s. Brown felt with Bird of Paradise plumes. Worn and given by Mrs C.M. Bradley. Right: John Galliano double-brimmed hat, 1987. Dark blue silk with bow. Given by Mr John Galliano. Centre: Eric hat, 1940s. Black felt with blue feathers and orange velvet ribbon. Worn by Miss Monica Maurice and given by her family. (T.213-1987, T.2E-1988, T.733-1995.)

PLATE 106. Men's traditional British hats. Left: Christy & Co. Ltd top hat, 1996. Black hare's hair. Given by Christy & Co. Ltd. Centre: Barbour deerstalker, 1990. Checked wool tweed. Given by J. Barbour & Sons. Right: James Lock hat, 1944-45. Grey felt square crown 'coke'. Given by James Lock & Co. Ltd. (T.311-1990, T.437-1996, T.145-1996.)

During the war Winston Churchill's wearing of a square-crowned 'coke' hat provided an alternative to the conventional bowler. This distinctive hat became central to his sartorial identity. Plate 106 shows a classic version dating from the mid-1940s, bought from James Lock & Co., the world-famous hat shop for gentlemen.

By the mid-1940s long-established traditions of hat-wearing were beginning to be eroded. In response to the threat to their livelihoods, British milliners and hatters staged a promotional campaign to get men to wear hats. Coining the oft-repeated slogan, 'Get a hat to get ahead', the campaign was featured in *British Millinery* in October 1948. As the magazine explained, it was aimed at men aged 18 to 35 years and would 'appeal to them on two main grounds – the desire to look well before their girlfriends, and the desire to get on in business'.

The design of men's headgear was predictably conservative in the post-war years, with the soft felt trilby (a generic term for a man's brimmed hat) being customary everyday wear. Available in a range of brim sizes, it could be worn at varying angles and sometimes featured a crease down the front of the crown. By the mid-1950s attempts were made to widen the market through design differentiation. A new style of trilby, with a narrow brim and a low crown, was introduced but it failed to attract many wearers. Bowler Hat Week was launched in October 1950 to celebrate 100 years of the wearing of bowler hats. Although this event was not an outstanding success, the bowler hat did make something of a comeback among British businessmen during the 1950s and '60s.

The exaggerated quiff hairstyles favoured by subcultural youth during the 1950s largely precluded the wearing of hats. Roger Stephenson of James Lock & Co. talks of 'the hatless generation' of this era. Despite this, in the years immediately following the war British millinery enjoyed a resurgence. The New Look for women precipitated a fashion for large hats, which balanced the full skirts of the period. Indeed, the Coronation year of 1953 saw a peak in British hat-wearing. Simone Mirman's design, created from black horsehair with pink fabric rosebuds, has the popular 'coolie' profile (plate 107). Mirman, who referred to her hats as 'objets d'art', was born in Paris but worked as part of the British fashion scene. She opened her own salon in London in 1947 and received her first royal commission in 1952, when she was asked to create a selection of hats for Princess Margaret. In 1965 Mirman was invited to design hats for the Queen.

Historical revival styles have proved a dominant influence upon post-war hat design in Britain. One of the most popular styles has been the picture hat, popularized by film stars such as Grace Kelly and Audrey Hepburn. Otto Lucas, the renowned British milliner of the 1950s, created the superbly crafted black straw and velvet hat typical of this style in about 1954 (plate 108). This nostalgia was an extreme contrast to the modernistic themes generated by space travel and science fiction which were also proving influential. One amusing and elegant example was that created by the House of Lachasse for Mrs Gordan-Gottschalk, to wear on her wedding day in 1955. This design, evocatively named 'Martian's claw', is a tiny metal-spangled headpiece with claw-shaped prongs

ABOVE:
PLATE 107. Simone Mirman hat, 1953. Black horse hair trimmed with pink rosebuds. Worn by Mrs Doris Langley Moore. (T.113-1980.)

reaching across the head (plate 109). For evening wear, women's hats of the 1950s were delicate and bejewelled, or extravagantly embellished with feathers, flowers and veils.

The social season was well served in this decade by milliners of the calibre of Aage Thaarup. Danish-born, Thaarup had set up his British business by 1932 and was favoured by royalty and society ladies. He was renowned for the wit and originality of his designs, and once made a hat for the future Queen Mother trimmed with plastic vegetables, much to the amusement of King George VI. The V&A has an ingenious Aage Thaarup hat in a pyramid shape, constructed from fabric daisies and wire (plate 110). Thaarup was the first British couture milliner to design for the wholesale trade.

ABOVE:
PLATE 108.
Otto Lucas
1954. Black
straw and
velvet. Given
by Mr Robin
Allanson and
worn by Mrs
Barbara
Allanson.
(T.218-1985.)

Milliners of this period also gained inspiration from sketches of the catwalk shows in London and Paris, which ensured that their designs complemented fashion trends. Mass-market manufacturers followed suit, adapting and simplifying catwalk creations to facilitate large-scale production and keep prices competitive. For those unable to attend the fashion shows, illustrations proved an invaluable stylistic resource. Francis Marshall, one of the most talented post-war British fashion illustrators, produced beautiful sketches of the catwalk as well as drawings of the British social season.

It seems that the strict dress codes demanded by the Season, the traditional 'coming out' for young society women, were decreasingly applied to hats. Alison Adburgham noted in a 1954 issue of *Punch* that a gathering of débutantes 'were reprehensibly hatless, a prevalent custom most distressing to milliners'.[6] However, some débutantes did continue to respect tradition by donning small elegant hats, perhaps topped by a spray or sprig of artificial flowers. Simone Mirman called these 'more than a coiffure, less than a hat'. The last débutantes to meet the Queen for a presentation at court in 1958 wore these discreet styles.

Designer boutiques of the 1960s provided the antithesis to the formal dress of the previous decade and young people no longer required the services of a bespoke milliner in order to wear a hat. Headwear was often purchased readymade from boutiques in colours and fabrics that complemented clothing. The fashionable large-brimmed floppy hats with minimal decoration were economical to make, did not require special fitting and were easy to wear. Accepted codes of hat-wearing were broken down by the most irreverent who wore their hats informally, irrespective of the occasion and time of day.

BELOW:
PLATE 109.
Lachasse
wedding headdress, 1955.
Spangled
'Martian's
Claw'.
Designed by
Michael of
Lachasse.
Given by Mrs
June Gordan-Gottschalk,
worn on her
wedding day.
(T.398-1988.)

LEFT:
PLATE 110. Aage Thaarup hat, 1950s. White organza daisies mounted on an organza covered wire frame. Worn by Mrs Blair Cok and given by her sister, Mrs B. Church. (T.252-1985.)

The vogue for high hairstyles and hairpieces in the 1960s created problems for milliners. A 1965 manual stated, 'For at least ten years now, the hairdressers and the hat designers have been at war...the woman who has paid as much for her new hair set as she would for her new hat understandably wants to preserve it as long as possible. Inevitable result: she goes hatless'.[7]

Despite this significant set-back, from the mid-1960s another group of hat-wearers was to emerge: fashionable young men had the option of revelling in peacock finery and hats played a key role. Indeed, Tim Glazier, designer at Herbert Johnson, declared hats to be 'potentially the most dramatic and expressive of all male garments', and dramatic broad-brimmed hats in deep colours appeared as 'instruments of amusement'.[8] Cecil Beaton regularly wore such a hat – a brown wide-brimmed trilby (plate 111) which he later donated to the V&A. It was at this time that film again proved an influence in hat design. Faye Dunaway in *Bonnie and Clyde* (1967) instigated a craze for berets in a wide colour range, made from a variety of materials. Retro styles such as the 'gangster' trilby of 1930s Hollywood also proved popular. Hats with a horticultural theme created much interest too: *Vogue* described a 'hat that's a

RIGHT:
FIG. 19. Pencil sketch of a woman wearing a floral hat at Ascot, 1950, by Francis Marshall. (AAD 1990/2/5/2.)

flower...like putting your head in an enormous chrysanthemum'.[9] The press coverage resulting from these exuberant and romantic floral fantasies provided a boost to British millinery.

By the 1960s the use of animal fur was a subject of great controversy, and fake fur became a popular and economic alternative. The use of feather trimmings (plate 112), even entire birds, in hat-making has also had a long and chequered history, resulting in rigorous protective laws. Feathers have been used extensively to trim hats throughout the post-war period and in recent years whole hat structures have been composed from feathers, such as the shocking pink hat by leading British milliner Philip Treacy.

According to influential milliner David Shilling, the 1970s witnessed a quiet but significant revival in women's hat-wearing. He believes that designer-level hats gained popularity due to greater interaction between the social classes. The mood of the time was for greater freedom of choice and embraced the wearing of hats. They became more comfortable to wear as more lightweight and flexible materials became available (plate 113). The 1970s fashion for pastiche styles of the 1940s saw the revival of pill-box hats for women, complete with tiny veils, as popularized by Greta Garbo. Hollywood films such as *The Great Gatsby* (1974) inspired designs based on historical precedents. These were cheap to produce and became fashionable at all market levels.

The 1960s vogue for unisex clothing, the feminist movement of the 1970s and the relaxation of fashion's dictates all contributed towards the erosion of gender-specific

ABOVE:
PLATE 111. Men's hats. Right: Herbert Johnson hat, 1965. Brown felt with wide brim. Worn and given by Cecil Beaton. Above Left: Fred Bare cap, 1995. Black-and-grey knitted wool 'beanie' with brown wool top knot. Given by Ms Carolyn Brookes-Davis. Below Left: Bernstock & Speirs hat, autumn/winter 1989-90. Brown felt with tassel. Given by Mr Paul Bernstock and Ms Thelma Speirs. (T.160-1980, T.167-1990, T.44-1996).

LEFT:
PLATE 112. Feathered hats. Right: Jo Gordan hat, 'Kiss of death', 1994. Black satin bonnet with pheasant feathers. Given by Ms Jo Gordan. Left: Frederick Fox hat, 1979. Black cap with bird and veil. Given by Mr John Bates. (T.139-1996, T.191-1980.)

LEFT:
PLATE 113. 1970s
Evening hats.
Above Right:
David Shilling
evening cap,
1979. Black
velvet with gold
coil. Worn by
Lady Diana
Cooper and
given by Yuki.
Below Right:
Graham Smith
(for Jean Muir)
evening cap,
1979. Black
sequins with
single plume.
Given by Miss
Jean Muir.
Left:
Simone Mirman
evening band,
1970s. Gold
lamé with black
fringed tassle.
(T.319-1980,
T.184-1983,
T.281-1980.)

BELOW:
PLATE 114.
Straw hats.
Right: Aage
Thaarup hat,
1960s. Natural
straw trimmed
with fabric
poppies and
cornflowers.
Given by Mrs B.
Church and
worn by her
sister, Mrs Blair
Cok. Left:
James Lock &
Co. Ltd. panama,
1994. Cream
straw with blue,
red and black
ribbon. Given
by James Lock
& Co. Ltd.
(T.261-1985,
T.144-1996.)

hats. Women incorporated trilbys and bowlers into their wardrobe and fashionable young men appropriated floppy felt hats. Ecological concerns also influenced hat designs: simple straw hats trimmed with fabric poppies and cornflowers were complemented by country tweed caps. An earlier example of this pastoral style using natural materials is illustrated by Aage Thaarup's straw hat (plate 114). The escapist, romantic look provided an antidote to the prevalent masculine styles of the trilby and fedora. However, fashion's landscape was to alter dramatically with the onset of the entrepreneurial spirit of the following decade.

From 1980 the media focus on Lady Diana Spencer, the patron saint of hats, placed British milliners in the international limelight. As the Princess of Wales she was frequently photographed wearing hats, during day and evening, creating an appealing and accessible endorsement both of hat-wearing and of the domestic milliners whose designs she favoured. Her honeymoon hat of 1981, a tricorne decorated with a single feather designed by London milliner John Boyd, generated up to six years of business for Luton hat manufacturers serving the huge demand for high-street copies. Before this time London milliners had found their greatest media exposure in the fashion reports of the seasonal collections.

London also saw the flowering of a new generation of highly talented, young, innovative and often iconoclastic milliners during the 1980s. Stephen Jones set up his own label in September 1980 after graduating in fashion design from St Martin's College of Art. Friends from the London club scene formed the earliest fans of his sometimes witty, always beautifully crafted, hats; soon he was creating couture-level millinery for top international fashion designers as diverse as Jean Paul Gaultier, Jasper Conran and Comme des Garçons. A fine example of Jones's work is the green and yellow silk 'twisted' hat with *coq* feathers (plate 115). This design was featured on the cover of the Christmas 1992 edition of *Tatler*, providing Stephen Jones with the first media exposure of his own-label couture designs.

Another young millinery talent to emerge during this period was Kirsten Woodward, whose surreal talents were spotted by Karl Lagerfeld, chief designer at the House of Chanel. Woodward's millinery subsequently enhanced many of Chanel's catwalk shows in the 1980s, which in turn won her huge international acclaim (plate 116).

British fashion designers catering for more radical markets also embraced hat design during the 1980s. In so doing they introduced hats to a new generation. Vivienne

LEFT:
PLATE 115. Stephen Jones hat, 1982. Green-and-yellow silk twist with black feathers. Given by Mr Bouke de Vries. (T.222-1989.)

RIGHT:
PLATE 116 Kirsten Woodward hat, 'Sex on the brain', 1989. Straw and esparterie covered with 'Russian' braid. Given by Ms Kirsten Woodward. (T.156-1996.)

PLATE 117. Philip
Treacy hat,
spring/ summer
1995. Shocking
pink goose
feathers. Given
by Mr Philip
Treacy. (T.182-
1996.)

Westwood's distressed 'hobo' hats from her spring/summer 1983 collection were enormously influential in this respect. Other designs, as in so many areas of British high fashion, have their roots embedded in British traditions. This practice found its most blatant
expression in Vivienne Westwood's affectionate subversion in 1986 of the crown, irrev-
erently made from Harris tweed and fake ermine. This design served humorously to dis-
tort traditional connotations of rank and privilege. As Colin McDowell has written,
'Royalty have always relied on ornamental accessories to induce in their subjects the
"willing suspension of disbelief"'.[10] By creating her own version, Westwood's crown
became a parody of the real thing.

The prominence of British milliners creating hats for both the traditional as well as
the more radical fashion markets, and the consequent mass-market spin-offs, saw British
hat-wearing rise by one-third between 1984 and 1990.[11] While royal patronage undoubtedly did much to fuel this, Frederick Fox also believes that the wearing of hats forms part
of fashion's cycle of peaks and troughs, stating that, 'Everything comes around in circles
if you wait long enough'.[12] Another determining factor in the success of contemporary
British hats is the international hat export industry. Export often supports a milliner's
couture hat-making, whose quality diffusion lines reach a wider audience. Thanks to
mass production, simple classic shapes such as the baseball cap, beret and 'brimmer' are
widely available.

Fred Bare Headwear, set up in 1982 by Carolyn Brookes-Davis and Anita Evagora,
operates a successful export side to their business. They combine traditional British
craft techniques with creative fabric treatments, including bleaching, appliqué and
other surface decoration. Carolyn Brookes-Davis believes that these skills are one of the
main reasons foreign buyers relish British hat design. Fred Bare's brown felt and wool
hat with tassel demonstrates these strengths superbly (see plate 111).

An exceptional couture milliner in his own right, Graham Smith is also responsible
for huge export success, in addition to large home sales, of Kangol hats. As consultant
design director, he produces two collections of exquisite millinery a year for the company. For these Smith employs a simpler design aesthetic than that of his tailored couture hats.

A further explanation for the resurgence in hat-wearing may be the very late introduction of millinery courses within art schools in the 1980s. A millinery course did not exist at the Royal College of Art until 1988, when it was created with the financial support of the entrepreneur and chairman of the British Hat Guild, Bill Horsman. Providing the money to remedy this absence of training in art schools, Horsman was investing in British talent.

Traditionally millinery was taught by apprenticeship within the industry and was subject to the necessary rigours of business. With the provision of training within art schools, students have been able to develop their creativity and freedom of expression, unhindered by market realities. Horsman, who believes that the British have an innate talent for accessories, agreed to sponsor Philip Treacy, whose postgraduate millinery collection at the RCA received a standing ovation.

Philip Treacy now creates modern hats for international fashion houses such as Chanel, as well as for his own highly successful couture range (plate 117). In 1996 these hats cost up to £1,000, while his diffusion line sells within department stores below £100. His unique talents are internationally admired. Italian designer Gianni Versace said of Treacy, 'Give him a pin, he makes a sculpture; give him a rose, he makes a poem'.[13]

Since 1947 British milliners and hatters have continued to serve an international demand for top-quality classic and high-fashion hats. From the early 1980s young art school trained designers have reworked traditional hat shapes and materials, finding favour with top international fashion houses and introducing a new clientele to the joys of hat-wearing. Sustained by a lucrative social season, hatmaking in Britain has maintained its superlative position in the post-war period, providing a yardstick against which the world's hats can be measured.

Acknowledgements

I would like to thank Carolyn Brookes-Davis (Fred Bare Headwear); Zoe Brown and Koula Constantinou (Vivienne Westwood); Christy & Co. Ltd; Mrs Clements (The British Hat Guild); Frederick Fox; Wayne Goodwin and John Boyd; Pippa Grimes (Stephanie Churchill PR); Shirley Hex and Marie O'Regan (RCA); William Horsman (Chairman British Hat Guild, Director Philip Treacy Ltd); Stephen Jones; Marion Nicholls, Principal Keeper, and Alison Taylor, Keeper of Costume and Textiles (Luton Museum); David Shilling; Roger Stephenson, Michael Braudy and Janet Taylor (James Lock & Co.); The Hat Shop, London; Philip Treacy.

Footnotes

1 Adburgham (1966).
2 Edwards and Beyfus (1956), p.113.
3 Frederick Fox, interview with author, April 1996.
4 David Shilling, interview with author, June 1996.
5 Harrison, Tom 'Mass Observation and the Nation's Hats', c.1940, Mass Observation Archive, University of Sussex.
6 Adburgham (1966).
7 Dariaux (1954), p.118.
8 Cohn (1971), p.105.
9 Probert (1981), p.72.
10 McDowell (1992), p.25.
11 Bawden (1992), p.7.
12 Frederick Fox, interview with author, April 1996.
13 The Daily Telegraph (18 October 1993).

Selected Bibliography

Adburgham, Alison A View of Fashion (London: Allen & Unwin 1966; printed in Punch 5 May 1954).
Bawden, Juliet The Hat Book: Creating Hats for Every Occasion (London: Letts & Co. 1992).
Clark, Fiona Hats (London: Batsford 1982).
Cohn, Nik Today There Are No Gentlemen: The Changes in Englishmen's Dress since the War (London: Weidenfeld & Nicolson 1971).
Dariaux, Genevieve Antoine Elegance (London: Frederick Muller 1954).
Debrett's Peerage Etiquette and Modern Manners (London, Debrett's Peerage).
Edwards and Beyfus Lady Behave: A Guide to Modern Manners (London: Cassell 1956).
Ginsburg, Madeleine The Hat: Trends and Traditions (London: Studio Editions 1990).
Hardy, William 'Head for Cover', London Magazine (November 1991).
McDowell, Colin Hats: Status, Style and Glamour (London, Thames & Hudson 1992).
McDowell, Colin A Hundred Years of Royal Style (London: Muller, Blond & White 1985).
Martin, Richard Fashion and Surrealism (London: Thames & Hudson 1989).
Marshall, Francis 'London West', Studio (London and New York, 1944).
Probert, Christine Hats in Vogue Since 1910 (London: Thames & Hudson 1981).
Shields, Jody Hats: A Stylish History and Collector's Guide (New York: Clarkson Potter 1991). 'Au Revoir, Belgravia Says Madame Mirman' The Standard (24 February 1982).
Thaarup, Aage Heads and Tails (London: Cassell 1956).
Time Out (10-17 January 1996).

Handbags

CLAIRE WILCOX

RIGHT:
PLATE 2.
Fassbender
handbag, 1940s.
Brown leather
with gold metal
clasp. Given by
Mrs P. Mines.
(T.43&A-1989.)

My mother's old leather handbag,
crowded with letters she carried
all through the war. The smell
of my mother's handbag: mints
and lipstick and Coty powder.
The look of those letters, softened
and worn at the edges, opened,
read, and refolded so often.
Letters from my father. Odour
of leather and powder, which ever
since then has meant womanliness,
and love, and anguish, and war.

(Ruth Fainlight, *Selected Poems*, Hutchinson, 1987)

Vogue welcomed in the New Year of 1947 with a plea for elegance, and suggested that until the 'aesthetic atmosphere' had returned women should concentrate on accessories. In this era of 'make do and mend', many women simply had their expensive pre-war handbags renovated or remodelled. Women of all incomes relied on accessories as a way of creating a new look, and there were numerous patterns available for those who wanted to make their own leather and fabric bags.

Wartime fashions had made a virtue out of a necessity: as everyone had to carry a gas mask a shoulder bag was obviously practical. But military and wartime associations were left behind when the overarm bag came in. The new fashion, as described in *Vogue* 1947, was for elongated bags in leather or satin, deep rather than wide and carried by slender handles. Bags moved down the arm from the shoulder, and were worn hooked over the elbow with the handles circling the wrist. Although jewellery, bags and evening hats

PLATE 120.
Group: H. Wald
& Co. for Rayne.
Waldybag, 1970.
Green silk satin
with gold and
diamanté acorn
clasp. Rayne bag,
1968. Pink silk
satin. Rayne bag,
c.1975. Purple
silk satin with
bow. Given by
Mrs J.Guinness.
(T.220A-1976,
T.218B-1976,
T.224A-1976.)

were still unrationed, by 1948 there was a 100 per cent purchase tax on leather goods, and metal was in short supply. A good-quality handbag could cost much more than the outfit it was worn with, especially if it was a Utility suit in need of 'lifting' by accessories. A cedar crocodile bag with matching cigarette case, compact and purse cost £32 10s. in March 1949; in the same year a tan-and-blue tweed suit by Jaeger Utility was £6 3s. 8d. In the late 1940s handbags in patent leather were fashionable, and leather with white top-stitching was common. Fabric drawstring styles were available in tweed and plaid. Gradually a wider range of colours became available: a double-handled Waldybag was featured in *Vogue* in August 1949 in red lizard skin. In contrast to practical wartime shapes, small rigid bags with loop handles were developed in a variety of forms, from a milk can shape to that of a miniature hatbox. Pigskin or hide shoulder bags with horse-brass fastenings were available, but these were clearly specified for country wear.

Evening bags were highly decorative, and became less inhibited as the British social scene was re-established. Cocktail bags were designed to dangle from the wrist, leaving hands free to deal with drinks and cigarettes in long holders. Materials and decoration varied from delicate petit point, teamed with a filigree silver clasp and chain on a bag by Duvelloroy, to snakeskin dipped in real gold as in a bag from Galeries Lafayette, and black satin piped in gold kid in a drawstring style by Bembaron. Aage Thaarup made matching hats and bags in brilliant bead embroidery in red on black. Women were reminded that accessories were unlimited if one had the funds, and there were no more excuses for 'making do'! In this optimistic post-war period *Vogue* (December 1949) fantasized about the contents of the fashionable woman's handbag. The list ran: 'pigskin cigarette case, square mock-gold compact, pantomime tickets for *Miss Muffet* at the Casino Theatre, gold-edged chiffon handkerchief, silver Dunhill lighter, tiny black-and-gold brocade-covered opera glasses by Asprey, silver heart-shaped key-ring, cigarette holder with gold trumpet'.

On a more prosaic note, in the same year a strictly tailored brown calf handbag from Revelation, with capacious two-sectioned interior for passports or ration books, cost £13.

There were many prominent British bag manufacturers between 1947 and the late 1950s, including Fassbender (plates 118 and 119), John Pound, Mohlo, Pissot & Pavy, Solrae, Lederer, Duvelleroy, Rowland Ward, Leathercraft, Lafarge, Derfield and Wald. A 1949 advertisement for H. Wald & Co. enthused that 'the art of gracious giving is best expressed in a Waldybag, the handbag to which every woman aspires...from about 5 gns'.[1] Established in 1914, the company's heyday was in the 1940s and '50s under Morris Wald, whose technical perfectionism and artistic flair embodied the philosophy that 'there was no effort to be spared on making the most perfect object'.[2] Until Rayne started producing handbags, shoes designed for the Queen were sent to Wald's art deco showrooms in the Tottenham Court Road and a handbag would be made to match. From the magnificent black crocodile handbag, finely lined in suede ('would last a lifetime' at £79 in 1952, an enormous sum at the time), to the painted pastel satin bags favoured by Princess Margaret, Waldybags were part of the established fashionable culture of the time (plate 120).

Prompted by the high cost of leather, a significant development from the late 1940s was the increased use of artificial materials in the accessory world. Plastic substitutes such as Vynide, PVC and laminated phenolics were originally developed for heavy industrial use, but their potential was soon realized in the luxury trades as they could be textured and patterned to reproduce expensive leathers and skins. Plastic bags were perceived initially as suitable for the young or those with 'limited incomes' (plate 121).

Fashion journalists recognized that plastics had become extremely sophisticated, and recommended readers to buy good plastic rather than poor leather. Freda Koblick in *Vogue* (October 1966) proclaimed, 'Central to the usefulness of plastics is the fact that with them we can manufacture large quantities of similar objects to an exacting standard at the lowest possible cost'. Although the purchase tax on leather goods was lowered in 1952 plastics were here to stay. Light and easy, they could be made in washable pastel shades to

RIGHT:
PLATE 121. Elgee handbag, 1950s. Red plastic with alloy frame and clasp. Given by Mr John Jesse and Ms Irina Laski. (T.235&A-1982.)

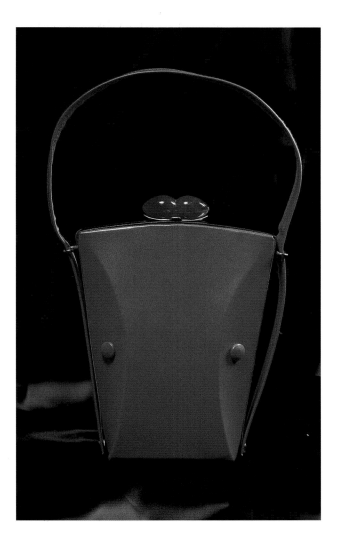

match new synthetic dress fabrics. Plastic filled the huge demand for cheaper goods in the next decades as the decline in skilled labour and craftsmanship in the leather trades and tanneries coincided with a boom in the population of young consumers.

For the affluent mature woman, low cost was not necessarily a major concern. The emphasis was still on having good matching accessories: 'It is a well-worn truth that it is far better to have a few well-made pairs of shoes, perfect gloves, one handsome handbag, than a rainbow of not-so-goods' stated *The Intelligent Woman's Guide to Good Taste* in 1958.[3] In the early 1950s, bags grew larger and pastels became fashionable: 'Carried unanimously...The new length handbag, roomy without being bulky...all the season's new fashion shades, including mauve, lavender, pale blue, grey etc.'[4]

The growth of boutiques in Paris at the beginning of the 1950s meant that top designers could sell fashionable accessories under their own names to a much wider audience. London soon followed suit. Matching ensembles were all the rage and demanded co-ordinating accessories: 'Matching goes to the length not merely of colour but of fabric; such as the gloves and the evening bags at Peter Russell'.[5] Edward Rayne was *the* name in matching shoes and handbags. As he stated, 'The total look's the point!'[6] In 1963 Rayne offered matching leather shoes and bag in a pink-and-green rosebud print. Sometimes complete outfits were made to match, such as a japonica pink nappa leather bag by Jane Shilton, which accompanied japonica pink shoes and a suit.

For the evening there were clutch bags from the costume jewellers Fior, in flowered blue or yellow Ascher silk for 39s. 6d: 'a beautifully ordered riot of colour, and especially lovely when applied to snowy white dresses' according to *Vogue* in June 1956. If money was no object, a black satin bag with an 18-carat gold frame set with diamonds was available for £430 from Asprey.

The various handbag shapes in Britain in the 1950s were designed to complement the fashionable silhouettes of the time: the slim, tailored look; the belted, full-skirted floral dress shape; and the new princess line, 'unbroken from bust to hem'. The manner in which the handbag was held was stylistically important. For formal day wear, the classic metal framed handbag was worn over the wrist or held by the handles. The smart and neat clutch bag or envelope was usually clasped close to the body. Bucket bags, a development of the open shopping bag that was typical of informal wear, were held in the crook of the elbow. Early types included a stiffened calf bag with an inner protective drawstring cover by Susan Handbags in 1952. A scoop-shaped model by Fior was studded in gilt and had an adjustable handle, while Revelation produced a bucket bag in tough hide and lined with check duster cloth for 55s. Open bucket bags, unlike handbags, were not subject to purchase tax.

In 1953 there was a brief craze originating in France for toy handbags, but by October 1955 handbag styles in Britain had polarized:

> Handbags have a new tailored dash – some tiny as a man's wallet, some big as briefcases. All give the final touch to a fashion plan; balance and reinforce it by line, texture and colour; give the tonic effect of a brilliant pink with black, alabaster with marigold.[7]

One of the most significant trends of the late 1950s was the popularity of huge handbags, needed to balance rising and widening hemlines. The 1958 December issue of *Vogue* noted that 'the bigger the better is the new philosophy for the handbag buyer'. Combinations of different materials, such as tweed and leather, were popular at this time, and matching bags and shoes in Irish linen or Swiss lace were summer favourites. The dynamic of the overarm bag with three-quarter length sleeves, slim wrists and gloved hands was essential to fashion in the 1950s. The relationship of bags to shoes was equally important as they were so often paired together.

Until the 1960s, bags had mirrored trends in shoes and were associated with the formal accessory-orientated fashions against which young people were then rebelling.

Confusion about bags and their place in the prevailing look led to them being virtually excluded in fashion shots between 1961 and 1966. Eventually this uncertainty was resolved by the liberating shoulder bag. The emphasis was on youth, and accessories were there to help, not to hinder the action.

Accessories began to be used in a less formal way, and sometimes deliberately challenged the unspoken rules of fashion. Mary Quant wrote in 1966:

> It is said that I was first with knickerbockers, gilt chains, shoulderstrap bags and high boots...I want to invent new ways of making clothes in new materials, with new shapes and new fashion accessories that are up to date with the changing ways of life.[8]

Quant's first handbags were round zipped or top-fastening shapes in patent with long thin straps, appliquéd with her ubiquitous daisy motif.

Other British handbag designers were emerging. The former actress Sally Jess designed bags that echoed the clean geometric lines and patterns of modern clothes, and used leather in a different, direct way. Her Cape handbag in white with a zig-zag of biscuit had no clasps and a top that narrowed to a handle. It cost £4 10s. from Kensington Church Street and was illustrated with hole-punched kid gloves, cut-out calf shoes, a crochet cloche and square white sunglasses, all from Top Gear in the King's Road. By early 1966 handbags had caught up with the space-age look launched by Courrèges in 1964. Plastic dresses in vinyl-coated aluminium, butyrate chain-mail dresses and bright, heat-welded PVC raincoats were startlingly futuristic. They were echoed by Roger Vivier's perspex shoes, Cardin's neon orange leather shoulder bag and Sally Jess's long silver pochette with a Perspex bar handle.

Not everyone could carry off this look and, for the older customer, Susan Handbags were still going strong. In June 1965 they made envelope bags to order, from the customer's own fabric to match flower-covered dresses, bras and shoes inspired by the all-pervasive Flower Power. Biba was packed with accessories such as bags upon which 'fantasy' flowers were scattered lightly on blonde linen, priced at 37s. 6d. Purple suede or shiny red satchel bags were available from Top Gear, but those who were better-off bought their 'super satchels' in black crocodile for £110 from Russell & Bromley. Rayne was the first to make shoes, boots and handbags in waterproof easy-care Corfam, which appealed to a young clientele.

Between 1969 and 1973 bags became much less structured to fit in with the prevailing layered and patterned ethnic look. It was quite appropriate to have, slung over the shoulder, a large untidy bag that could be filled with anything and everything – books, make-up, lunch – which made the traveller, even if she were only going to the King's Road, self-sufficient for hours. The natural hippie could have leather appliqué bags made by Nigel Lofthouse for Jean Muir, a squaw bag by Adrien Mann or Thea Porter's large embroidered and tasselled shoulder bags smelling exotically of patchouli oil. For summer there were Anna Balfour's smocked dresses and bags, and for winter matching leather bags and belts by Lesley Slight.

As the separates boom coalesced into a more classical look towards the middle of the 1970s, a clearer division emerged between youthful and mature styles. Satchel bags were upgraded into tiny sophisticated forms and sold by Lucienne Phillips; classics from Asprey and Rayne, the mainstay of many women's wardrobes, started to be carried more confidently. The 1970s rendition of the clutch bag, the 'purse', looked right with tailored clothes and pastels. Christopher Trill made large versions in ginger and cream striped leather, or there were flat maroon leather clutch bags from the Hardy Amies boutique in Savile Row. The English garden look of crêpe-de-Chine tea dress and straw hat was making a comeback, and was perhaps incomplete without an eau-de-Nil leather purse with quilted flower sides from Clive Shilton. A plain ensemble by Jaeger of 1971 with matching pale-green clutch bag by Roger Saul, the founder of Mulberry, was the anti-

dote to an excess of pattern. Butler & Wilson became known for antique evening bags to complete the 1930s retro look. The question of how to carry all the extras that did not fit into the clutch bag was solved by the tote or carrier bag. Clive Shilton made them to order in polished Pittard's leather.

An alternative to the handbag – tiny little fabric pockets or pocket-sized satchels worn diagonally across the shoulder – first became popular in 1975. Originally shown in Paris by Jap (Kenzo Takada) and in London at Joseph, they were soon followed by patch-work Tana Lawn versions by Liberty, leather pouch purses by the Chelsea Cobbler and pleated satin purses by Clive Shilton. In 1976 Bill Gibb made a broderie-anglaise evening jacket, which had matching padded fan 'pockets' suspended on thin gold pip-ing, to be worn around the waist or neck. Shoulder purses soon migrated to the belt, as in French designer Sonia Rykiel's 1974 collection, which featured a wool hip-wrapper with matching leather purse. In the 1980s, inspired by cycling gear, the purse was taken to the back of the body and became the bum bag.

The role of the countryside, so central to the British social calender and a dominant stylistic force in British fashion, has had a big influence on domestic handbag design. Tradition rather than fashion has ensured the longevity of companies such as Burberry and Simpson, whose Daks bag is shown in plate 122, and more recently Mulberry. Founded in 1971, the latter found its creative apotheosis in interpreting British traditions of saddlery. Mulberry's 1976 range, for men and women, derived from themes of hunting, shooting and fishing, and is still characterized by the use of embossed leather (plate 123).

A new design problem was created by the bagsize address book originated by Filofax. As large and heavy as a small clutch bag, it needed something large in which to carry it or was simply carried in the hand. In the 1990s this has been resolved by the Wonderbag, a personal organizer on a shoulder strap. Bags were often worn diagonally

across the body, including satchels with 'enough space for work – make-up, extra muffler, *The Times* and a tape recorder; enough for weekends – a slice of game pie, an apple and almost room for your folding Moulton'.[9] The new pliable look for bags was epitomized by the designs produced by the Italian company Enny, which were soon copied by many manufacturers.

In the early 1980s British designers such as Margaret Howell presented a soft, muted style which was complemented by natural suede bags. Reflecting the vogue for second-hand and ethnic garments, Naturally British made a huge carpet bag, like an outsize purse. Practical rucksacks became a fashionable style in 1984, and have remained popular ever since. In 1985 and '86 those with more exotic tastes embraced tasselled velvet purses. In July 1989 Henry's showed red-and-black quilted leather mini-bags with chains of twisted gilt and cord. The Queen is rarely seen without a handbag, and Launer & Co.'s handmade plain square handbags, with twisted gilt rope trims, remain a stalwart for her.

The businesswoman of 1986, in her Paul Costelloe houndstooth check suit, could wield her leather document case with gunmetal tinted clasp from Asprey like a weapon. Lady Thatcher's handbag was rigidly structured while Princess Diana clasped her clutch bag to her chest. The style of handbag that Princess Grace held to her stomach to conceal her pregnancy was named a Kelly bag after her by Hermès. Dressing to assert or protect oneself extended naturally to accessories, and the possession of status handbags was never so important as in the 1980s and '90s. The quilted Chanel bag with chains and gilt logo and the over-sized Kelly bags (which Hermès had been unable to sell only a few years before), were now only outdone by the Prada shopper: 'Like all the best objects of consumer fetishism, it is both a cult item and subliminally sexual: all black nylon and little zippers'.[10] A chic new swinger from chainstore British Home Stores for £12 was not quite the same.

ABOVE:
PLATE 123.
Mulberry
'Roger's brief-
case', 1996.
'Nile walnut'
brown leather.
Mulberry 'Grand
despatch' bag,
1996. 'Congo
teak' leather.
Given by
Mulberry
Company
(Design) Ltd.
(T.131-1996,
T.130-1996.)

Although British-made bags do not seem to inspire quite the same fetishistic delight, a number of designers have been highly successful in developing ranges of accessories (for example plate 124). Vivienne Westwood's cherubic Boucher print drawstring and clutch bags of 1992 (plate 125) and the doggy bag designed by Braccialini were reflections of her total look. London-based Nicole Farhi, Betty Jackson, Bruce Oldfield, Jasper Conran and Caroline Charles have all produced special accessories for their collections.

A number of the British handbag makers who have recently made a name for themselves are united by a concern for craftsmanship and innovative design. This group includes Bill Amberg, Lulu Guinness, Emily Jo Gibbs and Anya Hindmarch, whose first shop opened in Walton Street in 1993 and was full of 'evening bags as tiny and fizzy as a fruit drop and black pigskin carry-alls, big

ABOVE:

PLATE 124.
Zandra Rhodes
bag, 1983. Cream
pleated silk
with draw-string.
Given by Mrs V.
Parness. (T.225
B-1985.)

enough for an overnight stay, chic enough to deserve their cast-gold tassels'.[11] Her scarlet satin bag with rope handles and tailored 'poodle' bag of 1994 reflected the new ladylike look. In *Vogue* (January 1994) she stated that 'people want durable, classic bags now, and they're willing to pay a lot for them'. The new formality was given substance in Lulu Guinness's bags, such as the 'Florist's Basket' with rose-covered lid (plate 126). The clean lines of her small striped grosgrain box bags, shown with Capri pants and high-heeled ankle strap sandals, are an oblique tribute to the precision of 1950s tailoring.

Today it seems as if almost every young person is carrying on his or her back the once utilitarian but now highly fashionable rucksack. Often miniaturized and made in a mul-

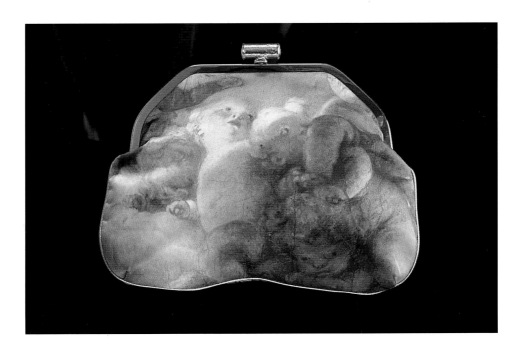

LEFT:

PLATE 125.
Vivienne
Westwood
clutch bag,
1991. Printed
silk Boucher-
inspired
cherubic
design with
gold plasti-
cised lining.
Given by
Mrs Vivienne
Westwood.
(T.29-1992.)

tiplicity of materials, this physically liberating bag of the past decade has been a great equalizer. Available at all market levels they are used by both men and women. A designer-level example, which subverts the original intention and stems from subcultural grunge styles, is Jamin Puech's 1994 crochet version for Ally Capellino.

Handbags have taken another sartorial turn recently with the advent of shoppers and bucket bags on short shoulder straps that sit just above the waist. These are made by Paul Smith Women among others. White patent has been revived from the 1960s, and bags in acidic colours with matching thin belts are widespread. The transparent vinyl bags designed by Patrick Cox, a reference to 1950s American box bags, have been accepted by the British women. Not normally known for their willingness to expose the contents of their handbags, British women were advised in April 1995 by *Vogue*: 'See-through bags put their contents on show so fill them with

ABOVE:
PLATE 126.
Lulu Guinness handbag, 'Florist's Basket', 1996 (1993 design). Black silk satin with red velvet roses. Given by Ms Lulu Guinness. (T.128-1996.)

glossy plastic purses'. For evening wear, glittery mesh bags by Katharine Hamnett dangle from the wrist, as they did in the 1950s.

Although bags accompany women everywhere, they are not contained by the body like shoes or hats. The advantage of the handbag's independence is that it can be placed discreetly on the floor, thus drawing attention to a well-turned ankle, or displayed on a tabletop, a detached and beautiful satellite of a fashionably clad body. The erotic element of the bag derives from the idea of secrecy. When so much today is laid bare and open, it is still something of a taboo to look into someone else's bag.

The ability to change a whole look endows handbags with great power. A handbag can have as many functions as women desire them to take on, determined by the role they play as part of a tradition – be it Romantic, Tailored, Country or Bohemian.

Essential and portable, handbags can be exquisite demonstrations of taste and fashion, becoming containers of private worlds in public places.

Footnotes

1 *Vogue*, December 1949.
2 Deborah Wald, interview with the author, 1996.
3 Chitty (1958) – from the chapter on accessories by E. Carter, p.30.
4 *Vogue*, July 1950, advertisement for Susan Handbags Ltd.
5 *Vogue*, September 1950.
6 Interview with Edward Rayne, *Vogue*, September 1972.
7 *Vogue*, October 1955.
8 Quant (1966), p.152.
9 *Vogue*, September 1976. A Moulton is a classic bicycle.
10 Irvine, Susan. 'Closet Fetishists', *Vogue*, July 1995.
11 *Vogue*, July 1993.

Selected Bibliography

Baclawski, Karen. *The Guide to Historic Costume* (London: Batsford 1995).
Chitty, Susan *The Intelligent Woman's Guide to Good Taste* (London: MacGibbon & Kee 1958).
Dooner, Kate. *A Century of Handbags* (Atglen, USA: Schiffer Publishing Company 1993).
Foster, Vanda. *Bags and Purses* (London: Batsford 1982).
Laver, James. *Costume and Fashion: A Concise History* (London: Thames & Hudson 1969).
Mulvagh, Jane and Mendes, Valerie D. *Vogue History of 20th Century Fashion* (London: Viking 1988).
Quant, Mary. *Quant by Quant* (London: Cassell & Co. 1966).
Sladen, Christopher. *The Conscription of Fashion* (Place: Ashgate 1995).

Shoes

TONY GLENVILLE

ABOVE:

PLATE 127.
Chelsea Cobbler
shoes: cream
leather with
brown and
green leather

'butterfly wings'
c.1971. Given by
Mr Paul Getty
Junior. (T.106-
1974.)

Going barefoot in the city in October was not simply the action of a crazy woman. She had always found shoes restricting and painful, but only in her seventies had she gained the confidence to shun them.

(Anne Sebba, *Enid Bagnold: A Biography*, Weidenfeld & Nicolson, 1986)

The wearing of footwear that complements both the clothes and the occasion has always been a matter of utmost importance to the well-dressed person. Even today, some people still consider it unacceptable to wear brown shoes in the city and black shoes in the country. Often cited but undeniably true is the generality that women tend to buy shoes on impulse to make a fashion statement, while men fastidiously purchase a few good pairs of shoes and demand extensive wear from these investments.

In many ways British shoemaking has led the field, and classic shoe types bear the names of famous British people and places. There are laced shoes called Oxford and Derby, boots that are termed Eton, Balmoral, Chelsea and Wellington, and Cambridge has given its name to a type of slip-on shoe.

Historically the apprenticeship to learn the 'trade, art and mystery of a cordwainer' took as long as seven years, but in spite of this shoemaking was a popular occupation.[1] (The term 'cordwainer' derives from Cordoba in Spain, which during the Middle Ages exported the finest leather.) The Worshipful Company of Cordwainers was formed in 1272 and is one of the oldest of the City of London guilds. The foundation of the Leather Trades School in 1887, now called Cordwainers' College, meant that shoemaking skills could be acquired through formal education as well as trade apprenticeships. June Swann has documented the social and technical contexts of shoemaking in Britain with meticulous attention to detail.[2]

In the mid-nineteenth century it became possible for sewing machines to work on leather, and the ability to stitch shoe uppers to the sole with a continuous chain stitch heralded the mass production of footwear. From this period many processes that were traditionally worked by hand, such as the cutting of leather, were mechanized. Various centres of production emerged: Northampton, Norwich, Bristol, Leeds and Street were all important to the industry. London, the fashion capital, was not the centre of shoemaking.

In spite of technological developments the top end of the shoe trade has remained a labour-intensive rather than a capital-intensive industry, and the dexterity with which shoemakers handle their materials has always been revered. Britain's custom of making top-quality handcrafted shoes has, since the 1960s, encompassed the advent of designer shoemakers who have ensured the survival of traditional craft skills.

The factors that determine the construction and design of a shoe are the wooden last upon which it is created, the heel and toe shape, the leather, skin and fabric that form the outer shell, and decorative details such as buckles. Good shoes and boots for men are still made primarily of leather, with styles defined by a series of design elements that vary only in detail. Much of women's footwear is also bound by tradition. Many post-war styles, such as brogues, mules, court shoes, and short elastic-sided and full-length boots, have been based on designs with historical precedents. Comfort is of paramount importance to British wearers, who have rarely subscribed to the philosophy that it is necessary to suffer to be beautiful; occasionally in town, but never in the country.

The evolution of fashion footwear since the Second World War has been a gradual process. Heavy wartime shoes with thick or high wedge heels were not transformed overnight into the light, poised shoes that characterize 1950s fashions. The late 1940s saw shoes of soft suede and leather with snub toes and high heels, a dramatic contrast to the stout styles characteristic of most Utility designs. The brown leather and suede lace-up shoes with the Utility mark are an example of this transitional shoe silhouette (plate 128).

Released from Utility constraints in the early 1950s, shoemakers started to refine heels, cut away high vamps, streamline heavily rounded curves and pare down toes to fine points in a quest for modern, streamlined shapes. As toes became increasingly pointed, fronts were cut lower to look less bulbous and heels were shaved more and more finely. Many women could now indulge in sophisticated and glamorous footwear, especially for evening. By 1956 heels were so thin that a metal spigot had to be inserted to stop them snapping. Holmes of Norwich placed advertisements in *Vogue* between 1950 and 1959 that variously described shoes as 'slim as a wand', 'light as a wisp of smoke' and 'the sharpest of toe points on a reed slim heel'. At its most extreme this style evolved into stiletto heels, an exaggerated fashion statement that many regarded as impractical and rather vulgar.

One of the leading designers and retailers of post-war high-fashion footwear was Edward Rayne. The Rayne company was founded in 1886 but it was not until 1918, when Edward's father took over, that it started to become fashion-conscious. When Edward took the helm in 1951 at the age of twenty-eight, the firm was still little known outside Bond Street, but soon the flowering of his special creative talent led Edward Rayne to become the most acclaimed shoemaker in Britain, patronized by royalty and high society. As well as producing his own seasonal ranges, he created special shoes to complement ensembles by top London couturiers such as Hardy Amies, Norman Hartnell and Digby Morton. A selection of shoes dating from the 1950s and '60s, from the Rayne archive, is shown in at the beginning of this chapter. They reveal the artistry and immaculate workmanship that was characteristic of the output of this top British company.

During the early 1950s easy-to-wear casual shoes, based on American designs, came on to the British market. These were promoted as comfortable walking shoes or as fun-to-wear junior sports shoes. Although successful in the high street, they did not encroach on the top end of the market where more formal footwear continued to be favoured. Traditional styles using stout, often brogued, leather remained highly popular for wear in the country. For town, the undecorated court shoe was a mainstay of the well-dressed. Over the past fifty years both these syles have subtly incorporated fashion changes while retaining their classic appeal. An advertisement for Lotus shoes (featuring clothes by Charles Creed) appeared in *Vogue* March 1952 stating, 'The English make the world's best court shoes...basic, indispensable, irreplaceable'. By 1957-58 lower heels had become fashionable and the fronts of shoes were extended – this was a foretaste of the 1960s revival of '20s styles. Although shoe designers such as Rayne continued to cater for a high-fashion clientele with traditional taste, the market was beginning to diversify.

RIGHT:
PLATE 129.
Above: Selby
evening shoes,
1962. Gold kid
leather. Worn
by Dame Edith
Sitwell and
given by Mr
Francis Sitwell.
(T.7C-1974.)
Below:
Johnny Moke
evening shoes,
spring/summer
1990. Silver kid
leather 'kissi'.
Given by Mr
Johnny Moke.
(T.234&A-1990.)

One of the most significant developments of the 1960s was the rise of designer shoe-makers. They met the needs of youthful fashionable tastes by creating innovative designs in limited editions, which were supplied through their own outlets as well as expensive boutiques. Designer Richard Smith and Mandy Wilkins started Chelsea Cobbler in 1967, creating unique and distinctive designs for celebrity clients such as top models Twiggy and Verushka from their studio. They later opened the Chelsea Cobbler shoe boutique in Draycott Avenue, south-west London. An example of their extraordinary footwear is the winged mules dating from 1962 (plate 127).

In the early 1960s toe shapes became distinctly square while heels thickened, a dramatic change of profile matched by an emphasis upon elaborate materials and decoration. A multiplicity of ethnic, 'retro' and military styles provided inspiration for 'swinging London' fashions, including shoes. By the mid-1960s stage footwear sold by top theatrical and dance shops, such as Anello & Davide and Gamba, entered the forefront of fashion. Particularly successful were tap dance shoes with bars and ribbon bows that could be customized by the wearer. In 1962 Dame Edith Sitwell commissioned a pair of gold kid evening shoes that reflected her highly individual bohemian syle of dress (plate 129).

ABOVE:
PLATE 131. Jimmy
Choo sandals,
1996. Red patent
leather sling-
backs with
'kitten' heels.
Given by Mr
Jimmy Choo.
(T.155:1&2-1996.)

Boots were one of the major fashion footwear statements of the 1960s, first worn with mini-skirts and then towards the middle of the decade with maxi-skirts. They remain a favourite today. Sold by shoe shops and fashion boutiques, boots became available in a dazzling array of synthetic and natural materials and in many colours. The knee-length tightly fitting boots sold at Biba were so coveted that girls knew when the delivery van was due to arrive and would queue for hours to be sure of acquiring a pair. Made from fabric as well as leather and suede, these boots were dyed in the same mouthwatering, muted hues of plum, claret, chocolate brown and bottle green as the distinctive Biba clothes.

As early as 1967 shoe designers started to revive 1940s platform styles. By 1971-72 platform soles had been elevated to between two and three inches high, although in a streetstyle context they reached staggering heights. Some designers exploited the vogue for platforms with a modernist vision, while others sought romantic refuge in retro styles. Barbara Hulanicki, owner and designer of Biba, looked back to shoes worn by the Hollywood film stars Betty Grable and Carmen Miranda, which she re-interpreted in a contemporary idiom. Disco and futuristic fantasy fuelled the extrovert platform designs of Terry de Havilland, who exploited metallic leathers and sparkling synthetic materials. His shoes were designed to accompany glamorous clothes by designers such as Antony Price. Perhaps ironically, the bell-bottomed trousers worn by fashion purists were so long that they concealed these extravagant shoes. An alternative, more understated option was wedge heels, which were often featured in magazines like *Vogue* to complete outfits by Bill Gibb, Jean Muir and Zandra Rhodes.

In 1971 Manolo Blahnik opened his Chelsea shop and for over twenty-five years has made highly seductive shoes for an international clientele. Renowned for his use of the most supple leathers, luxurious silks and laces, with exquisite decorative beadwork, embroidery, ornate buckles and clasps, Manolo Blahnik's shoes have occasionally been provocative, but have always been innovative and highly influential. In addition to his own collection, he designs for top international fashion houses. The 1996 example from Manolo Blahnik's own range of shoes in the V&A collection (plate 130) reveal his

LEFT:
PLATE 130.
Manolo Blahnik
evening shoes,
1996. Cream
beaded silk
satin. Given
by Mr Manolo
Blahnik.
(T.157:1&2-1996.)

RIGHT:
PLATE 132.
Patrick Cox
shoes, spring/
summer 1987.
Black-and-
white leather
'Roll Tongue'.
Given by Mr
Patrick Cox.
(T.230 &
A –1990.)

refined aesthetic and meticulous craftsmanship. Although of Czech and Spanish parentage, it is difficult to imagine Manolo Blahnik practising his craft anywhere but London. Always dressed as the quintessential English gentleman, he acknowledges an aesthetic debt to the late Cecil Beaton. Joan Juliet Buck, now editor of the French edition of *Vogue*, wrote in 1977 that 'He is one of the few people in the fashion world who with his European sensitivity can remind you of the real value of English tradition.'[5] His creations are frequently inspired by the Bohemian and Romantic styles and have a special escapist appeal.

Romantic styles became popular at the end of the 1970s and prevailed during the early 1980s. The work of Clive Shilton, with its emphasis upon delicate ornament, came into its own and he was chosen to make the wedding shoes for Lady Diana Spencer in 1981. Decorative shoes in ornate fabrics with historically inspired Louis heels, embroidered pumps, gilded mules and Turkish slippers served the British love of dressing up. A

new generation of British shoe designers led by Johnny Moke, Jimmy Choo (plate 131), Emma Hope and Patrick Cox (plate 132) blossomed during this period. Their handmade, bespoke and limited edition shoes injected a lively new impetus into high-fashion footwear. Claire Norwood (plate 133) and Diane Hassall (plate 134) are now becoming known for their special occasion shoes. Dr Martens, the company founded in 1960 to provide utilitarian shoes for workmen, has exerted an enormous influence upon fashion footwear. First appropriated by subcultural skinheads, by the early 1980s Doc Martens shoes had for a few seasons been elevated to the international catwalks.

After years of dangerous and exhausting wartime duty, men of the armed forces longed for footwear without military connotations and clothes that bore no resemblance to uniform. However, these desires were thwarted by the continuation of rationing, acute shortages of materials and the fact that, for many men, war-related duties were not completely over. There was no New Look to revitalize men's fashion and, for the typical British male, the very word 'fashion' remained an anathema. Indeed, it was widely considered that overstated designs in footwear were worn by those who were 'cads', 'bounders' and 'gigolos'. Even such minor variations as the use of suede were usually regarded as unacceptable, to the extent of signifying homosexuality. Such insular attitudes have lessened, with the younger generation becoming more adventurous, but none the less the classic British brogue has remained the dominant shoe style for men over the past 50 years.

Constructed from several pieces of leather or suede, each punched and serrated round the edge, with punched toe sections, brogues are versatile and ever-present. Dinah Hall wrote in *The Times* on 11 June 1991: 'The country gent treats his brown

PLATE 135. Group:
Manfield Utility
brogues, 1940s.
Brown suede.
Given by Mrs
Goddard.
(T.116&A-1985.)
New & Lingwood
brogues, 1989.
Made from 18th-
century brown
Russian calf-
leather. Given by
New & Lingwood
Ltd.(T.216&A-
1989.) Alan
McAfee brogues
c.1980. Black
leather. Given by
Ms Lisa Monnas.
(T.278&A-1989.)

brogues rather like his labradors: works them hard, pampers them and buys exactly the same sort when they die. The city gent is not so different, except that his are black'. This description would have been as applicable in 1947 as it remains today. By merely changing the colour of his shoes, the English gentleman has little need to pay attention to the vagaries and whims of fashion. The V&A includes a pair of brown suede 1940s Utility shoes, black polished leather city classics by Alan McAfee and a pair of brown leather brogues by New & Lingwood (plate 135). These last shoes are made from Russian calf retrieved from the wreck of a Danish brigantine sunk in Plymouth Sound in 1786. In 1996, Sebastian (Predrag Pajdic) re-worked this classic style for the high-fashion market (plate 136).

British hand-crafted shoes are considered to be among the best in the world. Hardy Amies recalls, 'One of the first facts I learned about London life was that for shoes it had to be Lobb'.[4] John Lobb Ltd, established in 1866, enjoys an international reputation for its work, which is guided by the proved success of tradition. A pair of their luxurious shoes can take up to six months to make and involves the skills of many craftsmen. The 'fitter' measures the client's feet, then the 'clicker' selects the skin or hide. At least eight

RIGHT:
PLATE 136.
Sebastian
brogues, 1996.
Black leather.
Given by Mr
Predrag Pajdic
(Sebastian).
(T.184:1&2-1996.)

BELOW:
PLATE 137. John
Lobb evening
shoes, c.1960.
Black patent.
Worn and
given by Cecil
Beaton.
(T.155&A-1980.)

pieces of top-quality skin are used for each shoe. Wooden lasts, which replicate the exact size of the client's feet, are carved by the 'last-maker'; the 'closer' cuts the leather and the 'maker' completes the operation by attaching the sole and the heel.

Stylistic developments in men's shoe design since the war – even the most fashionable – have invariably been based on classic designs: the Victorian elastic-sided boot, heavy workwear boots, sporting shoes such as those worn for golf, the brogue and the American loafer. Even Cecil Beaton and Kenneth Tynan, amongst the most flamboyantly attired of British men, wore classic shoes. The most extreme examples of men's footwear during the 1950s were Italian-style winklepickers, popular with subcultural youths, but even these were based upon traditional black leather lace-ups.

Since the 1960s the two-tone corespondent shoe has been widely regarded as a classic. When it first appeared, however, refined taste considered the style rather 'showy', and an element of this conservative attitude persists to the present day. The co-respondent shoe is most acceptable when complementing white linen or 'picnic look' clothes, at events such as the Henley Regatta. The style has been taken up by modern designers including Patrick Cox, who featured them – with a twist – in his summer 1987 collection (see plate 132).

The slipper style of man's shoe, with a neat flat bow in grosgrain, has been appropri-ate formal and dance wear since the late eighteenth century. Reserved for special occa-sions, men often wear such evening shoes over a period of many years. The V&A has a pair of the very finest gentlemen's evening shoes worn by Cecil Beaton and made by John Lobb Ltd (plate 137). While many British gentlemen are restrained in the footwear they wear in public places, in the private confine of the home, tastes can tend towards the exotic. Decorative slippers such as those made of luxurious black velvet with embroi-dered pheasants on the uppers with red quilted lining, by New & Lingwood, exemplify this style (plate 138).

In the 1960s a group of top-level shoemakers allied themselves to various fashionable trends. Fashion took hold in two main areas: the neat unadorned loafer style of shoe for casual wear, and the boot that became known as the Chelsea boot, with its characteris-tic elastic side inserts (plate 139). More extreme variations exploited the heels. These flamboyant styles went perfectly with clothes by Mr Fish and Tommy Nutter. Fashion fads like brightly coloured leathers and styles such as high boots, cowboy boots, winklepick-er toes, cuban heels and platform soles primarily belong to the realm of street styles.

Some footwear, originally designed for active sports, has assumed a high-fashion identity. For example, fashion editor Michael Roberts regularly featured equestrian styles in the influential pages of the *Tatler* during the mid-1980s. The green wellington boot (descended from the knee-length boot introduced by the Duke of Wellington in the early nineteenth century) acquired a certain fashion cachet. 'Green wellies' were turned into an amusing 'Sloane Ranger' style statement by Peter York.

Throughout the 1990s traditional styles have continued to dominate men's footwear. At the exclusive level of hand-made footwear, shoemakers adhere to traditional formulae while designers reinterpret tradition to give it a fashionable edge.

Although British shoe design from 1947 to 1997 is distinguished by its variety, certain national characteristics can be pinpointed. The British harbour great respect for tradition and utility, which is offset by a leaning towards romance and the unconventional.

Footnotes

1 Thornton (1979), p.9.
2 Swann (1982).
3 Joan Juliet Buck writing in *Ritz* newspaper, March 1977, p.13.
4 V&A cutting: Colin McDowell obituary for Eric Lobb, 1991.

Select Bibliography

Swann, June. *Shoes* (London: Batsford 1982). See also Northampton Shoe Museum publications.
Thornton, John. *From Cottage Industry to Factory: The Shoe Show – British Shoes Since 1790* (London: The Crafts Council 1979).
Vogue magazine, 1947-1997.

LEFT:
PLATE 139. Trickers Chelsea boots, mid-1970s. Brown leather with elastic insets. Given by Mr Stephen M. Craggs. (T.116 + A-1989.)

Underwear

MAXINE SMITHERAM

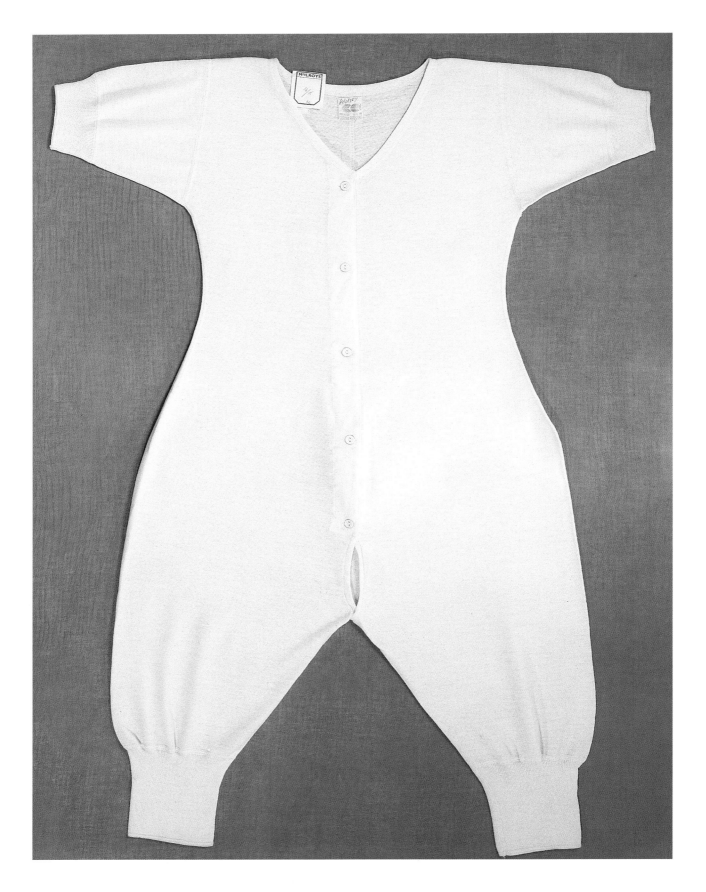

In contrast to the stormy history of women's underwear, men's underwear has diversified almost unseen. It was as if keeping men's underclothes plain and functional could secure male bodies as a bulwark against unrestrained sexuality.

(Jennifer Craik, *The Face of Fashion*, p.131)

PREVIOUS PAGES:
Left: Mary Quant body-stocking, late 1960s. Cream synthetic jersey, sheer white nylon cups. Right: Mary Quant pantie girdle, late 1960s. Black synthetic jersey. Given by Mrs M. Wilson MacDonald. (T.443-1988, T.442-1988.)

LEFT:
PLATE 140.
Ladies' Utility combinations by Wolsey, 1940s. Cream wool jersey. Given by Ms Lyn Healy. (T.107-1989.)

ABOVE:
PLATE 141.
Utility slip and French knickers, 1940s. Pink floral printed rayon. (T.204:A-1982.)

Attitudes to underwear are affected by its intimate associations with the body, arousing conflicting notions of propriety and erotic or fetishistic pleasure. As Jennifer Craik has noted, a person wearing only underclothes can be seen as 'simultaneously dressed and undressed'.[1]

Women's underwear has its own specific history, closely related to that of fashionable outerwear. Throughout the post-war period women's dress and underwear have, with varying degrees of exaggeration or subtlety, been sympathetically amalgamated to create an array of fashionable silhouettes in pursuit of changing ideals of femininity. Indeed, women's underwear is integral to the artifice of fashion and its proffered images of beauty, fantasy and sexuality.

Conversely, underwear has not generally been used to redefine men's bodies. Men's underwear has tended to follow the natural shape of the body and to mimic the mainly simple, tailored lines of outerwear. This has been despite innovations in masculine dress since the 1960s, and the fact that men's underwear design has become more overtly sexualized as the twentieth century has progressed.

Underwear manufacture recovered slowly during the austere post-war years – shortages of essentials, such as wool, cotton, rayon, steel, rubber and elastic, had curtailed its production during the war. The use of silk, which had long been associated with hand-made luxury lingerie, had been banned from garment-making in 1942. Utility styles prevailed until the end of the 1940s, and underwear remained expensive for most of the population. Underwear bearing the CC41 label in the V&A's collection includes Wolsey combinations (plate 140), celanese lock-knit garments, and matching rayon slips and French knickers with a tiny fabric-conserving repeat floral design (plate 141). As with outerwear, the garments are short and quite slim-fitting, with narrow hems, little elastic and no trims. Underlining economic priorities in 1948, high-quality woollen pants and

vests made by the Scottish firm of Pringle carried the caption: 'Exquisite Undies. NB: the more we export the sooner *you* will be able to buy more freely'.[2] In the same year *The Lady* advised potential middle-class brides, 'with a longing for lace insets and a fragile candle-light look', to make their 'own precious trousseau items', including long, full taffeta petticoats from old evening gowns. The cost of a hand-made model camisole-petticoat, when available from a specialist shop, was greatly inflated.[3]

Male undergarments worn between 1940 and 1950 included mid-thigh trunks and buttoned V- and round-necked vests. Utility garments made from cotton actually improved the quality of men's underwear. Although sleeveless singlets had been worn since the 1930s, low-necked versions with sleeves, as well as straight-fly underpants, appeared around 1948. In 1949 new 'glamour trunks' in Celnet, with shaped legs and reinforced fronts, were advertised by Morley. Long johns were winter staples and supportive Y-front underpants were introduced in about 1937.

In the late 1940s the use of merino wool, silk blends and cashmere in men's underwear was a mark of luxury, as exemplified by the underclothes produced by John Smedley and Braemar, both well-established makers. In December 1951 a Braemar advertisement in *The Field* for expensive, hand-finished underwear targeted British gentlemen, whose wardrobes consisted of bespoke tailored garments and traditional sporting clothes. It played up the need for warmth as well as good fit underneath the city suit. Today, as in 1947, good-quality men's underwear tends to be white, pastel or quietly striped, while advertising has continuously stressed men's athleticism (as in Wolsey's Knights and Jockey styles).

It was not until 1946, eight years after the Americans, that British manufacturers began to produce much-desired nylon stockings, replacing the pre-war silk and sub-standard Utility rayon varieties. Fine, seamed flesh-toned 'nylons' became an essential adjunct to the formal co-ordinated high-fashion demands of the 1950s. Unseamed stockings were introduced in 1953. In 1955 Ballito's range of hosiery for different occasions and times of day was 'colour banded' to aid good dressing. In total contrast, women aspiring to the avant garde wore thick black or dark coloured stockings in the mid to late 1950s. Mary Quant's late 1950s clientele wore black stretch stockings, which were expressive of the mood of Bohemian Chelsea.

In Britain many aspects of corsetry manufacture were subject to government controls until 1955, yet the ultra-feminine silhouette of the 1947 New Look required a severely sculptured midriff. Fashion-conscious women achieved this by wearing the stiff belt-like 'waspie', a much diminished laced corset either worn alone or with a roll-on. The process was aptly described as 'waist cinching'.

Corsetry was enthusiastically promoted in the 1950s.[4] Magazines referred to the 'foundation wardrobe' and stressed the importance of well-fitting undergarments. Members of the Incorporated Society of London Fashion Designers worked with Berlei, showing corsets in conjunction with couture garments. *Décolleté* couture evening dresses inspired copies and the wearing of strapless bras, basques and tiered nylon petticoats. The Spirella Company of Great Britain trained corsetiers countrywide to measure women in their own or the fitter's home – a more discreet option than buying in a department store, even though lingerie departments aimed to entice customers with an intimate and relaxed environment.

Madame Illa Knina, who had trained as a sculptor, was a leading and much-publicized corsetier creating exclusive made-to-measure corsetry from her Mayfair studio. Her undergarments, which celebrated feminine curves, are represented in the V&A's collection by sets of long-line bras and girdles that combine elements of modernity and glamour. In brightly flowered nylon, they feature decorative lacing, satin straps and suspenders (plate 142). Madame Knina also designed master patterns for Marks & Spencer and for the Soviet Union.

Foundation garments of the 1950s followed the body's natural curves, but shaped it to the hour-glass silhouette that fashion decreed. They incorporated new light and highly tensile nylon elastic nets as controlling panels, which

reduced boning. Innovations included high-line zipped and step-in girdles and corse-lettes (combined bras and girdles). In harmony with the prevailing fashion, new sup-portive bras included plunge, half-cup and underwired designs. A selection of beautifully crafted nylon lace bras of the period (plate 143) were made by élite corsetiers Rigby & Peller. Padded and inflatable bra cups, and bra inserts referred to as 'falsies', were worn to achieve the right contours. Whirlpool, circular-cup stitching formed the tilted, pointed bustline.

Throughout the 1950s there was much competition between American and British manufacturers of mass-produced foundation wear, with the former often leading inno-vation. British brand names, such as Court Royal and English Rose, indicate British sen-sibilities. The 1953 season was marked by Berlei with a 'Coronation' controlette in red, white or royal blue. From the mid-1950s, manufacturers sought to attract the teenage market with suspender belts, panty girdles and camisole bras and petticoats in broderie

anglaise. In 1956 the Silhouette Company produced an outstandingly successful cinema film to advertise its 'little X' two-way stretch girdle. Aimed at 16 to 24 year-olds, it featured an 'exu-berant' girl enjoying the garment's light-weight abdominal support. Youthful elements were reflected in the candy pink, red and black fabrics, trimmed with gold Lurex. This British product was subsequently made under licence in 32 countries.[5]

The 1950s saw the introduction of underwear using nylon and consequently underclothes with a slimmer cut, such as women's briefs and spun-nylon trunks for men. Nylon was promoted as a material that kept its shape, was easy to launder and light to pack for holidays, and it appealed to a wide consumer market even though it was machine made. Prettiness was preserved as sheer nylon could be pleated, gathered or given a soft 'brushed' texture, and it dyed and printed well. Interestingly, the taste for coloured underwear has been analysed as a blatant expression of the erotic impulse.[6]

Although the dynamic, youth-orient-ed fashions of the 1960s precipitated the need for less structured styles of underwear, those with more sophisticated tastes and the more mature continued to wear pull-on hip-length girdles and corselettes with suspenders, often worn with full slips. Similarly, while plain and printed body-defining nylon briefs without a fly-opening became a fash-ionable style of underpants for men, they co-existed with conventional underwear.

During the 1960s elastomeric, the artificial elastic fabric invented in 1958 and now known as Lycra, redirected foundation and underwear design, as had earlier textile inno-vations. Extremely light, with great stretch and recovery properties, this fabric was attributed with 'natural control' and sleekness.

Advertising has commonly linked notions of beauty and health with underwear. By the mid-1960s, with fashion's greater emphasis on slimness, *Vogue* was recommending the benefits of firm-fitting bras and long-legged pantie girdles in Lycra, reminding its readers that 'the adaptability of girls for reshaping is indubitable'. It further advocated

LEFT:
PLATE 143. Rigby & Peller group, 1950s. Above: wired corset brassiere, black machine-made lace, black nylon backing, 'Divorce' style. Centre: wired bra, pink syn-thetic lace, pink satin trim. Below: Wired bra, black machine-embroidered tulle, black nylon backing. Given by Mrs Kenton, Rigby & Peller. (T.634-1995, T.604-1995, T.599-1995.)

dieting, exercise and 'a spell at a health or beauty farm to start the new sculpture'.[7]

The stretch nylon bikini briefs and bras which complemented the adolescent boutique fashions of the 1960s were extremely minimal. Examples in the V&A's collection include multicoloured striped hipster briefs and a synthetic jersey bodystocking by Mary Quant in cream and black, with her signature daisy motif (see pages 176-177).

Bodystockings created an unbroken flat line and the sheer and lacy versions were often worn under transparent outergarments. Bra design was influenced by the 'no-bra-bra' prototype, which consisted of soft triangular cups mounted on a narrow band with thin, stretch shoulder straps. Gossard's Glossies range (still made in 1996), provided extremely unobtrusive bras and bikini pants in a gauzy, shimmering, clinging synthetic fabric.

Youthful underwear, which included the new bra-slip and sets of pants, bras and petticoats, was often printed with vivid designs that echoed the materials used for fashionable outerwear. Bold paisley patterns, or multicoloured flowers sprinkled on a dark background, represent two contemporary trends. Plain fabrics included strong oranges and purples, and psychedelic prints permeated late 1960s underwear.

RIGHT:

PLATE 144. Right: Keturah Brown camisole and French knickers 1996. Pale pink silk georgette and satin, cream nylon lace. Left: Janet Reger mini slip, 1996. Ivory silk satin, ivory-and-pink synthetic lace. Keturah Brown underwear given by Keturah Brown Ltd. (T.436:1-2-1996.) Janet Reger slip given by Mrs Janet Reger. (T.129-1996.)

Stockings continued to be worn throughout the 1960s, although they were gradually replaced by seamless tights, which were more practical and decorous to wear with mini-skirts. By 1965 tights were an integral part of the complete fashion look. At the top end of the ready-to-wear market, very long knitted or jersey stockings, and tights made by Women's Home Industries, co-ordinated perfectly with dresses and accessories and were relatively expensive. Patterns included tattersall checks, diamonds, florals and paisley. Textured white or lacy tights, appliqué stockings and fishnet and silver metallic tights were also contemporary choices.

The decision taken by some women in the late 1960s to discard their bras prompted reactions that were both embarrassed and sexist. Dubbed 'bra-burning', this gesture was part of the wider political struggle for emancipation, and opened up debates about fashion constraints and concepts of what was natural. However, this same period saw the launch by Gossard in 1969 of the Wonderbra, which enhanced the bustline by pushing the breasts upwards and together to create an exaggerated cleavage. This style of bra remained influential and when the company's licensing agreement for manufacture ceased in December 1993, it was immediately replaced by their similar Ultrabra range.

Janet Reger's sensuous colour co-ordinated designer lingerie, incorporating silks, satins and lace appliqué, perfectly fitted the 1970s mood for nostalgia and glamour. Then, as now, her favoured styles included seductive wide-legged French knickers and suspender belts. An ivory satin bias-cut mini-slip with lavish lace insets (plate 144) testifies to the continuing romantic appeal of such garments for the wealthy home and international markets. Biba's underwear in rich dark colours, such as terracotta, represented the other extreme of 1970s glamour design.

Good-quality Marks & Spencer underclothes, which were bought by a wide sector of the market, illustrate the general trends in women's mass-produced underwear during the 1970s. New garments for gentle, elegant control included Lycra body and bottom shapers, and moulded, seamless bras and briefs. Developed in the late 1970s, the latter generally replaced previous known forms of foundationwear. As an alternative, the store also offered lacy polyester lingerie, and sets of bras and bikini briefs. In contrast to the 1960s, underwear fabrics tended to be plain in the 1970s. Many women gave up slips and any form of corsetry.

In the 1970s men's underpants in hectic colours were advertised by Meridian and Lyle & Scott. In 1975 the latter produced a patterned range with contrasting white bands and 'Y' construction. The advertising for this novelty placed the female and male models in a 'Tarzan' scenario, indicating the more relaxed social mores of the era as well as the increasing eroticization of men's underwear.

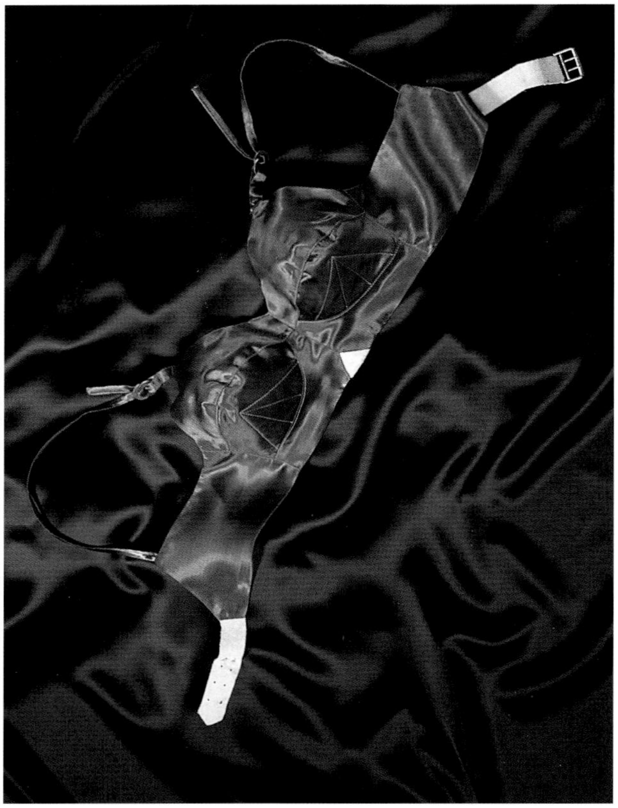

At the end of the 1970s fashion's demand for Lycra sports and dancewear produced parallel designs in underwear. Footless tights and women's bandeau-style sports bras and stretch 'bodies' are lasting examples. Spandex 'bodies', which are closely related to leotards but with convenient fasteners, have been worn extensively during the 1980s and '90s as casual garments by the body-conscious. In dressed-up form, with bra-cup under-wiring and in velour or textured fabric, bodies have been worn for more formal occasions and sometimes replace blouses under tailored suit jackets. They have been diversely made by Pineapple dancewear, John Smedley and Rigby & Peller, as well as by many other underwear designers.

The pluralistic nature of underwear from the 1970s onwards relates to wider choices in outerwear. In the early 1980s androgynous underwear, such as printed unisex boxer shorts, and women's cotton singlets and pants with outerseams, topped with high elastic waistbands and modelled on men's styles, entered all levels of the market. Simultaneously, men's more streamlined underwear was increasingly advertised by younger men 'striking provocative poses'.[8] To a degree, these changes reflect both the exploitation and breakdown of gender.

Vivienne Westwood's controversial introduction of underwear as outerwear in an ensemble for her autumn/winter 1982 Buffalo Collection has widely influenced other designers and consumer taste. Layers of visible underskirts worn over patterned leggings and body, topped with a retro-style tan satin bra, comprised this innovation (plate 145). In 1991 Marks & Spencer's Fortuny Pleat underwear range was reported as serving 'the increasing desire for lingerie that will work both as under *and* outer-wear'.[9]

Concurrently, and surviving into the late 1990s, an interest in fluid romantic underwear prevailed during the 1980s with a revival of styles such as camiknickers, also known as 'teddies'. A late 1980s boudoir set consisting of hand-made and painted camiknickers

LEFT:
PLATE 145. Vivienne Westwood 'outer' bra, Buffalo Collection, autumn/winter 1982-3. Brown synthetic satin, brown cotton, brown leather. Given by Mr Patrick Moore. (T.238-1985.)

and deep-fringed shawl, in pale blue silk satin with intricately appliquéd red poppies, was bequeathed to the V&A by Ian & Marcel. These luxurious and languid one-off garments evoke the feel of 1920s lingerie.

Goug Wilcox, the owner and designer of Keturah Brown, describes the nuance of her work of 20 years as softly romantic. Her high-quality garments, which are hand-cut, finished with French hems and infilled with English laces, earned a British Fashion Industry Award for Women's Nightwear and Lingerie in 1983. An exquisite ice-pink set of silk and georgette French knickers and a matching camisole with filigree lace was donated to the V&A in 1996 (see plate 144).

The high status of Rigby & Peller has been confirmed by a succession of royal warrants since 1960. The company still experiences a demand for élite made-to-measure corsetry, particularly for special occasion wear, and receives commissions from the performing arts. However, in step with the times, the present owner and designer Mrs June Kenton has produced a collection of ready-to-wear lingerie and control garments in the finest laces, silks and stretch fabrics. While the maintenance of a specialist shop is an important facet of business relations for companies such as Rigby & Peller and Janet Reger, with the concept influencing 'the destination department' philosophy of mass-market retailing, selected items from both the above collections are now sold by top British department stores as well as abroad.

From the late 1980s, matt black 40 or 70 denier opaque tights became a commonplace accessory to the vogue for black outerwear across the fashion categories. In the late 1990s tights, and stockings mainly worn with suspender belts, are available in many weights, textures, shades and prints, while finer denier tights, colour co-ordinated with outerwear, continue to accessorize tailored dressing.

Since the late 1980s there has been a resurgence of interest in historical women's underpinnings, which has been explored by radical British designers Vivienne Westwood and John Galliano. Westwood's work has translated the crinoline into the collapsible 'mini-crini' (1985), the bustle into lightweight *derrière* pads (1995), and made reference to traditional corsetry in many *décolleté* concoctions. John Galliano has re-created the eighteenth-century man's fencing jacket as a female basque. In 1996 Alexander McQueen showed corsets made by Mr Pearl, a London-based male designer who wears a corset.

In the 1990s the work of these designers can be assessed as being witty or confrontational, objectifying or liberating. Ideas relating to this couture work have filtered into the wider market for underwear, fuelling a demand for 'bespoke' as well as mass produced, underwired and orb-forming balconette bras, boned bodices and corselettes, basques and bustiers (the last commonly marketed as wedding wear). However, Karl Lagerfeld, commenting in 1994 on the revival of the voluptuous bust at the latest Paris fashion show, cited the Wonderbra as 'the single most important feature of fashion in the past 10 years'.[10] Claims for modern corsetry stress that it contours without physical harm or pain, while many female erogenous zones are accentuated.

At the beginning of the 1990s advertising recommended that women own underwear in a diversity of styles, from seamless bras to wear under T-shirts to the Slim-slip with integrated knickers created by Rigby & Peller to be worn under a short tight skirt. Accelerating the growth of the lucrative 'intimate apparel' industry into the 1990s, department and chain stores usually offer an individual fitting service and display a multiplicity of women's undergarments. These include stretch-control alternatives to the highly structured designs mentioned above, in the form of figure-following Lycra bras and racer-back sports bras. Knickers are cut to enhance a range of fashionable lines and can be full, high-legged or reduced to 'G-strings'. Much underwear incorporates Lycra or complex Lycra laces. A new nylon fibre called Tactel, which allows the skin to breathe, is used alone or blended with natural yarns. Cotton, promoted as pure or under ecological labels, remains a popular underwear choice. Colours span the spectrum, although white is still perceived by some as innocent and black as sexy.

PLATE 146. John
Smedley group,
1996. Right: crop
top and knickers,
black Sea Island
cotton jersey.
Centre: long
vest, white Sea
Island cotton
jersey. Given
by Mr Tony
Langford, John
Smedley. (T.441-
1996, T.442-1996,
T.443-1996.)

The need for practical warm women's underwear for everyday and winter sportswear is met at the top of the market by the firm of John Smedley, who produce long johns, vests and bodies in plain and lace materials made from natural fabrics (plate 146). Damart's widely patronized range, which includes spencers and bodies, has harnessed the plastic fibre thermolactyl. Modernizing its design image in 1991, Damart offered a body with marabou feathers at the neck and sleeves. Apart from thermal fibres, thick ribbed cotton underwear and knitted silks are insulating.

Marks & Spencer, which offers a huge range of underwear, currently holds approximately 35 per cent of the women's lingerie market in Britain, and 77 per cent of its garments are British-made.[11] The successful British companies Gossard and Charnos compete with American and European top-selling lingerie brands.

The underwear/outerwear equation continues at the level of high fashion. Bras and knickers, blatantly visible beneath ultra-sheer garments, are presented as part of the whole fashion statement while simultaneously insinuating *déshabillé*. Westwood's fig-leaf and printed penis tights have confounded many fashion commentators, while the bias-cut slip dress in chiffon or satin, resembling lingerie of the 1930s, is a more obvious, yet enduring 1990s outerwear fashion.

At the end of the 1990s women's underwear, especially corsetry, is regarded by many as sensual (although no longer mysterious), to be enjoyed by a new generation of women and men, distanced from the past disadvantages of structured styles. Agent Provocateur, based in London's red-light district and owned by Vivienne Westwood's son Joseph Corré, feeds this notion which is mixed with the possibly questionable ethos of empowerment. The shop sells vintage 1950s corsets and Westwood's *derrière* cage knickers. Crotchless and bottomless pants, baby-doll lingerie and tight, cropped stretch T-shirts celebrate underwear's fetishistic potential. Fabrics range from leopard-skin prints to garish coloured nylon and garments are trimmed with fake fur and nylon lace. The antithesis of the functional, many of the garments double as *outré* outerwear.

In contrast with the above, along with the open display of women's underwear in department stores, men's underwear is usually discreetly packaged. Many men simply buy underwear to stock up when they purchase new clothes. At the top end of the range, traditional male styles similar to those in existence in the 1950s are sold by London department stores such as Harrods, Harvey Nichols and Simpson's. John Smedley has continued to produce long pants, trunks, briefs and vests in Sea-Island cotton and wool and silk mixes. Sunspel-Boxer Ltd, part of a long-established Nottingham company, manufactures good-quality cotton boxer shorts with an additional back panel for comfort. These underpants in plain dyes and prints sell to a faithful British and export market. Since 1936, Sunspel Menswear has made a range of traditional fine cotton and cellular garments and thermal wear in merino wool. Paul Smith has recently joined these makers: classic cotton-jersey pieces include high-cut slips, briefs with a key-hole opening and A-line fronted trunks. Knitted boxers have button-fly detailing and singlets include high crew-neck styles. The colour range is navy, white, black and grey.

Tangas (pouches on waistbands) and Lycra briefs are late 1990s alternatives to conventional garments. Although many young men have substituted the T-shirt for vests, obvious designer labels represent status for others. Marketing focuses on the relationship between the well-toned male body and the snug fit of garments. Men's underwear, even the recently revived and revamped combination, has the potential to be 'ephemeral, sensual and desirable.'[12]

At the end of the 1990s, as with outerwear, underclothes are chosen by many as an expression of preference for tradition or their desire to embrace modernity. There is much scope in the field of underwear design for both the wearer and the maker to experiment freely with many strands of fashion.

Acknowledgements

I would like to thank the following for their assistance with this chapter: Braemar; Charnos; Gossard and Janet Hurton; Goug Wilcox of Ketura Brown; Sue Sadler, Corporate Press Officer, Marks & Spencer; Mrs June Kenton of Rigby & Peller; John Smedley and Poppy Eliot; the press office at Paul Smith; Sunspel-Boxer; Triumph International; Janet Reger; Warner's and Loraine Carter.

Footnotes

1 Craik (1995) p.119.
2 *Tatler and Bystander*, 3 March 1948.
3 *The Lady*, 8 April 1948.
4 Sales of corsets doubled between 1948 and 1958, and the first National Corset Week was held in 1952.
5 Archive of Art and Design, AAD/1994/21, Silhouette (Salop) Ltd.
6 Cunnington and Cunnington (1992), p.236.
7 *Vogue*, 15 October 1965.
8 Explored in Craik (1995).
9 *Daily Telegraph*, 29 July 1991.
10 *Daily Telegraph*, 1 August 1994.
11 Marks & Spencer corporate figures, April 1996.
12 Craik (1995), p.133.

Bibliography

Ash, J. and Wilson, E. (eds) *Chic Thrills, A Fashion Reader* (London: Pandora Press 1992).

Bernard, B. *Fashion in the 60's* (London: Academy Editions 1978).

Craik, J. *The Face of Fashion: Cultural Studies in Fashion* (London and New York: Routledge 1995).

Cunnington C. Willett and Cunnington, Phillis. *The History of Underclothes* (London: Faber & Faber 1981; Dover Publications Inc. 1992).

Ewing, E. *Dress and Undress: A History of Women's Underwear* (London: Batsford 1978).

Hawthorn, R. *Knickers: An Intimate Appraisal* (London: Souvenir 1991).

Page, C. *Foundations of Fashion: The Symington Collection, Corsetry from 1856 to the Present Day* (Leicester Museums 1981).

Wilson, E. and Taylor, L. *Through the Looking Glass: A History of Dress from 1869 to the Present Day* (London: BBC Books 1989).

Wood, M. 'We wore what we'd got': Women's Underclothes in World War II (Warwickshire Books 1989).

Designer Interviews

COMPILED BY AMY DE LA HAYE

Leading designers working in the British fashion industry between 1947 and 1997 were invited to describe their career developments; their own distinctive market niche; to what extent they use UK textiles; why they show in London or abroad; their perception of Britain's fashion identity and to what extent 'Britishness' determines the design and marketing of their own collections.

Their responses are gathered together below, with each designer listed according to when they started working in the British fashion industry. This date is indicated in brackets after each designer's name in question 1.

Did you undertake a formal fashion training – either within the industry or at a college?

JOHN CAVANAGH (1932): I started within the industry when I was 18, working with Edward Molyneux in his Grosvenor Street premises. I had been to see him eight months earlier, having seen an announcement in the *Evening Standard* that he was in London. He told me I needed to acquire drawing skills, which I did at one of the LCC colleges. Molyneux then offered me a job. By working day and night, and learning from my mistakes, I became responsible for overseeing his models made up in London. I then went to work with him in Paris, as his assistant, where I learned every stage of production.

HARDY AMIES (1934): No, I did not have a formal training.

MARY QUANT (1955): I studied at art school and learned pattern cutting and millinery at evening classes.

GINA FRATINI (1956): Yes, at the Royal College of Art.

CAROLINE CHARLES (1960): I studied at Swindon College of Art and then served an apprenticeship with Michael Sherard.

FRANKA (1961): I went to college in Zagreb where I studied fashion design. I then joined the studio of Madame Stepinska, a leading designer of her time, in Zagreb. I came to London in 1961 via Paris, and started working in the British fashion industry right away.

CHARLES AND PATRICIA LESTER (1966): 30 years apprenticeship – self taught. We are very proud of the fact that we have taught ourselves all our techniques from dyeing and printing through to manufacturing. This has meant that our work tends to be more original as we have not been cluttered by convention. Too many people in the industry say you cannot do this or that, basically because college said so.

ZANDRA RHODES (1968): I studied lithography and printed textiles at Medway College of Art (NDD) 1959-1961, and printed textiles (not fashion) at the Royal College of Art (Des.

RCA): First Class Honours.

PAUL SMITH (1970): No. I learned by 'doing it', turning my ideas into reality by trial and error. I set up a small business when I was 24 years old and designed clothes which I then had to have manufactured. I slowly learned my trade as I went along.

MARGARET HOWELL (1970): I studied fine art at Goldsmith's College, London. I had always made my own clothes, so the enjoyment of choosing the fabric and adapting the pattern to what I wanted was my training. The 4 year Dip Ad course was an invaluable training in colour, proportion and design. I started my own company in the early 1970s. It hardly felt like working in the British fashion industry as with no formal training I was unaware of the importance of fabric fairs (PV, Moda In etc.) or creating full collections. I concentrated on men's shirts and building up a room of skilled machinists for most of the '70s, then added a jacket and a trouser etc.

VIVIENNE WESTWOOD (1971): No.

MANOLO BLAHNIK (1973): I started in college, but most of my training has been within the industry.

BRUCE OLDFIELD (1973): Ravensbourne College of Art, 1971-2.

RICHARD JAMES (1976): No. My fashion training was solely via retail – as a sales assistant, then as a Menswear Buyer.

DAVID SHILLING (1976): I have had no 'formal' fashion training, although I have lectured in colleges and acknowledge their importance. When I was a child my grandmother and my mother did take me to fashion shows in France and England, like other boys might have been taken to football matches by their fathers. And that's where I learned to love fashion. (Formal training is obviously not essential, but without a college behind you it seems more dangerous, lonelier, and you have to try harder all the time, but you do retain an individualism that sometimes gets lost during college.)

CATHERINE WALKER (1977): (completed on her behalf) Catherine Walker is self taught. She spent the first five-

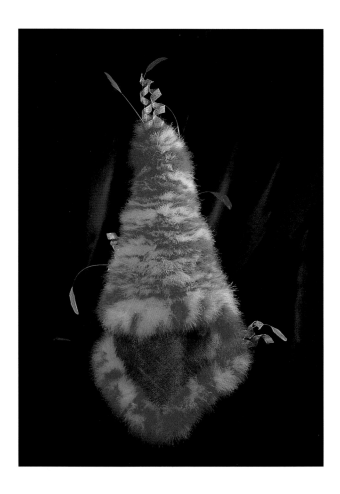

ABOVE:

PLATE 147 David Shilling hat, summer 1996. Multicoloured marabou feathers with metal visor, L.E.D. light system. Given by Mr David Shilling. (T.456-1996.)

year period of her business as a non-profit making exercise to acquaint herself with the basics of pattern cutting, sewing and of course commerce.

PATRICK COX (1984): I did the Footwear Design Course at Cordwainers Technical College, Mare Street, Hackney. It was a 2 year course (Sept. 83 – July 85). Shoes, however, are a craft that are best understood through experience working with factories; college taught me very little. My first year in college I worked with Vivienne Westwood, in the second year – Bodymap.

JOHN GALLIANO (1985): I did a four year Fashion and Textiles course at St Martin's School of Art.

PHILIP TREACY (1990): I studied fashion at the National College of Art and Design in Dublin and then won a scholarship to go to the Royal College of Art, where I learnt hat design in my final year. I was really interested in developing my creativity and although we were taught business studies, nothing prepares you for running your own business. I certainly consider it to be an advantage having trained with fashion designers, because I now know how they work.

SHIRIN GUILD (1992): No.

HUSSEIN CHALAYAN (1993): Yes, at Central Saint Martins.

With whom did you first work and when did you launch your own label?

JOHN CAVANAGH: I started by working with Molyneux. After serving in the army for six years, I worked with the Parisian couturier Pierre Balmain. I launched my own label in 1952.

HARDY AMIES: Lachasse. I launched my own label in 1946.

MARY QUANT: We launched on our own in 1955, i.e. Alexander Plunket Greene, Archie NcNair and myself.

GINA FRATINI: I worked with the Katherine Dunham Theatre Group (American company) for 2 years, before starting Gina Fratini Ltd in 1964.

CAROLINE CHARLES: My first job was with Mary Quant in 1961, and I set up my own label in 1963.

FRANKA: My first job in London was with Norman Hartnell, where I worked from 1962-64. I launched my own label in 1967.

CHARLES AND PATRICIA LESTER: Ourselves in 1963.

ZANDRA RHODES: On leaving college, I taught 2 days a month and designed on a freelance basis (1964-67 prints for Foale & Tuffin and Bellville Sassoon). Set up a company with Sylvia Ayton called: Sylvia Ayton & Zandra Rhodes. 1968-69 retailed Sylvia Ayton & Zandra Rhodes through our own outlet: The Fulham Road Clothes Shop. I launched my own company, Zandra Rhodes, in 1969.

PAUL SMITH: Me. I had my own shop from 1970 to 1976 and designed some of the clothes myself. I launched a wholesale label in October 1976.

MARGARET HOWELL: I was always self-employed. Apart from my husband joining me and growing the business together, I did have a working relationship with Joseph Ettedgui for several years. He opened franchise shops – one in Paris and one in South Molton Street, London. From the very beginning, I had a printed label and later progressed to the woven label with the signature and 'walkers' trade mark.

VIVIENNE WESTWOOD: Self-employed. Together with my partner Malcolm McLaren I opened a shop in 1970 called 'Let it Rock'; this was the name of our first label. Since then we had various different names/labels for our clothes. In 1987, being for some time independent of McLaren, I used my own name.

MANOLO BLAHNIK: Ossie Clark and Zandra Rhodes. I launched my own label in 1973.

BRUCE OLDFIELD: Freelance – collection for Henri Bendel, New York, 1973. I launched my own label in 1975.

RICHARD JAMES: Browns of South Molton Street. The Richard James label, based in Savile Row, was launched in 1992.

DAVID SHILLING: I first worked with David Shilling – the worst and best boss you could ever imagine! We've been together ever since! The David Shilling label began in 1975. Because I had already created the hats for my mother to wear at Ascot each year, which created so much attention while I was still at school, my first commercial designs were scarves and blouses. After two seasons I opened my shop in Marylebone High Street, selling blouses, wedding dresses etc. but dominated by hats arranged centrally in urns.

CATHERINE WALKER: Catherine Walker has only ever worked alone. In deference to her initial inexperience she first called her company The Chelsea Design Co. During the past four years she has changed her label to Catherine Walker.

PATRICK COX: I first worked with Vivienne Westwood, while in my first year at college (February/March 1984). My flatmate at the time was her design assistant, David Smiles. 4-5 weeks before the show in Paris they realised no one had done the shoes yet. David suggested that I could help…I had a meeting with Vivienne (who was my hero and half the reason I'd moved to London) and everything went well…I even modelled in the show! Immediately after graduation I set up my own label which will be eleven years old as of spring 1997. The Patrick Cox shoe collection (including the 'Wannabe' range) arrived in shops for spring/summer 1986. The Wannabe Clothing collection was launched for spring/summer 1995. The PC's shoe collection was also launched for spring/summer 1995.

JOHN GALLIANO: Myself. I began my own label immediately after my final year collection at St Martin's.

PHILIP TREACY: Myself: I went in to business straight from college in 1990.

SHIRIN GUILD: No-one in the fashion industry. I launched my own label in spring 1993.

HUSSEIN CHALAYAN: Timothy Everest – the tailor. I launched my own label on 29th March 1994.

How would you describe, in a few words, your style and position in the fashion market?

JOHN CAVANAGH: I designed a wide range of clothes to accommodate the social life of my (mainly British and American) clients. I made tailored suits, day dresses, cocktail outfits, evening gowns and wedding dresses. However, I don't ever remember making a débutante dress. I hope that my work reflected my Paris training – I had lived and worked there and it is perhaps inevitable that my clothes looked more French than British.

HARDY AMIES: The one remaining *truly* couture house in Great Britain. Worldwide licensee operation – over 50 in 14 countries.

MARY QUANT: Mid to high price-range fashions. The look: sport-chic. Fashions, undies, bags, belts, swimsuits, make-up (120 eye colours, 101 lip colours, 80 nail colours), Skincare and Bodyline.

GINA FRATINI: Romantic – clothes for special occasions – clothes to make women feel very special – in wonderful colours and beautiful fabrics.

CAROLINE CHARLES: Style – plain shapes, fine details, eclectic fabrics – made well to suit the modern woman. Position – ready-to-wear.

FRANKA: I consider my position to be one of the leading couturiers in England today, with an international following of clients from all over the world. My design endeavour has always stretched across several generations. Some designs are aimed at individual clients' needs, but they are always feminine and flattering to a woman's body. I like bold, strong jewel colours, and use black a lot. I design a lot of very intricate beadwork for my eveningwear. I am lucky to be able to work with a beadier who beads entirely by hand, so I am able to achieve unique designs.

CHARLES AND PATRICIA LESTER: We have established our own identity and do not follow rules, trends and predictions. Our product is aimed at customers who are aesthetically orientated, not fashion conscious.

ZANDRA RHODES: Unique personal style based around flowing fabrics, especially printed chiffons. A self-taught way of cutting and draping. Textile-led: a Colourist. Developed a way of cutting around the print on fabric, the garment and its shape developing from this point.

PAUL SMITH: Top end of the ready-to-wear market. I have a respect for tradition and craftsmanship which I combine with a sense of humour and a love of 'the Street'.

MARGARET HOWELL: I arrived in the fashion market in the early 1970s, the end of the '60s funky throw-away fashion. There was a new wave of young retailers, mostly American, who were looking for more classic, interesting English clothes. I took traditional fabrics such as linen, Harris Tweed and fine shirtings and made them into softly constructed (or what was known as unstructured) modern tailoring. My style could be described as understated quality; updated modern classics.

VIVIENNE WESTWOOD: My style is recognized world-wide as innovative and is entirely connected with the importance of researching design from the past. I am the only designer who really does this today. As a result I have added to the oeuvre of fashion technique. All this is perceived more abroad than in England, as seen in fashion editorial, though here I do have the support of many good fashion journalists and people like yourselves in the V&A.

MANOLO BLAHNIK: I guess I am a different phenomena from everyone else who designs shoes. I am totally individual in that I never follow trends.

BRUCE OLDFIELD: A designer of couture and deluxe ready-to-wear – an old hand. A survivor. A classicist with a fondness for curves and sensuality.

RICHARD JAMES: I have led the field in making traditional British tailoring relevant and modern, and have led the reaction away from the high fashion of a few years ago and back to a spirit of individual style.

DAVID SHILLING: At a time when hats weren't being worn by the young or the fashionable, I made them instantly desirable again. People still think of hats and David Shillling as being synonymous, although I've expanded into other areas. The Shilling style is always glamorous, witty, sexy, fun, with attention to detail and quality, whatever I am designing.

CATHERINE WALKER: Catherine Walker occupies the only position in the British fashion market of true couturier. The British Fashion Awards recently advised her that they could not make an Award to her as a couturier because they need a choice of six nominees, and there was really no one else to choose from in Britain.

PATRICK COX: The words most often used to describe my work are: young, hip, modern, clean, British and Credible.

JOHN GALLIANO: Intelligent.

PHILIP TREACY: Modern millinery with a British influence, aimed at an international clientele.

SHIRIN GUILD: Simple, comfortable clothes for women with personal style. I am not in the 'fashion' market.

HUSSEIN CHALAYAN: Designer, experimentally and conceptually orientated.

Do you only show your collections in London? If not, can you briefly explain the reasons you show abroad and where.

JOHN CAVANAGH: I showed once in Paris and New York, but otherwise in London.

HARDY AMIES: Yes, only in London.

MARY QUANT: We show to our own shops internationally.

GINA FRATINI: I showed in London and New York because they were my main selling markets.

CAROLINE CHARLES: Press show in London. Promotional shows anywhere in the world to support the brand.

FRANKA: I have always shown my principal collections in London. The main reason being that my clients come to me, and I have not aimed for a large *prêt-a-porter* market.

CHARLES AND PATRICIA LESTER: No, not any more. It used to be our only venue, but London has now lost its pull. Our buyers do not come here any more. The majority do not have businesses that cater for street fashion. This is the image that has been heavily promoted for London with less attention paid to the quality, individuality and style of the designers and we do not fit into the shriek and freak category.

ZANDRA RHODES: I have mainly shown all over the USA. Some big charity shows, but mainly 2-3 day trunk shows all around America: Los Angeles, Houston, Dallas, Boston, NY etc. For some reason, the American tastes found a niche for me so I kept going by travelling to my market.

PAUL SMITH: We sell in 38 countries and have showrooms in Milan, Paris, Madrid, Munich, New York, Tokyo and London. We show our menswear in Paris and do not have shows of the women's fashion. I show in Paris because all the world's press and buyers are there. There isn't an equivalent event in Britain.

MARGARET HOWELL: We show the women's collection on the catwalk in London. We also show in Paris at SEHM. We have shown men's and women's collections in Japan where we have a large licence company.

VIVIENNE WESTWOOD: I show ladieswear in Paris. I did this after showing 3 collections in London. I moved because there were no strong designers here and I wished to show with my peers. I showed again in London at a time when Conran, Galliano and Ozbek were strong here and moved back to Paris when this nucleus collapsed. Of course I am seen as essentially British but my level is more importantly international. I show men in Milan for these same reasons.

MANOLO BLAHNIK: I show my collections in London, New York, Paris. In this way I get to reach more people.

BRUCE OLDFIELD: Yes.

RICHARD JAMES: I only show in London at my premises in Savile Row.

DAVID SHILLING: When I first started I realised the enormous value of showing collections. We always showed at *haute couture* time, that is close to the beginning of the complimentary season, and I created a total look each time that every client could relate to. To my knowledge no other hat designer was showing collections in that way then. Today I don't see the same ben-

efits of annual shows; the idea seems out-of-date and misdirected, so we don't. On the other hand, one-off presentations to introduce my work abroad seem very relevant. I'm currently enjoying a 'world-tour'…everything from a show for Los Angeles County Museum to the first ever Miss USSR contest in Moscow.

CATHERINE WALKER: Catherine Walker does not show at home or abroad because (a) she does not wholesale, and (b) she does not licence or produce ancillary goods such as perfume.

PATRICK COX: I don't do any fashion

ABOVE:
PLATE 148
Franka evening dress, spring/summer 1996. Green silk satin and black lace with sequins, beads and pastes. Given by Baroness Stael von Holstein (Franka). (T.439-1996.)

shows at all – it's not something I believe in. The shoe collections are shown at fairs in Paris and Düsseldorf and through agents in Italy, America and Japan. Fashion today is a Global Market – we show where we see the Maximum Press and Buyers.

JOHN GALLIANO: I show both my own collection and my collections for Givenchy in Paris. There is a massive international audience of buyers and press, and showing in Paris allows you to reach this audience.

PHILIP TREACY: I choose to show my own collections in London, because people understand hats here, and clients come from abroad because England is the home of the hat. Furthermore, I've enjoyed fantastic support here. London also has something special, a creative edge, that you don't find anywhere else.

SHIRIN GUILD: Paris – because international buyers all come to Paris.

HUSSEIN CHALAYAN: We only show in London as part of London Fashion Week.

To what extent do you use UK fabrics?

JOHN CAVANAGH: Each season fabric representatives brought me textile samples, which were international. I selected on the basis of the best designs, often they were British. There were some marvellous British companies, such as Sekers.

HARDY AMIES: As much as possible, but foreign countries produce beautiful fabrics we cannot find in Britain.

MARY QUANT: I use fabrics from France, Italy and Japan – some developed for us. Knit and jersey and tweeds are from Britain. Our designs for furnishings and bed linen are printed in this country and in Japan.

GINA FRATINI: Wish I could have used more – always tried, and did whenever possible.

CAROLINE CHARLES: UK fabrics used

where possible – wool crêpes and blends from Scotland and Yorkshire.

FRANKA: Sadly, I rarely find useable UK fabrics. It is a question of design and quality. The market simply isn't here, particularly with printed silks and quality plain silks.

CHARLES AND PATRICIA LESTER: Very little. Suitable fabrics are not often made in the UK. We do, however, all our own processing, so in this respect it is British, although the basic cloth is imported.

ZANDRA RHODES: Whenever possible, but except for velvets and very basic suiting cloths, most come from Italy, France, or Germany.

PAUL SMITH: Wherever possible I have a loyalty to British mills and always use some British fabric in each collection; the percentage varies from season to season. I have tried to nurture some of the more traditional mills to come up with fashion fabrics and new yardage – encouraging them, for example, to work with new dyes, finishes or synthetic yarns – to be more adventurous. However, many are still locked into a certain type of production and are reluctant to change, sometimes their product is relevant and other times it is out of key.

MARGARET HOWELL: In the early days we used only UK fabrics. Now it is probably 60% Italian and some French fabrics. Some of our most successful fabrics are UK.

VIVIENNE WESTWOOD: As I produce most of my collections in Italy it is becoming more difficult to use British fabrics, because of the links between my producers and Italian companies, and also because the British fabrics I like are of an expensive quality. The process of mass-manufacture results in a corruption of taste, and people prefer cheap quality because it enables them to buy more – sadly. However, it is incredibly important to work with some British fabrics for every collection to maintain standards of excellence, and manufacturers here are very efficient and flexible. It should be government policy to support these wonderful manufacturers, as in Italy where there is an infrastructure and garment producers see the importance of working with creative people. In England there is an unbridgeable chasm between cottage industry (that is the way I started, DIY) and the kind of people who produce for Marks & Spencer. It is impossible to grow in England.

MANOLO BLAHNIK: I use a lot of classic UK fabrics e.g. flannels, tweeds, silks, hardy leathers.

BRUCE OLDFIELD: *Very* limited – mainly for tailoring or for small runs of artisanal fabrics and embroidery.

RICHARD JAMES: Almost all of the fabrics I use are British – especially for tailoring.

DAVID SHILLING: My criteria when I choose fabrics is that they are the best for the job. I could use British fabrics more but UK textile manufacturers don't show any more enthusiasm for me to use their fabrics than any other mills abroad. At the moment social issues are becoming more important to me. Child slavery is particularly abhorrent to me, and I hope to my clients as well. Being certain that textiles are in no way damaging, both environmentally and socially, is increasingly important.

CATHERINE WALKER: Catherine Walker uses British fabrics whenever possible not only because she supports British industry but also because of the logistics of obtaining a suit length at short notice. However, many of the fabrics she requires are not available in the UK in the quality and are sourced from companies such as Agnona in northern Italy.

PATRICK COX: With the footwear we use exclusively Italian leather. With the clothing we sometimes use British wools, otherwise 90% of the fabrics are Italian, Spanish or French.

JOHN GALLIANO: I use Noble British fabrics every season.

PHILIP TREACY: Straw and felt are the main materials used in hat-making and unfortunately I buy these from the Far East and the Czech Republic. However, I do use a feather factory in Devon.

SHIRIN GUILD: Completely – 100%.

HUSSEIN CHALAYAN: Very little.

LEFT:
FIG. 21
Manolo Blahnik drawing of sandals, with fabric swatch, 1979 (for 1980). (E1335-1979.)

Do you think that Britain has a national fashion identity? If so, can you describe what you believe it to be?

JOHN CAVANAGH: The tailored clothes are wonderful and also the very grand evening dresses, which are so much a part of British social life. There's no point designing garments for which there is no occasion to wear them.

HARDY AMIES: Too diluted – needs co-ordination.

MARY QUANT: What the French call Style Anglais and Style Anglaise: style sporty – hunting, shooting, fishing, cricket, polo, golf. Male and female.

GINA FRATINI: Britain certainly has a very strong fashion identity. British fashion is quite unique and hugely creative – I believe 90% of new trends originate from Britain. Sadly, as in all creative people, we are not good at marketing ourselves.

CAROLINE CHARLES: British fashion identity: (i) Streety/club – youth; (ii) Sport /country – classic; (iii) Social/work – modern luxury

FRANKA: I think the British fashion identity has two extremes. There is the traditional element of country tweeds of normal clothing, and the trend-setting fashion of punk and grunge. England seems to plunge from the outrageous to the innovative. There are some exceptions like Jean Muir, who had her own very special fashion statement linked to British manufacturing.

CHARLES AND PATRICIA LESTER: Street and Classic. Britain is noted for quality eveningwear and sophisticated Savile Row tailoring.

ZANDRA RHODES: Individuality and original ideas from where whole themes are started. The British art school system is the best in the world. It helps to build individuality, which is *not* the same as commercialism.

PAUL SMITH: It is fair to say that Britain has the biggest talent in the world.

The sad thing is that we don't know how to use it – management don't know how to use designers. If there is a style, it's freedom of thought and ever-changing styles, which explains street fashion and young people wanting to express their own identity through their dress. Britain is also famous for high quality Yorkshire cloth, Savile Row tailoring and good quality shoes, and finally for the high standard of clothing available in the high street.

MARGARET HOWELL: There is a strong divide. It still has its established identity of craftsmanship and quality, the English style of Burberry, hunting, fishing, tweed, country clothing, hand-made shoes etc. but also the creative extreme looks of the younger designers.

VIVIENNE WESTWOOD: The identity is one of tradition founded in the time of the Empire/Industrial Revolution of which Savile Row and our wonderful fabrics remain. On the DIY end we have street fashion which you could buy in such places as Hyper Hyper, though as I haven't been there in years I don't know where this is now sold. I deplore the negative aspects of the bad teaching in our colleges.

MANOLO BLAHNIK: Britain stands alone for eccentric fashion and street cred, and is the nursery of ideas for many countries.

BRUCE OLDFIELD: More steeped in the menswear traditions. The women's tends to be classic 'apparel' for mass markets or cutting edge witty, with no areas for meeting in the middle – a pity.

RICHARD JAMES: Britain is best at making beautiful classic clothes, and at updating beautiful classic clothes.

DAVID SHILLING: Britain has not just one national fashion identity, but two! I call this 'Monarchy and Anarchy'. Monarchy is the classic look, in which ladies in hats still figure as do men in formal tailoring: the traditional British look. Anarchy is the experimental free-spirited look in which Britain excels, whether seen through 'pop' or 'streetstyle', or commercially interpreted by a whole range of design tal-

JEAN MUIR
LONDON

Autumn 1977

LEFT:
FIG. 22
Jean Muir pen-
and-ink sketch
of blouses for
her autumn/
winter 1977
collection.
(E.141-1978.)

ent from market stall to international market-place. The look is funky, eccentric, often humorous, and above all innovative.

CATHERINE WALKER: Catherine Walker believes that Britain has an identity abroad of being eccentric. Apart from this there has always been a strong British tradition in bespoke tailoring which is not at all eccentric, and very highly regarded worldwide.

PATRICK COX: British youth are very tribal. They create new movements to belong to, new music and new fashion. The fashion identity of the British is very experimental and youth-orientated.

JOHN GALLIANO: There are two aspects of British Fashion. Britain is known for both its classic tradition and wild creativity – from Burberrys to Kensington Market. Since the 1960s British fashion has been seen as creative and daring. Music has played a strong part in shaping British Fashion since the 'Swinging Sixties' to punk, the new romantics and the house/techno scene.

PHILIP TREACY: People are not afraid 'to go for it' in this country. There is a gutsy attitude to creativity that other fashion capitals are slower to adhere to. Part of the talent abroad is also British grown – many of my fellow students are now working in major fashion houses abroad.

SHIRIN GUILD: I think the identity is menswear. I love the fabrics – traditional.

HUSSEIN CHALAYAN: Yes, British fashion tends to be more extreme, expressive, experimental and apparently influential.

To what extent do you draw upon British culture and clothing traditions in your design and marketing?

JOHN CAVANAGH: Because of my training and life in Paris, virtually not at all. I believe that a suit or dress should look equally good in London, Paris or New York.

HARDY AMIES: We create clothes to fit in with our customers' way of life – cultured and knowledgeable. We know their lifestyles and design accordingly.

MARY QUANT: A lot – Noël Coward, Prince of Wales, riding. Knicker-bockers, knitwear. Evening dress – 'smoking' came from riding clothes. Billiards – waistcoats. Cardigans. Plus fours. Spencers. Liberty bodice. Norfolk jackets

GINA FRATINI: I draw upon all cultures – the world is so small now, I find so much to be inspired by. Design must come first. Once you have the product, then you find the way to market it.

CAROLINE CHARLES: How women lead their lives is the main drive behind our design work. The culture of British social life is now firmly enmeshed with working life.

FRANKA: It is inevitable that one draws on English culture and tradition. You have to be able to create clothes that fit into the British society lifestyle, which is perhaps a more traditional style. My ultimate aim when designing is to make a woman feel so good that she forgets the clothes she is wearing, and to let her personality show through. As my clients usually buy with a specific function in mind, I design to suit the occasion.

CHARLES AND PATRICIA LESTER: We do not draw on British culture, except when considering our marketing strategy. We gear our selling to cultural events such as Glyndeborne and study the migratory pattern of the rich and cultured!

ZANDRA RHODES: I am what I am because I am British. Several of my collection themes have been particularly British in both their theme and concept: Slashed, Cut Silk and Smocking, 1971 – based on V&A slashed silk bodice. Conceptual Chic, 1976. The Renaissance Gold collection, autumn/winter 1981 – heavily based on the Elizabethan period. The Fairy collection, spring/summer 1982 – using prints with their source idea coming from

the Flower Fairy Books of Cicely Mary Barker – with their fairy poems. Fantastic Flower Garden, spring/summer 1986. Queen of Hearts, autumn/winter 1989.

As such, British clothing traditions spring mainly from the 1960s. England has always been known to breed individualists from out of the blue, especially in the innovative art world of textiles with such greats as William Morris, Voysey, Ascher and Libertys. In clothing itself, there was Charles James, but since him it took until the 1960s for a British clothing 'look' to take shape.

PAUL SMITH: A respect for craftsmanship and tradition. Use of tradition with a modern twist seen through humour and a modern approach. A traditional suit with hot pink lining, odd buttons, such as the pinstripe suit with white T-shirt and plimsolls in the V&A collection.

MARGARET HOWELL: I would say quite a lot as I love well-made, crafted and traditional things. They are often an inspiration. Something that lasts and endures time is the essence of good design, as is something that is relevant to its time. That is why my collection will always have the trenchcoat, the shirt, the pinstripe suit, but it is giving that classic item a certain character that is desirable for now. That is the task. Some of the more obvious influences have been a love of our countryside, the climate and colours, the English country house sustained by the National Trust, the Ealing films and the 1960s 'kitchen sink' films, the English tea room and cottage gardens.

VIVIENNE WESTWOOD: Fashion as we know it is the result of the exchange of ideas between France and England, and I still adore what remains of the British tradition in clothes.

MANOLO BLAHNIK: Certain aspects of British culture are very evident in my work, such as the extensive use of traditional British fabrics.

BRUCE OLDFIELD: I try not to, except from an attitude of Britishness purveyed on screen (Joan Fontaine in *Rebecca*) –

mousey but endearing and enduring. Or the more theatrical techni-colour brooding sexiness in films by Powell and Pressburger (*Black Narcissus*). It's probably the only way for people to know that we *had* a clothing tradition – Vivienne Westwood does it best?

RICHARD JAMES: Everything in my work is based on the spirit of being British, and on the history and traditions of British tailoring and Savile Row in particular. I manage to make traditional British tailoring modern and younger.

DAVID SHILLING: Working and living within ten minutes walk of where I was born, in the centre of London, I am obviously very influenced by my Britishness but only in an international context. I am also influenced by other cultures I know of worldwide, especially through my most recent travels, but people are always referring to the 'Britishness' of my look, so it must be winning through. I hope there is no conscious use of British Tradition in our marketing – I hate the 'Olde Curiosity Shoppe' look to death. I design with a respect for the past whilst reaching into the future. Happily there's no need to choose between the two, when we can all have both. Schizophrenics should have twice the fun! And twice the wardrobe!

CATHERINE WALKER: There are traces of British culture throughout Catherine Walker's work. This is probably to do with the environment in which she works and her customers. Her handwriting is usually viewed as somewhere between the unstructured Italian and very formal French. Although there is no conscious attempt on Catherine Walker's part to follow this, it inevitably shows in the delicacy of embroidery, pastel colouring, silhouette...Catherine Walker uses bespoke tailoring in every collection. There are very, very few tailors in the UK who use traditional handcanvas methods. Catherine Walker has about six such tailors who she has found during the past fifteen years and who work exclusively for her. A

jacket of this type would take a workroom over a week to make and puts the retail price well over £1,000. However for those who want the best there is no compromise and Catherine Walker continues to use this traditional skill year in and year out.

PATRICK COX: Living in London is my main source of inspiration...the scene. The attitude of the British youth, the flea markets, the pop music industry, current creativity in magazines and the monarchy. The Mods are my current big influence.

JOHN GALLIANO: I always research a large part of the Galliano collection in

ABOVE:
PLATE 149
Vivienne
Westwood
'Watteau'
evening dress,
'Les Femmes'
collection,
spring/summer
1996. Given by
Mrs Vivienne
Westwood.
Photo: Niall
McInerney.
(T.438:1-3-1996.)

Britain. I go to museums and libraries in London like the V&A and the National Art Library, but also find going to British clubs equally as important a form of inspiration to my work. The energy and passion generated by music in British clubs is awesome. I also love to wander around places in London like Camden and Portobello – not just for the markets. Britain has a very rich 'street culture' and it's as much the attitude of people that is inspiring as the appearance. My clothes can be understood within the context of English gamesmanship and a tradition of service. In some ways I can also be seen to carry on a British tradition begun by Worth – being a British couturier at the head of a French Couture House.

PHILIP TREACY: The Tower of London, Big Ben and hats: throughout the world people associate hats with Britishness. I am very partial to the age old tradition of hat-making, and its wealth of techniques which could disappear. The hat industry is more entwined with British culture than fashion itself. Ascot, for example, is a celebration of hat-wearing as well as horse racing. This occasion provides people with an opportunity to wear their very best hats – I have clients come from all over the world. They plan their hats two months in advance and approach us in a very conscientious way, bringing the clothes they want to wear with them to my studio. If Ascot didn't exist, it would be detrimental to the hat industry. The royal family also play an important role – the Princess of Wales brought a lot of attention to hat-wearing. People see the essence of what I do as British, and buyers come here for that reason.

SHIRIN GUILD: I do not draw upon British culture at all, but I am influenced by British clothing traditions such as men's fabrics, tweeds and stripes, men's English shirting, and knitwear such as Fair Isle – the best translates.

HUSSEIN CHALAYAN: The influences of British culture are subconscious, for me it's about the melting point of cultures which Britain currently epitomizes along with the freedom of expression, realism and honesty which one can witness generally in Britain.

Selected Glossary of British Designers 1947-1997

TONY GLENVILLE, FIONA ANDERSON AND EMMA DAMON

This glossary provides details of a number of British fashion designers, tailors, boutiques and classic brand names that have shaped the history and successes of British fashion in the latter half of this century.

Note: Dates of birth are included where possible, but some were unavailable at the time of going to press. The numbers after each heading indicate page references, italic numbers indicate an illustration on that page, bold indicates an entry in the Designer Interviews section.

ALLY CAPELLINO 161
Label launched by Alison Lloyd (b.1956, studied fashion at Middlesex Polytechnic, first worked at Courtaulds Design Studio) with her partner Jono Platt in 1979 – Capellino means 'little hat' in Italian. In 1986 she held her first London showing of menswear and womenswear and in 1990 launched her Hearts of Oak diffusion collection. She creates stylish restrained clothes.

AMBERG, BILL (b.1962) 160
Born in Northampton, the centre of Britain's leather trades, and worked with leather as a child. Apprenticed to a cobbler and saddle-maker. In 1982 launched design consultancy business in London, and quickly enjoyed commissions from top international fashion designers. Opened shop to retail own-label goods in 1996. Creates stylish modern bags, which combine the finest leather craftsmanship with a minimalist aesthetic.

AMIES, HARDY (b.1909) 14, 16, 17, *17*, 25, *25*, 27, 34, 40-41, 45, 47, 52, *52*, 65, 69, 72, *72*, 78, 90, 124, 125, 157, 166, 172, **188-200**
Trained at W. & T. Avery in Birmingham and then from 1934 at Lachasse, where his mother was employed. Became managing director at Lachasse, followed by a brief spell at Worth (London) Ltd. Set up own couture house in 1946. Dressed the Queen from 1948 and received a royal warrant in 1955. Launched ready-to-wear in 1950 and menswear in 1962. Knighted 1989. Famous for understated tailoring and regal ball gowns. Author of *Just So Far* (London: Collins 1954); *Still Here* (London: Weidenfeld & Nicolson 1984).

ANDERSON & SHEPPARD 48-9, *48*
Established in 1906. One of the 'old guard' of Savile Row, known for the softness of their tailoring. Extremely popular with Americans. Royal Appointment to the Prince of Wales.

ANNACAT
Top-level designer boutique opened 1965 by Janet Lyle and Maggie Keswick. Zany and romantic clothes. Made much use of printed fabrics by Ascher and Liberty. Launched wholesale label in 1970 and engaged talents of designer Leslie Poole 1970-74 (RCA 1958-61).

ANOUSKA HEMPEL 34, 87-8, *88*
Trading under the name Anouska Hempel, Lady Weinberg opened her couture house in London in 1988. Rapidly gained a reputation for elegant evening and special occasion clothing. Her garments and millinery are exquisitely made and sometimes dramatically sculptural in form. She is patronized by a prestigious clientele including the British royal family.

AQUASCUTUM 28, *44*, 122, 129
Founded in 1851. The company name means 'watershield' in Latin. Introduced showerproof woollen rainwear. Aquascutum provided trenchcoats for the British services in both world wars. This protective wear became assimilated into civilian wardrobes. From the mid-1950s introduced greater colour range and fashionable cuts. Classic British ready-to-wear brand name.

ARBEID, MURRAY (b.1935) 27
Aged 15 took a basic pattern-cutting course; then worked as an assistant cutter for a couture company. In 1952 went to work for Michael Sherard. Opened own business in December 1954. Progressed from making clothes solely for private clients to selling wholesale. Cocktail and evening dresses were a speciality. Closed 1992.

ARTWORK
Founded in 1977 by Jane and Patrick Gottelier. Specialize in handknits: eminently wearable up-dated British classics and innovative one-off designer sweaters. Revived the practice of printing on knit.

ASHLEY, LAURA (1925-85) 29, 127
Born in Wales, she was a self-taught designer. Formed company with her husband in 1953 selling printed scarves, table mats and T-towels. In 1969 launched clothing range of simple aprons, smocks and dresses. 1961 moved to Wales and opened first shop. By the late 1960s Laura Ashley was highly successful, with retail outlets throughout UK and abroad. Captured the sustained mood for romantic, escapist pastoral styles.

AVISON, CATHRYN (b.1969) 88, *89*
Trained at Cumbria College of Art and Design, University of Ulster and RCA. Established her own business on leaving college with a Crafts Council grant in 1995. New Generation Award BFC 1995-96. Ethereal, cutwork and embroidered clothes in hand-dyed silks.

AZAGURY, JACQUES (b.1956)
Born in Morocco. Apprenticed to a wholesale clothing company. Undertook two years study at the London College of Fashion and then transferred to St Martin's School of Art. Aged 20, introduced own label – survived only one year – but successfully re-launched in 1978. Specializes in glamorous evening clothes.

BACCARAT 126, *126*
Fashionable 1960s and 1970s wholesale company, founded by Claire and Monty Black to distribute clothing by young innovative designers including Bill Gibb. Based at 40 Great Marlborough Street, London. The Baccarat range was united by a soft romantic

look, and Baccarat boutiques appeared in leading department stores throughout Britain. In 1974 they linked up with Wetherall to produce a range of re-styled mix and match clothes.

BAKER, MAUREEN (b.1925) 28
Head designer for Susan Small 1943-78. Launched her own label company in 1978.

BANKS JEFF (b.1943) 21
Born in Wales. Trained as a painter and studied textiles at St Martin's School of Art. Ran Clobber boutique 1964-74 selling own designs and those of other young designers. Became widely known in the mid-1970s when he launched the Warehouse chain, followed by the 1980s mail order firm Warehouse Utility Clothing Company. Now has his own label and design licenses. A great supporter of the British fashion industry, instigator and presenter of the first mainstream fashion programme on British television, *The Clothes Show*.

BARBOUR 122, *123*, 129, *140*
Established in 1890 by John Barbour, producing waterproof, thornproof jackets. The company's signature waxed cotton jackets have become known simply as the 'Barbour' and are the emblem of the modern country gent. The company is by Royal Appointment to both the Duke of Edinburgh and the Prince of Wales.

BARNETT, SHERIDAN (b.1951) 29, 57, 128
Trained at Hornsey and later at Chelsea Schools of Art. First job as pattern grader with Ossie Clark and Celia Birtwell at Quorum 1975. Launched his own label with Sheilagh Brown 1976. Re-launched on his own 1980. Has also worked for Salvador and Reldan. Meticulous tailored clothes, often devoid of decoration and made in high-quality British wools.

BATES, JOHN (b.1938) 21, 26, 28, 97, *97*, 127
Trained as a journalist. Aged 19 was apprenticed at couture house of Herbert Sidon. John Siggins and a partner backed the launch of Jean Varon in 1959 and appointed Bates as designer. Launched own label in 1974. An innovator, who exploited modern fabrics and daring cut. Dressed many actresses – especially known for his designs for cult television series *The Avengers* and for pop stars.

BELLVILLE SASSOON 19, 27, 30, 79, *79*, 80
Founded 1953 by Belinda Bellville (whose grandmother was a couturier in the 1920s) as Bellville et Cie. In 1958 David Sassoon joined straight from the RCA (1955-58). After 24 years working together, Belinda Bellville retired in 1982. Lorcan Mullany (who trained with Bill Gibb and Hardy Amies) joined the company in 1987 – it has been renamed Bellville Sassoon Lorcan Mullany. Much admired for romantic and exotic eveningwear.

BENDER, LEE (b.1939) 21
Trained at St Martin's School of Art, 1955-57, then spent one year at the London College of Fashion. Opened her first Bus Stop boutique with husband Cecil in 1968. Sold adventurous appealing youth fashions. Closed late 1970s.

BERNARD WEATHERILL *48*, 49
Established in 1912, this leading equestrian specialist is the only Savile Row tailor with a Ladies Department. The company retains its own identity despite sharing premises with Kilgour, French & Stanbury since 1969. Has a clutch of royal warrants.

BIBA 21, 52-3, *53*, 126, *127*, 157, 169, 183
Label created by designer Barbara Hulanicki (born in Poland in 1936, trained at Brighton College of Art and worked as a freelance fashion illustrator) and her husband Stephen Fitz-Simon. Launched Biba mail order boutique in 1963 and first tiny shop in Abingdon Road, London. 1964 moved to larger premises at Kensington Church Street. 1973 took over the Derry & Toms department store in Kensington High Street. Closed 1975. Innovative youth fashions, which exploited Hollywood glamour and art deco pastiche. Renowned for skin-tight clothes and palette of muted colours. The Biba label was re-launched by a new company in 1996. Hulanicki currently has a successful retail business in New York. Author of *From A to Biba* (London: Hutchinson 1983).

BLADES 47-8, 105, *105*
Influential Savile Row tailor, opened in 1962 by designer Rupert Lycett Green. Catered for the 'New Dandies' of the 1960s, producing flamboyant, innovative high-quality tailoring. Have subsequently become more conventional.

BLAHNIK, MANOLO (b.1943) *168*, 169-70, **188-200**
Born in the Canary Islands to Spanish mother and Czech father. Studied literature in Geneva and the Ecole du Louvre, Paris. Came to London in 1971, opened Chelsea shop in 1973, and another in New York in 1979. Refined, ornate, romantic and exotic shoes crafted in luxurious materials.

BOATENG, OSWALD (b.1967) 61
Trained at Hepworths in Milford Haven, then worked for Tommy Nutter in Savile Row. Describes himself as a 'couture tailor'. Produces bespoke tailoring as well as ready-to-wear. Shows in Paris, though based in London.

BOYD, JOHN (b.1925) *136*, 147
The doyen of London milliners. Served an apprenticeship at Aage Thaarup. Opened his business 1946 and caters for royal and society clientele. He created the tricorne hat to complement the Bellville Sassoon dresswhich the Princess of Wales wore as her going-away outfit.

BURBERRY 28, 122, 129, *130*, 131, 158
Drapery business opened in Basingstoke, Hampshire, in 1865 by 21-year-old Thomas Burberry. In conjunction with a cotton-mill owner, he produced waterproof gabardine raincoats. Launched wholesale business in London in 1900. Coats originally designed for sportswear; worn by services during First World War and then assimilated into civilian wardrobe. The company launched womenswear in 1910 and Thomas Burberry, a more youthful collection, in 1988.

CAMPBELL, PADDY (b.1940)
Trained within the industry – started by working on the shop floor, then organising fashion studios, before designing own label. Opened first shop in 1979, Beauchamp

Place premises in 1984. Designer of top-level, ready-to-wear, streamlined contemporary classics.

CARTMELL, ADRIAN 57
During the late 1970s and early 1980s his elegant and stylish clothes were worn by high society and regularly featured in the pages of glossy magazines. He later moved to New York.

CASELY HAYFORD, JOE (b.1956) 34, 84, *84*, *114-15*, 131, *131*
After working in Savile Row, he enrolled at the Tailor and Cutter Academy in 1974 and then studied at St Martin's School of Art, graduating in 1979. Stylish ready-to-wear, initially with streetstyle influences, moved to a sophisticated look. Also renowned for styling music business personalities from Mica Paris to U2.

CAVANAGH, JOHN (b.1914) 18, 22, 27, 45, *45*, *46*, 69, *69*, 124, **188-200**
Born in Ireland. At 18 was working for Molyneux in London, and then in Paris. Served in the army during the Second World War. From 1947 to 1952 worked for Balmain in Paris. Launched own London house at 26-27 Curzon Street in 1952. A couturier who created elegant, impeccably made chic, tailored daywear and evening clothes. Royal commissions included the Duchess of Kent's wedding dress of 1961. Establishment closed in 1974.

CHALAYAN, HUSSEIN (b.1970) *8-9*, 21, 34, **188-200**
Trained St Martin's School of Art 1989-93. Sold graduation collection to Browns. Briefly worked with tailor Timothy Everest, and launched own label in 1994. Renowned for innovative fabrics, including photographically printed, washable paper, as well as unorthodox techniques such as burying textiles in his garden prior to use.

CHARLES, CAROLINE (b.1942) 58, *59*, 160, **188-200**
Born in Egypt. Trained at Swindon Art School 1958-60. Apprenticed to Michael Sherard, then worked for Mary Quant. Launched her own label 1963, providing stylish modern clothes for her customers, including British and American pop stars. Opened Beauchamp Place retail outlet in 1977. Beautifully cut, eminently wearable clothes, executed in the finest fabrics.

CHELSEA COBBLER *164*, 167
Designers Richard Smith and Mandy Wilkins started Chelsea Cobbler in 1967, initially as a studio and later as a boutique. Inventive, crafted shoes.

CHOO, JIMMY (b.1961) *169*, 171
Trained at Cordwainers College, and became a shoe design consultant to Bally, Switzerland, before launching his own label. He was joined by Gee Wee Lai, who trained at Wellingborough Technical College. Designs own range of modern, sophisticated shoes, as well as producing special ranges for fashion designers.

CHRISTY & CO. LTD. 139, *140*
Founded in London in 1773 by Miller Christy. Company moved to Stockport, Cheshire, in 1826. One of Britain's oldest surviving hatmakers. Christy's supplies

international clientele with traditional hats including fur-felt trilbys, top hats, bowlers and dressage riding hats. They sell to major retailers and export to 30 countries. The finest traditional hatmakers in Britain.

CIERACH, LINDKA 34

Working in the traditions of the court dressmaker, she was commissioned to make the wedding dress of the Duchess of York, Sarah Ferguson. Continues to make made-to-measure clothes for high society.

CLARK, OSSIE (1942-96) 19, 21, 26, *27*, 28, 80, 108

Trained Manchester College of Art 1957-61, RCA 1961-64. Married to Celia Birtwell, influential fabric designer (trained Salford Art School). Designed under own name and for Quorum. A truly innovative designer who exploited Op Art textiles, metallic leathers and snakeskins. By the late 1960s was celebrated for soft tailoring and romantic eveningwear made in fluid floral fabrics, often crêpes and chiffons designed by Celia Birtwell.

CLIVE (John Quentin Evans, b.1933) 26, 27, 78

Studied medicine, then spent two years in the Royal Navy. Attended Canterbury School of Art. Trained at Cavanagh, Lachasse and Michael. Opened his own couture house and ready-to-wear business in 1962. Smart, youthful designs. Closed 1971 to become a design consultant.

CONRAN, JASPER (b.1960) 30, 32, 58, 147, 160

Trained Parsons School of Art and Design, New York 1975-77. Worked briefly for Fiorucci in New York and Wallis in London. Produced first collection 1979, aged just 19 years. From the outset Conran's precision-cut, refined and linear clothes were a great success. Respected for his fine workmanship, attention to detail and use of distinctive textile designs, many his own. Recently diversified into the more experimental area of costume design for ballet and theatre. British Designer of the Year 1986.

CORDINGS 121, *121*, 122, *123*

Opened in the Strand in 1839 by Mr John Charles Cordings and moved to their present site in Piccadilly in 1890. They produce top-quality classic country tailoring and sportswear in superb British fabrics. Introduced the covert coat.

COSSERAT, KAY (b.1948)

Studied textiles and embroidery at Goldsmiths College, and weaving and knitting at the RCA from 1970-72. Began working as a textile designer. Launched her own company in 1972.

COSTELLOE, PAUL (b.1945) 26, 57, 159

Born in Ireland of Irish and American parents. Trained at the Chambre Syndicale school in Paris 1967-69. Assistant to Jacques Esterel 1969-71, freelance in Milan, London and New York 1972-79. Launched his own label in 1979. Modern classics, often made in Irish linens and tweeds.

COX, PATRICK (b.1963) 60, 161, *170*, 171, 173, **188-200**

Born in Canada. Trained Cordwainers College, 1983-85. As a student designed shoes for Vivienne Westwood, Body Map and later for John Galliano. His own collection

became available from 1987 and his fleur-de-lis logo soon became recognized as a sign of elegant, fashionable and sometimes quirky design and top-quality workmanship. The diffusion range Wannabe, launched spring/summer 1995, has added to his international commercial success.

CREED, CHARLES (1909-66) 15, 45, 124, 166

Born in France. Creed was a tailoring firm established London 1710 and Paris 1850. Launched womenswear early 1900s. Charles Creed served apprenticeships in Vienna and at Linton Tweeds in Cumbria. He later took over Paris womenswear. In 1946 set up on his own at 31 Basil Street London; the house closed on his death. Understated, classic tailoring. Author of *Maid to Measure* (Norwich: Jarrolds 1961).

CROLLA, SCOTT 30, *106*, 107, 111

During the 1980s became a key designer, in the opulent, dandy mode. His menswear exploited exotic fabrics and drew on ethnic and historical styles. For a number of seasons joined forces with Georgina Godley. He now works in Italy for Callaghan.

DAGWORTHY, WENDY (b.1950) 19, 128

Trained at Medway and Hornsey Schools of Art. Worked as a freelance designer for one year and launched own label in 1973. Easy, loosely tailored often layered clothes in natural fabrics, for men and women. Closed her business in 1988 to run the BA fashion course at St Martin's School of Art.

DAKS-SIMPSON LTD 158, *158*

The House of Simpson tailoring establishment was founded by Simeon Simpson in the late 19th century. In 1917 his son Alexander joined the business. Introduced Daks (an amalgam of Dad and slacks) trousers in 1934, which eliminated need for braces. Opened Piccadilly store in 1936. Clothes manufactured in Larkhall, Scotland. Introduced a new era of sportswear based on the founder's philosophy of 'comfort in action' for men, using British fabrics. Introduced classic womenswear late 1930s.

DEBORAH CLARE 108, *108*

Fancy and exotic shirtmakers of the 1960s and 1970s, with boutique in Beauchamp Place.

DELANGHE, ANGÈLE

Member of the Incorporated Society of London Fashion designers, who created soft, feminine tailored clothing, and beautiful romantic eveningwear and wedding gowns.

DUCKWORTH, SUSAN

Self-taught knitwear designer. Known for colourful designs which often exploit garden flowers such as pansies and roses. Hand-knitted garments by commission and ready-made. Author of *Susan Duckworth Knitting* (London: Century Hutchinson 1988).

EDELSTEIN, VICTOR (b.1946) 27, 34, 84, *85*

Born into the rag trade, of Russian parentage. During the early years of his career worked for Alexon, Clifton Slimline, Nettie Vogue and Biba. In 1970 he opened his own business, which went bankrupt. Spent three years at Christian Dior, London. In 1977 he established his own label and from 1982 produced solely *haute couture*. Was especially celebrated for his luxurious, elegant,

restrained and flattering eveningwear and wedding dresses. In 1993 he closed, stating that there was no longer a market for luxurious couture clothing.

EMANUEL (Elizabeth b.1953 and David b.1952) 30, 72, *73*

Trained at Harrow School of Art, then RCA 1975-77. Launched own label 1977, introducing *haute couture* in 1979. Split up in the early 1990s and now work separately. Their clothes epitomized the early 1980s vogue for romantic, historic revival styles. Most famous design was Princess Diana's wedding dress. Co-authors of *Style for all Seasons* (London: Michael Joseph 1983).

(HELEN DAVID) ENGLISH ECCENTRICS 26, 100, *101*

Founded in 1982 by Helen Littman, (b.1955) Judy Littman and Claire Angel as English Eccentrics. Printed textile based collections. Helen David (née Littman) trained in fashion at Camberwell School of Art and at St Martin's. Eclectic and extrovert designs inspired by the paintings of Gustav Klimt, mosaics, astrology, heraldry and foreign travel. Publication: McDermott, Catherine, ed. *English Eccentrics – The Textile designs of Helen Littman* (London: Phaidon 1992).

FARHI, NICOLE (b.1946) 160

Born in France. Studied at Studio Bercot, Paris. Worked for French ready-to-wear house, Pierre D'Alby. Moved to England in 1973 working for the French Connection label. Launched own label in 1983 and added menswear in 1989. Stylish, understated modern clothes.

FASSETT, KAFFE (b.1937) 29, 128, *128*

Born in Canada, came to England early 1960s. Originally an artist but fell in love with yarns on a trip to Scotland with Bill Gibb and became an influential knitwear designer. Famous for his painterly designs, tapestry and fabrics and innovative blending of colours. Also worked for Bill Gibb, and for the Italian knitwear company, Missoni. Author of *Kaffe Fassett at the V&A: Knitting and Needlepoint* (London: Century Hutchinson 1988).

FAVOURBROOK 112, *112*

Founded 1989, London (Jermyn Street) and Paris. Top-quality 'dandyish' menswear – and some womenswear – in a selection of 2,500 fabrics, often embroidered and inspired by historical designs.

FEWLASS, ANNE

With a background in fashion, Fewlass creates elaborate, richly coloured knitwear and for a time explored medieval themes.

FIELDEN, DAVID

Studied for the theatre and became a choreographer for Ballet Rambert. Started fashion career selling antique clothing and then went on to create own-label ball gowns, bridal and eveningwear.

MR FISH 50, 108, *109*, 111, 174

Londoner Michael Fish was a delivery boy to a haberdasher, became a salesman at Sulka and then a designer at Turnbull & Asser. Launched own label and shop in 1966, backed by Barry Sainsbury. Created flamboyant clothes in colourful, often patterned fabrics.

FLETT, JOHN (1964-91) 100
Graduated from St Martin's School of Art in 1985. Freelanced then launched his own label 1988-89. Innovative youthful fashions. Worked for Claude Montana on Lanvin couture, Paris, then at Enrico Coveri, Italy. Planned re-launch of own label before premature death.

FOALE & TUFFIN (Marion Foale b.1939 and Sally Tuffin b.1938) 19, 21, *21*, 102, *102*, 127, *127*
Both studied at Walthamstow School of Art followed by the RCA. Launched label in 1961. Fun, youthful clothes. Highly talented colourists, they often combined patterned fabrics, including prints by Bernard Nevill and Susan Collier. Partnership dissolved in 1972. Sally Tuffin went on to design children's clothes. Marion Foale has become a knitwear designer. Author of *Marion Foale's Classic Knitwear* (London: Pelham Books 1985).

FOX, FREDERICK (b.1931) 138, *144*, 148
Born in Australia, made hats from the age of 12. At 17 went to work in a hat factory in Sydney. Came to England in 1957 and launched own label when he took over the old-established millinery firm Langee in 1963. Milliner to Queen Elizabeth II since 1969.

FRANKA 27, 34, **188-200**
Baroness Stael von Holstein was born in Yugoslavia, went to college in Zagreb and then joined the studio of Madame Stepinska. Came to London in 1961; worked at Norman Hartnell 1962-64, and then at Madame Vernier, the milliner. Launched the Vernier/Franka label in 1967. Working under her own name, from her Mayfair premises, Franka designs *haute couture* clothing for royalty and high society. Luxurious evening gowns in dramatic rich colours are a speciality.

FRATINI, GINA (b.1931) 19, 28, 80, *81*, 96, 97, *97*, 124, 127, **188-200**
Born in Japan, came to England as a baby. From age 7 lived in Canada, Burma and India. Returned to school in England and trained at the RCA 1950-53. Costume designer for the Katherine Dunham Dance Company 1953-55. Freelanced for stage and films, before launching own label in 1964. Romantic clothes, sometimes with ethnic inspiration, and speciality wedding dresses.

FREUD, BELLA (b.1961) 30, 53
Spent childhood in North Africa, educated in England. Aged 16, worked in Vivienne Westwood and Malcolm McLaren's Seditionaries shop. Trained at Academia di Costuma e Moda, Rome, and at the Institutto Mariotti. Returned to work with Vivienne Westwood as her personal assistant. Launched own label in 1990. Saucy tailored suits and knitwear in pastel colours and re-worked British classics.

GALLIANO, JOHN (b.1960) 30, 32, 34, *34*, 39, 60, *62-3*, 84, *86*, 87, 91, *139*, 185, **188-200**
Of Spanish-Gibralterian parents, came to London aged 6. Studied at St Martin's School of Art, and graduated in 1983 with a collection based on French Revolution costume which was sold to Browns. First professional collection, presented under his own name, in October 1984. Moved to Paris in 1990. He has been backed to create his own collections by Peder Bertelson, Faycel Amour and John Bault. He is now part of the LMVH group, France, which owns Givenchy, for whom Galliano designed both the couture and ready-to-wear collections. In October 1996 he was appointed designer at Christian Dior. He is a fantasist who is inspired by historical dress and legends. British Designer of the Year 1987, 1994 and 1995.

GASTER, OWEN (b.1959) 34
Trained Epsom College of Art and Design, graduated 1992. Launched own label 1993 and made catwalk début February 1994. An experimental cutter who works with unusual fabrics. His spring/summer 1997 collection included heat-resistant textiles which changed colour, looking like oil on water.

GHOST 34
Established by Tania Sarne (b.1947) in 1983. Initially importing Peruvian knitwear and then fashion sportswear, Ghost is now famous for fluid flattering ready-made fashions in interesting fabrics, often in muted colours. Ghost now shows as part of the New York collections.

GIBB, BILL (1943-88) 28, 29, 80, *80*, 96, *96*, 119, *119*, 129, *129*, 158, 169
Born in Scotland, trained at St Martin's School of Art 1962-66 and Royal College of Art 1966-67. He achieved immediate success with buyers and the press. Designed for Baccarat 1968-71 and then launched Bill Gibb Ltd with Kate Franklin. In 1975 they opened a retail outlet. Inspired by the rich diversity and volume of ethnic costume as well as Scottish Highland dress, he created layered clothes, often in contrasting patterns, colours and materials with ornate trimmings. In conjunction with Kaffe Fassett he designed a range of machine-knitted separates. His signature motif was the bee (B for Bill), which often featured in his stylish daywear as well as his romantic and fantasy evening clothes. Late in his career, he introduced a *haute couture* line.

GIEVES & HAWKES 50
Gieves was founded by Mel Meredith, opening his first establishment in Portsmouth in 1785, primarily to meet the tailoring requirements of the British Navy. Thomas Hawkes was founded in 1771 in Soho. In 1974 Gieves acquired Hawkes, opening a flagship store at the prestigious address of No.1 Savile Row. They continue to cater for a military clientele, whilst producing bespoke tailoring and top-level ready-to-wear.

GODLEY, GEORGINA 30
Trained at Wimbledon and Brighton Art Colleges, working in sculpture, painting, 3-dimensional design and fashion. Worked with Scott Crolla and later launched her own label. Since working under her own name, she became known for boldly confronting conventional notions of femininity and challenging mainstream fashion trends.

GRACHVOGEL, MARIA (b.1969)
Self-taught designer predominantly known for bias-cut satin, *devoré* and richly decorated eveningwear. Fashion partnership was established in 1988, and in 1991 she launched her own label. Has developed links with Liberty who invited her to use an exclusive Liberty print in her 1996-97 collection.

GUINNESS, LULU (b.1960) *150-1*, 160, *161*
Self-taught handbag designer. Started her business in 1989. First London show in 1990. Has also designed bags for the catwalk shows of Norman Hartnell, Caroline Charles and Tomasz Starzewski. In particular, her 'Florist Basket' design has won widespread acclaim.

GUILD, SHIRIN (b.1946) 30, 99, *99*, **188-200**
Born in Tehran. Launched her own label in 1993. Largely self-taught except for six months' instruction from a St Martin's School of Art tutor. Loose, layered, easy-to-wear clothes and knitwear, in square shapes, made in luxurious British fabrics and yarns.

HACKETT 122, *122*
Jeremy Hackett (who had worked for John Michael in Savile Row) and Ashley Lloyd Jennings (who had worked for Browns and Yves Saint Laurent) met through their interest in top-quality second-hand gentlemen's clothes. Founded own shop in 1982 and expanded to create their own collections of classic menswear. The company now has several branches and its own bespoke tailor.

HAMNETT, KATHARINE (b.1948) 27, 32, 161
Educated at Cheltenham Ladies College and trained in fashion at St Martin's School of Art. Freelanced for various companies including Tuttabankem and launched her own label in 1979. Youthful, sometimes rebellious, sexy clothing and up-dated utilitarian styles in luxury fabrics. Brought ecological issues to fashion's forefront with her 1983 'Choose Life' collection. Has at times presented collections in Paris and Milan. British Designer of the Year 1984.

HARTNELL, NORMAN (1901-79) 14, 18, 22, 27, 34, 43, 45, *64*, 66, *68*, 69, 71, 74, 75, *75*, 78, 80, 82, 90, *90*, 96, 166
Trained at Lucile. Opened his couture house at 10 Bruton Street, Mayfair 1923 and moved to No. 26 in 1934. From 1938 became royal dressmaker. Launched ready-to-wear in 1942. Knighted in 1977. Especially famous moments in his career include the all-white wardrobe for Queen Elizabeth, the Queen Mother, in 1938 and the current Queen's Coronation gown in 1953. Winterhalter style, beaded, crinoline evening gowns were a speciality. Author of *Silver and Gold* (London: Evans Brothers 1955).

HASSALL, DIANE (b.1964) 171, *171*
Luxurious special occasion shoes in silks and kid leather, often beaded and embroidered. Sold through Hassall & Carlow in Islington, London.

HENRY POOLE 39, *67*
In 1806 James Poole opened a linen drapers. On joining the Volunteer Corps he had to provide his own uniform, and it was greatly admired. Set up as a military tailor in Savile Row in 1846. Henry took over the company and it has kept his name to this day, with a tradition of making special uniforms and ceremonial clothing as well as being a top-level gentleman's tailor.

for their suits and separates with crisp clean lines.

MATTLI, GUISEPPE GUSTAVO (1907-82) 14, 27
Swiss-born. Came to London to train as a tailor and learn English, then worked for Premet in Paris. Returned to London and launched his couture house in 1934. Stopped producing *haute couture* in 1955. After his retirement, the ready-to-wear side continued for some seasons but closed in the early 1970s. Famous for his suits, cocktail dresses and understated eveningwear.

MAXFIELD PARRISH
Launched in 1972 by Nigel Preston (born in 1946, trained at Dartington Hall in painting and graphic art, then freelanced) who by the end of the 1960s was specializing in suede and leather.

MCCANN, GERALD (b.1931) 19
Trained in fashion at the RCA and graduated in 1953. Influential youth designer, whose signature fashions included dresses made in denim and Liberty's Tana Lawn, military-style coats and fake fur clothes. Sold designs through Mary Quant's Bazaar, and was instrumental in founding the Top Shop boutiques. Expanded into the American market, with his own departments in leading stores such as Bloomingdales. Returned to London 1990.

MCQUEEN, ALEXANDER (b.1969) 34, 39, 40, 185
Trained at Epsom and then St Martin's School of Art, graduating in 1992. Pre- and post-college worked for Romeo Gigli, Koji Tatsuno, and at Savile Row's Anderson & Sheppard. Launched own label in March 1994. A bold, confrontational designer with creative vision, who enjoys a worldwide reputation. In October 1996 he was appointed designer at the Paris fashion house Givenchy, taking over from John Galliano. British Designer of the Year 1996.

MICHAEL, JOHN (b.1931) 34, 48
John Michael Ingram opened his menswear business in the King's Road, London, in 1957. It became the nearest male equivalent to Mary Quant's Bazaar. Formed a precursor to the explosion of young, British fashion boutiques of the 1960s.

MICHAEL, MICHAEL DONÉLLAN 11, 27, 45, 50
Born in Ireland. Spent several years with Lachasse before opening own couture house in 1953. He was then heralded as one of the most stimulating designers working in London. Also known as Michael of Carlos Place. Renowned for stylish tailoring and strong uncluttered design statements. Was recorded by *Vogue* as having been called 'the Balenciaga of London'.

MIRMAN, SIMONE 124, 141, *141*, 142, *145*
Art school trained, she worked for Schiaparelli in Paris. Came to London in 1947 and started a millinery business, briefly working from an attic before opening her couture millinery outlet. Made hats for Princess Margaret from 1952, and the Queen and Queen Mother from the 1960s.

MOKE, JOHNNY (b.1945) *167*, 171
Self-taught shoe designer, has created innovative, stylish shoes with an emphasis on craftsmanship since the late 1970s. Since 1988 has shown in London and Paris, and

has produced individual collections for many top British fashion designers.

MOLYNEUX, CAPTAIN EDWARD (1891-1974) 13, 14, 15, 25, 78, *78*
Born in London to Irish parents. Studied art and trained at Lucile. Became an army captain during the First World War. Opened own couture houses in 1919, in London and Paris. A highly respected designer renowned for his tailoring, bias-cut and use of oriental styling. In the 1930s designed costumes for leading actresses including Gertrude Lawrence and Ina Claire. He returned to London in 1940, retired in 1950, made a comeback in 1964 and finally retired in 1969. John Tullis continued to run Studio Molyneux, a deluxe ready-to-wear line, until the house closed in 1977. Designed costumes for the stage and for Hollywood films.

MORTON, DIGBY (1906-83) *10*, 14, 16, *38*, 124, 166
Born in Ireland, trained at the Dublin Metropolitan School of Art and then at the Polytechnic Art School, London. Designer at Lachasse from its opening in 1928. Launched his own couture house in 1930, and introduced ready-to-wear in 1939. Specialized in fashionable tailoring and country clothes in tweeds which he sometimes teamed with Aran knitwear. Worked in America 1953-57. In 1958 he became Design Director of the London firm Reldan-Digby Morton, which produced casual classic sportswear. Retired 1973.

MOSCA, BIANCA 16
Of Italian origins, she worked for Schiaparelli in Paris before moving to London to direct the studio at Jacqmar in 1939. She opened her own couture house in 1946.

MOSS BROS 34, *49*, 49, *66*
Founded in the 1850s by Moses Moses. Currently most well-known for their hire facility, which offers formal day, evening and occasion wear. The largest proportion of their business still comes from selling ready-to-wear men's tailoring. The Moss Bros Group now incorporates Cecil Gee, The Suit Company, Savoy Taylor's Guild and Beale & Inman.

MUIR, JEAN (1933-95) 28, *28*, *29*, 53, 58-60, *60*, 75, *77*, *145*, 157, 169
Trained within the industry: 1950 worked as a sketcher for Liberty studio, 1956 worked at Jaeger, 1962 appointed designer for Jane & Jane. Launched own label in 1966, which continues in her name. A highly skilled dressmaker and tailor, renowned for her precision cut clothes and meticulous attention to detail. Signature fabrics are jerseys, matt crêpes and supple suedes, and standard colours are navy-blue and black. Unadorned clothes, often accented with precious handcrafted accessories. Publication: *Jean Muir* (Leeds City Art Galleries 1980).

MULBERRY 157, 158, *159*
Company founded by Roger Saul (b.1950, trained at Westminster College) who was a trainee at John Michael where one of his roles was accessory buyer. In 1971, with his mother Joan Saul, he started Mulberry as an accessory company. Began producing belts,

then bags in the saddlery tradition, as well as more ephemeral fashionable designs. Expanded into garments in 1975. Known for their classic designs, with subtle fashionable styling, Mulberry continues to retain its emphasis upon traditional leather goods, classic sports and leisure wear, while at the same time breaking into the fashion market with a sharper, more sophisticated, look.

NEW & LINGWOOD 172, *172*, 174, *174*
Founded 1865 in Eton by a Miss New, who married the proprietor of Mr Lingwood's hosiery shop. Opened in Jermyn Street, London, in 1922. Since 1972 has incorporated Poulson Skone (shoe and boot makers), Haines & Bonner (pyjamas and nightshirts), and Bowring Arundel & Co. (bespoke shirtmakers). Top-level gentleman's outfitter, supplying bespoke and ready-made shoes and shirts with a full range of accessories.

NORWOOD, CLAIRE (b.1964) 171, *171*
After completing a degree in business studies, Claire Norwood undertook the two-year shoemaking and design course at Cordwainers in 1991. Understated designs in metallic organzas and soft suedes. Her signature designs are shoes with banded uppers.

NUTTER, TOMMY (1943-92) *36-7*, 50, *50*, *51*, 55, 105, *111*, 112, 174
Born in Wales. Studied architecture at Willesden Technical College but at 19 abandoned his studies to work for Ward & Co., traditional London tailors. Launched own name Savile Row premises in 1969, funded by Cilla Black and Peter Brown of Apple (the Beatles' record company). Tommy Nutter revolutionized menswear tailoring by introducing high fashion to Savile Row.

OLDFIELD, BRUCE (b.1950) 30, 33, 87, *87*, 160, **188-200**
Fostered by tailor and dressmaker Violet Masters. Trained at Ravensbourne College of Art 1971-72 and then worked as a freelance designer. Launched his own ready-to-wear label in 1975 and couture in 1978. Famous for pretty and glamorous eveningwear. Author, with Georgina Howell, of *Bruce Oldfield's Seasons* (London: Pan 1987).

ONG, BENNY (b.1949)
Born in Singapore. Moved to London and trained at St Martin's School of Art, graduating in 1968. Worked freelance before launching his own label in 1974. Graceful eveningwear in beautiful fabrics.

OZBEK, RIFAT (b.1953) 32, 58, *98*, 99
Born in Turkey. Originally studied architecture but changed to fashion. Trained at St Martin's School of Art and was subsequently appointed designer at Monsoon. Launched his own label in 1984, producing influential and eclectic collections inspired by ethnic and historical dress and the London club scene. He is noted for his skilled cut, use of colour and surface decoration. A designer with international appeal, he has shown in London and Milan but now presents his collections in Paris. British Designer of the Year 1988 and 1992.

PABLO & DELIA
Design duo from Buenos Aires. Founded

fashion workshop in London *c*.1970. Colourful, youthful, hand-painted appliquéd felts, leathers and suedes were a speciality. Their romantic, rainbow and fairy-tale imagery perfectly captured the prevailing fashion mood for hand-crafted clothing with a hippie influence.

PATERSON, RONALD (b.1917) 18, *43*, 45, *45*, 78, 124
Born in Scotland, he moved to London in 1936 and trained at the Piccadilly Institute of Design. Launched his own couture house in 1947 and became a highly successful British fashion talent. Closed in 1968 and then worked in films, before retiring.

PEARCE FIONDA 34, 40, 57, *57*
Launched in 1994 by Andrew Pearce (b.1967) and Reynold Fionda (b.1964), who both trained at Trent Polytechnic. Andrew went to the RCA and Reynold to St Martin's School of Art. Had their first solo catwalk show at Liberty's in 1995. Meticulous, fashionably styled tailoring.

POLLEN, ARABELLA 29, 30, 58
A self-taught designer who, after making clothes for herself and friends, was backed to launch her own label by Naim Attallah. She was later backed by Courtaulds but having come to prominence in the early 1980s, failed to survive the 1990s.

PRICE, ANTONY (b.1945) 19, *53*, 55, 87, *87*, 169, 180
Trained at RCA 1965-68. Designer at Stirling Cooper 1968-1974 and at Plaza 1974-79. He was at the forefront of early 1970s glam-rock style and designed clothes for Bryan Ferry and Roxy Music. Launched own label in 1979. Famous for his wonderfully cut and constructed overtly glamorous eveningwear and bold, tailored clothing.

PRINGLE OF SCOTLAND 28, 29, *117*, 118, 132
Founded in Hawick 1815 by James Pringle, this knitwear company also specialized in performance wear and supplied knitwear to the army in the Second World War. In the 1930s their Austrian-born designer Otto Weisz introduced the twinset, which became an instant British classic. Also famous for sportswear and argyle patterned knitwear. Pringle is a subsidiary of Dawson International, the major processor of raw cashmere.

QUANT, MARY (b.1934) 20-21, 26, 43, 47, *47*, 79, *79*, 80, 127, 157, *176-7*, 181, 183, **188-200**
Trained in Fine Art at Goldsmith's College, and learned pattern cutting at evening classes. Worked with the milliner Eric. Opened first King's Road boutique, Bazaar, in 1955, with husband Alexander Plunket Greene and business partner Archie McNair. This was an immediate success. Stylish and innovative youthful fashions. Opened other boutiques in 1957 and 1967; started to design for J. C. Penney in New York 1962; launched wholesale Ginger Group 1963; introduced cosmetics in unprecedented colour range in 1966. Subsequently diversified into accessories and household designs. In 1994 opened Mary Quant Colour Shop. She has been a major design force in British fashion. Author of *Quant on Quant* (London: Cassell 1965).

RAHVIS
Raemonde (b.1918) and her sister Dorothy Rahvis were born in South Africa. From 1935-41 Raemonde worked as a freelance modelliste. Dorothy joined her to open the couture house Rahvis Soeurs in 1941 at 19 Upper Grosvenor Street. Specialized in supremely elegant eveningwear and tailoring. In the 1950s and 1960s they dressed many top film stars and remained open until the 1980s.

RAYNE *154*, 155, 156, 157, *162-3*, 166
Founded as H. & M. Rayne in 1889, catering exclusively to the acting profession. In 1920, the company opened a shop in Bond Street. In the post-war period Edward Rayne, the founder's grandson, transformed the company into a high-fashion label including, in 1959, commissioning Oliver Messel to re-design the Bond Street shop. Top-level, stylish, meticulously crafted fashion shoes, sometimes with matching bags.

REGER, JANET (b.1935) 183, *183*, 185
Trained at Leicester College of Art & Technology, Reger originally worked as a freelance beachwear designer. Her name has since become synonymous with glamorous silk lingerie including silk nightdresses and satin pyjamas. In 1978 she created a beribboned waspie. Sold her company to Berlei in 1983, bought it back in 1986. Author of *Janet Reger – Her Story* (London: Chapman 1991).

RHODES, ZANDRA (b.1940) 21, 26, 27, 28, 80, 82, *82*, *94*, 96, 124, *160*, 169, **188-200**
Her mother worked at Worth in London. Zandra trained at Medway College of Art and then studied textiles at the RCA, graduating in 1966. She and Sylvia Ayton launched Rhodes & Ayton and in 1967 opened the Fulham Road Clothes Shop to sell their work. First solo collection was in 1969. Her fabrics, shapes, colours and themes are unique and innovative. She is especially well-known for her ethereal special occasion clothing, with screen-printed and hand-decorated textiles. Author with Anne Knight of *The Art of Zandra Rhodes* (London: Jonathan Cape 1984).

RICHMOND, JOHN (b.1961) 34
Graduated from Kingston Polytechnic in 1982. Immediately began to work under his own name, as well as designing freelance for Emporio Armani, Joseph Tricot and Fiorucci. In 1984 he formed a partnership with Maria Cornejo and together they gained cult status for their uncompromising body- and street-conscious fashions. Since 1987 he has worked under his own name, producing a mainline collection and two diffusion ranges. One of his signature garments is the leather jacket printed with a tattoo design.

RIGBY & PELLER 182, *182*, 184, 185
Founded in 1946 by Mrs Rigby and Mrs Peller, and bought in 1982 by Mrs June Kenton. Exclusive and luxurious readymade and bespoke underclothes and lingerie. Caters for wide-ranging demands from the Queen to those of fashion designer John Galliano.

ROBERTS, PATRICIA (b.1945) 29, 104, *104*
Trained in fashion at Leicester Polytechnic, with knitting as a subsidiary subject. Worked for IPC magazines in the early 1970s. Saw a gap in the market for interesting hand-knits and set up as a freelance knitwear designer. Her earliest work was sold to Browns. Opened her first London shop in 1976, and has published many knitting pattern books since this time. Innovative, fashionable designs exploiting a bold use of colour, contrasting textures and decorative stitches.

ROCHA, JOHN (b.1953) 32
Of Chinese-Portuguese parents, born in Hong-Kong. Trained at the London College of Fashion. Moved to Ireland after using Irish fabrics for his graduation collection. Lives and works in Dublin and has shown in Paris. Designs softly tailored mens and womenswear in interesting fabrics, often Irish linens. British Designer of the Year 1993.

ROECLIFFE & CHAPMAN
Couture and top-level ready-to-wear house much in vogue in the 1940s and early 1950s. Created beautiful, predominantly romantic special occasion and eveningwear.

RONAY, EDINA (b.1945) and **STENGARD, LENA** 29, 128, *128*
Trained at St Martin's School of Art and RADA, Edina was a model and actress before she became interested in antique clothes. Launched knitwear company in the 1960s with Lena Stengard, named Edina & Lena, which specialized in nostalgic knitwear inspired by 1930s and 1940s designs. After the partnership was dissolved Edina Ronay launched her own fashion label in 1984, which conveys a classic line with a taste for glamour.

RUSSELL, PETER 14, 15, 16, 78, 124, 156
Farmed in Canada, fought in France in the First World War, and ran a rubber plantation in Malaysia, before launching own couture house. Specialized in sports and travel clothes during the 1930s and 1940s. When he closed in 1953 his establishment in Carlos Place was taken over by Michael.

SEARLE, PATTI 119, *119*
Launched her own company in 1975, designing sophisticated restyled classics with a twist.

SHERARD, MICHAEL 18, 78
Launched his couture house in 1946 and created elegant eveningwear and neat, tailored suits. Closed in 1964 when demand for *haute couture* declined. Subsequently taught at London College of Fashion, bringing the same high standards to teaching as he had to design.

SHILLING, DAVID (b.1953) 55, 138, 144, *145*, **188-200**
From the age of 12 designed the extravagant creations that his mother wore to Ascot each season. With no formal training but an eye for millinery, he launched his own label in 1975 and opened his own shop in 1976. He continues to amaze with his inventiveness. Author of *Thinking Rich – A personal guide to luxury living* (London: Robson Books 1986).

SMITH, GRAHAM (b.1939) *145*, 148, 161
Trained at Bromley College of Art and the RCA, graduated 1958. Worked for one year at